BEAT
SUGAR
ADDICTION
NOW!
COOKBOOK

THIS IS NO LONGER THE
PROPERTY OF
KING COUNTY LIBRARY SYSTEM

JAN   2012

JAN 16 2012

BEAT SUGAR ADDICTION NOW!

COOKBOOK

RECIPES THAT CURE YOUR TYPE OF SUGAR ADDICTION AND HELP YOU LOSE WEIGHT AND FEEL GREAT!

Jacob Teitelbaum, M.D.,

and Chrystle Fiedler

Recipes created by Deirdre Rawlings, Ph.D., N.D.

FAIR WINDS

PRESS

© 2012 Fair Winds Press

Text © 2012 Jacob Teitelbaum, Chrystle Fiedler, and Deirdre Rawlings

First published in the USA in 2012 by

Fair Winds Press, a member of

Quayside Publishing Group

100 Cummings Center

Suite 406-L

Beverly, MA 01915-6101

www.fairwindspress.com

All rights reserved. No part of this book may be reproduced or utilized, in any form or by any means, electronic or mechanical, without prior permission in writing from the publisher.

16 15 14 13 12   1 2 3 4 5

ISBN: 978-1-59233-489-6

Digital edition published in 2012
eISBN: 978-1-61058-179-0

Library of Congress Cataloging-in-Publication Data available
Book design by Kathie Alexander

Printed and bound in Canada

The information in this book is for educational purposes only. It is not intended to replace the advice of a physician or medical practitioner. Please see your health-care provider before beginning any new health program.

DEDICATIONS

JT: To Laurie, my beautiful lady, my wife, my sweet best friend, and the love of my life. To my children David, Amy, Shannon, Brittany, and Kelly, who already seem to know so much of what I'm trying to learn, and to my beautiful grandchildren, Payton and Bryce. To my mother, Sabina, and father, David, whose unconditional love made this book possible; and to my patients, who have taught me more than I can ever hope to teach them.

CF: To Valerie Boergesson: a great sister, an even better friend.

DR: To the health and happiness of people who suffer from the wide array of disorders stemming from imbalanced blood sugar levels. May the recipes and information in these pages support your return to good health and help you to feel good.

CONTENTS

CONTENTS

12 RECIPES FOR ALL SUGAR-ADDICTION TYPES   192

Introduction

You are what you eat. And with food processors adding more than 140 pounds of sugar to our diets each year, plus another 18 percent of our calories coming from white flour (which acts like sugar in our body), we eat a lot of sugar!

I understand why you reach for a quick sugar fix to keep you going. I've done it myself. But even though that piece of chocolate cake, brownie, doughnut, or energy drink perks you up and gives you energy, that initial high is replaced by a dip in blood sugar that leaves you wanting more. I like to say that sugar acts as an energy loan shark. In effect, it takes away more energy than it gives. Eventually, your "credit line" runs out, and you find yourself exhausted, anxious, and moody.

Since recovering from chronic fatigue syndrome driven by sugar addiction more than 30 years ago, I have counseled thousands of patients who have felt the disastrous effects of sugar consumption on their health, including:

- Chronic fatigue syndrome and fibromyalgia
- Chronic pain of many kinds
- Decreased immune function
- Chronic sinusitis
- Irritable bowel syndrome and spastic colon
- Autoimmune disease
- Metabolic syndrome with high cholesterol and hypertension
- Heart disease
- Hormonal problems
- Anxiety and depression
- Candida and yeast infections
- ADHD

The good news? These conditions are all treatable. It's just a matter of taking charge of what you eat. This is a lot easier to do once you've treated what is driving your sugar addiction, as we discussed in *Beat Sugar Addiction Now!*.

EATING TO BALANCE BLOOD SUGAR

As a physician, it has always amazed me how the body can feel great if given the nutritional support it so desperately needs. When you eat in a way that balances your blood sugar and give your body the right vitamins, minerals, and nutrients it craves, you can eliminate the sugar roller-coaster and feel energized all day long. For example, the omega-3 essential fatty acids found in cold freshwater fish such as salmon improve brain function and elevate your mood, so you don't need sugar or caffeine for a lift. Eating walnuts improves heart health, repairing some of the damage a high-sugar diet can do to your cardiovascular system. Broccoli improves immune function, offsetting sugar's immune-suppressing effects. I think eating healthfully is fun, delicious, and makes you feel your best. That's what you'll find the *Beat Sugar Addiction Now! Cookbook* is all about.

In *Beat Sugar Addiction Now!* you learned the importance of kicking sugar addiction and how to do it by first identifying which type(s) of sugar addict you are. You then learned how to get off of the sugar roller coaster by using a combination of diet, vitamins and minerals, other supplements, and simple lifestyle changes.

The four sugar addiction types are:

Type 1: Sugar as an Energy Loan Shark. Chronically exhausted and hooked on quick hits of caffeine and sugar.

Type 2: "Feed Me Now or I'll Kill You." When life's stress has exhausted your "stress-handling" adrenal glands.

Type 3: The Happy Ho-Ho Hunter. Sugar cravings caused by yeast/candida overgrowth (often associated with nasal congestion, chronic sinusitis, or spastic colon).

Type 4: Depressed and Craving Carbs. Sugar cravings caused by your period, menopause, or andropause.

This cookbook will teach you all about which nutrients are the most important to healing your particular type(s) of sugar addiction. You'll discover how these nutrients work in the body, what specific foods contain them, and to how to create meals using the recipes here.

The 120 delicious, nutritious recipes created by the wonderful holistic nutritionist Deirdre Rawlings, Ph.D., N.D., and the specific information she gives about each one, will help you beat sugar addiction by keeping your blood sugar levels balanced and ensuring you get the nutrients you need to help you avoid or recover from sugar-related health problems. These delicious and satisfying recipes will supercharge your recovery and enable you to eat well, without excess sugar, as a natural part of your healthful lifestyle.

Lose Weight by Breaking Sugar Addiction

In addition to feeling great, looking great is a "side effect" of this program. Many people find that by cutting out sugar, they are finally able to lose weight. Instead of the usual yo-yo dieting, where you lose 50 pounds and gain 100, this program will help restore a healthy metabolism so your weight comes off gradually—and stays off! In addition, I've created a BSAN Weight Loss supplement program for each sugar addiction type to make dropping excess pounds easier.

Once you have treated your type of sugar addiction for three months using the recipes in the corresponding section of this cookbook, your metabolism will usually return to a healthy-enough place that you can enjoy all of the recipes in this book. Once your sugar addiction has cleared, if you would like to lose a little more weight, you can follow a simple "Can-Do" diet my wife, Laurie, offers at the end of the book. You can also use it intermittently whenever you want to shed a few pounds.

HOW TO USE THIS BOOK

We know it's easy to get overwhelmed when making dietary changes, so take it slow. Choose one or two recipes for your specific type that appeal to you and try them out. Once you've added them to your meal rotation, try a few more. Before you know it, you'll be eating to balance your blood sugar all day long! In the back of the book you'll also find recipes that all four types can use to keep blood sugar in check.

Start by reviewing Sugar-Free 101 in the next chapter, which outlines the basic foundation for your recovery. After that, you'll learn the ins and outs of eating to balance your blood sugar. Next, you'll move into the core of the book, the blood sugar–balancing recipes for all four types. Ideally, you have already read *Beat Sugar Addiction Now!* to identify which type or types you are and have begun making lifestyle changes. If not, you can take the handy quizzes in the beginning of each section of this cookbook, focus on the recipes for your type, and circle back to the additional recommendations in *Beat Sugar Addiction Now!* to help you complete your recovery. Once you've effectively treated your sugar-addiction type, in addition to feeling much better (and most likely looking trimmer), you'll be able to use the recipes for all four types, giving you a total of 120 delicious new low-sugar recipes to choose from every day!

Ready to take control of your health and eat delicious foods that balance your blood sugar, tame your sugar addiction, and help you feel great? Let's get started!

Love and blessings,
Jacob Teitelbaum, M.D.

CHAPTER 1

Sugar-Free 101: The Basics for Breaking Your Sugar Addiction Now!

The *Beat Sugar Addiction Now! Cookbook* is a powerful tool in kicking your sugar addiction for good. But before we get started, let's review the sugar-free basics you learned about in *Beat Sugar Addiction Now!* that will form the foundation for your recovery.

DIETARY CHANGES

Stop Eating Sugar

The most important thing you need to do is a real no-brainer: stop eating sugar. Eating sugar just fans the fires of your addiction and keeps you stuck in a vicious cycle. You don't have to quit cold turkey, though. Start by getting rid of high-sugar foods in your diet, including fast food, processed food, soda, and fruit drinks. Read ingredients labels and learn to recognize sugar synonyms, including sucrose, glucose, fructose, dextrose, corn syrup, evaporated cane juice, honey, lactose, maltodextrin, malt syrup, maple syrup, and molasses, among others. As a rule of thumb, if sugar in any form is in the top three ingredients of a package label, don't eat it, or look for a similar product with less added sugar.

When it's convenient to do so, you'll also want to decrease the white flour found in bread, pasta, and pizza, since your body rapidly turns it into sugar. Make a gradual switch over to whole grains over a period of two to three months to give you time to adjust to the taste.

Strike a Balance between Good Nutrition and the Occasional Treat

Although some people will find they need to avoid added sugars entirely, most people can have sugar and white flour in moderation, where it gives the most pleasure. This is not an "all or nothing" approach, which makes it much easier to make these changes into habits that you will happily live with. A good rule of thumb is to focus on cutting out the high-sugar foods that give you the least pleasure. If you have a food that you especially enjoy, give yourself permission to keep that one, but in small amounts. Then savor it, without guilt! For example, skip that 48-ounce (1.4 L) soda when you're at the local convenience store (that's 36 teaspoons [170.8 g] of sugar!), but have a bite or two of high-quality dark chocolate when you get home. Or give yourself permission to occasionally have a slice or two of pizza with white flour crust when you are out with friends, if you are eating whole grains most of the time.

Cut Out Excess Caffeine to Soothe Symptoms of Sugar Addiction

Caffeine makes the symptoms of sugar addiction worse—after it wears off your energy plummets, which makes you crave sugar for another energy boost—so you also need to moderate your intake. Limit yourself to just one or two cups (8 ounces [235 ml], or 1 shot of espresso) of regular coffee or tea a day, and then switch to decaffeinated coffee or tea. Note: If you are drinking more than four cups of coffee a day, cut the amount in half each week until you get down to one cup a day. This decreases the risk of caffeine withdrawal headaches.

Withdrawal from Sugar Addiction

When you begin to change your diet, by stopping eating sugar, and moderating your caffeine intake, you may temporarily become cranky, moody, and irritable. The good news is that these withdrawal symptoms will pass in a week or so (even faster if you apply the treatment plans found in *Beat Sugar Addiction Now!*).

If you are really struggling, simply cut back on your sugar and caffeine intake more gradually. Better yet, allow yourself a healthy snack of fruit or even one or two squares of high-quality dark chocolate (savor each bite!), which you can enjoy without guilt. This will make it easier for you to stick with the program. It's important to look at the big picture: flexibility in the short term may help you achieve your lifetime goal of enjoying sugar in healthy moderation. After being "off" sugar long enough to see how much better you feel, you'll notice how lousy you feel after a sugar binge. Let this experience of feeling great by eating healthfully—not guilt—be what guides and motivates you!

Try Sugar Substitutes

Sugar substitutes can satisfy your sweet tooth without the side effects. Some are very healthy and some are, frankly, not. Let's take a look at some of the more common substitutes:

Stevia This excellent sugar substitute is safe and natural. It has been used worldwide for decades and was recently approved by the FDA for use in food processing in the United States, so stevia-sweetened foods and beverages are becoming more widely available.

Stevia comes from leaves of the stevia plant, an herb in the chrysanthemum family that grows wild as a small shrub in parts of Paraguay and Brazil. The leaves contain an extract (called a stevioside) that may be 200 to 300 times as sweet as sugar, but with no calories. It can be used in cooking and as an excellent overall sugar substitute. It is even safe for diabetics.

However, unless it is properly filtered, stevia has a nasty bitter licorice aftertaste. So if you try a brand that does not taste good, it was not properly filtered. Simply switch brands. One excellent version is a clear liquid from Body Ecology (www.bodyecology.com or 1-800-4stevia). Add one drop per ounce to whatever you are drinking. If you prefer a convenient powder form, look for Sweet Leaf, which is available in individual use packets and can be found in most natural food stores and in many health-conscious restaurants. Other good brands include Truvia and PureVia, which are made of stevia plus a natural sugar alcohol called erythritol (see below). Both are available at grocery stores nationwide.

Sugar alcohols These are also safe and healthy sugar substitutes. The most common one is maltitol, used in sugar-free chocolates. Its only downside is that it can have a mild laxative effect, causing gas and loose stools in some people. If you find this problematic, simply eat less of it. Another good alternative is a sugar alcohol called erythritol, which is less likely to cause this problem and is starting to become more popular. Other sugar alcohols include inositol and any other substance ending in the letters "-ol."

Whey Low This is a powdered natural sweetener made from whey that has one-quarter the amount of sugar by weight as granulated sugar. You can substitute it for sugar in a one-to-one ratio in all food applications, including baking. Because it still has some sugar, however, use it in moderation. Available for purchase at www.wheylow.com.

Chemical sweeteners You'll want to avoid these when you can, since some holistic experts contend that all chemical sweeteners are toxic (you may want to start carrying some Sweet Leaf packets with you). The three main brands of chemical sweeteners are:

Sweet'N Low (saccharin). It has the best and longest overall safety record. I consider it safe in moderation.

Splenda (sucralose). A relative newcomer, the jury is still out regarding its long-term safety in large amounts, so I recommend using it in moderation. For example, most sugar-free ice creams are made with Splenda, and I consider these okay to enjoy.

NutraSweet (aspartame). It's surprising to me that this sweetener ever received FDA approval for use. Aspartame has nearly one hundred associated side effects, including brain fog, migraine headaches, skin allergies, insomnia, pain and inflammation, and many others. There is some evidence that aspartame may even suppress thyroid function, making sugar addiction and some of its related health problems worse.

The bottom line? Use stevia as first choice, followed by Truvia, erythritol, maltitol, and Sweet'N Low. Whey Low is an option for use in baking. If your only choice is between products with Splenda or Nutrasweet, opt for those with Splenda. With all these options, you'll never miss sugar again!

Choose Whole Foods to Balance Blood Sugar

The next step is to add in healthy foods that help keep you off the sugar roller coaster. The best way to do this is to choose whole foods (unprocessed fruits, vegetables, grains, and meat). Most of these foods are also low on the glycemic index, so they won't fuel your sugar cravings.

What is the glycemic index (GI)? The GI tells us which foods raise blood glucose fastest and highest. This is especially important to keep in mind when it comes to sugar addiction. Pure glucose is given a GI score of 100—all other foods are then measured in relation to glucose. A food with a GI over 85 raises blood sugar almost as much as pure glucose, but a food with a GI lower than 30 does not raise blood sugar much at all. You also need to take portion size into account. The term *glycemic load* combines these factors.

You'll find a glycemic index in Appendix B, which will guide you to make healthy choices. How high a score is acceptable depends both on your sugar addiction type (you'll find recommendations for you in individual treatment chapters), as well as the protein, fiber, and other healthful substances (like vitamins and minerals) contained in the food. Remember, the best approach is to simply listen to your body by noticing what foods and combinations leave you feeling the best.

LIFESTYLE CHANGES

Take a Multi to Manage Sugar Cravings

Most people—especially sugar addicts and people on a diet—can benefit from taking a daily multivitamin. That's because inadequate levels of nutrients will trigger food cravings (especially for sugar in people who have fatigue or adrenal exhaustion) as your body instinctually seeks to obtain the vitamins, minerals, and other nutrients it needs. I recommend vitamin powders that you can dissolve in liquid, because one of these drinks can replace over 35 tablets of supplements. There are several good brands available (see appendix A).

Stay Hydrated to Reduce Your Reliance on Caffeine and Sugar

You will have a tougher time kicking sugar if you don't stay hydrated. Water helps the machinery of the body function and helps rid the body of toxins. Being dehydrated can also leave you fatigued and craving sugar. Instead of reaching for a soda to pick you up, try drinking 8 to 12 ounces (235 to 335 ml) of cold water for a lasting energy boost. How much water should you drink a day? Check your mouth and lips every so often. If they are dry, you are thirsty and need to drink more water.

When you can, drink water that is purified by reverse osmosis and carbon block filtration. For good home water filters, see "Pure Water" in Appendix D.

Get Enough Sleep to Help You Shun Sugar

It's important to get seven to nine hours of sleep a night. Not only does this optimize energy, it decreases your appetite and slashes sugar cravings. You'll find the basics for a great night's sleep below. If you need help for insomnia, please refer to Chapter 5 of *Beat Sugar Addiction Now!*

- Go to bed and wake up at the same time each day. This will set your internal clock (circadian day/night rhythm) to a healthy pattern. Your body loves routine.
- Don't drink an excessive amount of alcohol right before bedtime.
- Cut off your caffeine at 2:00 p.m. It's okay to have one or two cups of tea or coffee in the morning, but switch to decaf after 2:00.
- If you frequently wake up to urinate during the night, limit your fluid intake near bedtime.
- Keep your bedroom cool, around 65°F (18.3°C).
- Don't exercise within an hour of bedtime.
- Put your clock out of arm's reach and facing away from you so you can't see it. Looking at the clock frequently aggravates sleep problems.

Ask for Help If You Need It

If you feel like you need more support in changing your eating habits, organizations like Overeaters Anonymous (www.overeaters.org) and Overeaters Anonymous Primary Purpose (www.oapp.info) have helped many people break free from emotional and stress eating. Food Addicts Anonymous (www.foodaddictsanonymous.org) specifically focuses on removing sugar and white flour from your diet and has a more stringent eating plan. All of these groups may have meetings in your area and/or phone meetings. You may also want to speak to a trained professional who specializes in eating disorders. Remember, seeking help is a sign of strength, not weakness. If you feel you need to reach out to change your life in a positive way, do it!

Let's move on the nuts and bolts of eating to balance your blood sugar!

CHAPTER 2

Eating to Optimize Blood Sugar Balance

In this chapter you'll learn about the primary ingredients in the recipes that follow for Sugar

Addiction Types 1, 2, 3, 4, and All Addiction types. These ingredients are packed with health

facilitators—protein, fat, carbohydrates, fiber, enzymes, vitamins, and minerals—that are all

essential to beating sugar addiction. Each recipe in this book includes an easy-to-use chart (see

an example on page 35) that shows which heath facilitators are included and their effectiveness

in balancing blood sugar. You'll also learn how to maximize the blood sugar–balancing

effects of each recipe by adding certain nutrients. First, let's take a quick look at the role of

macronutrients and micronutrients in your diet.

WHAT THE BODY NEEDS TO RUN

There are three key macronutrients: protein, fat, and carbohydrate. They provide calories, or energy, necessary for growth, metabolism, and other body functions. Macro means large, and macronutrients are called such because your body needs these nutrients in large amounts and because they supply the bulk of our calories. You need smaller amounts of micronutrients (vitamins and minerals), which help your bones and organs grow and work properly.

Like hardware on a computer, which is constructed of solid materials such as metal and plastic, your body parts—muscles, tissues, hormones, nerves, bones—are built from protein, fats, minerals, vitamins, and water. These are the building blocks your body needs to replenish itself and replace worn-out cells, and they are critical for keeping sugar addiction and its related health problems at bay. For example, foods high in protein trigger the release of glucagon, a hormone that helps balance the excess insulin released when you eat too many carbohydrates.

Carbohydrates, on the other hand, are more like software that runs the programs and applications—they are your body's fuel. Your body breaks down carbohydrates into glucose and stimulates your pancreas to release insulin, which transports the glucose (energy) into your cells. Eating too many high-glycemic, starchy carbohydrates, however, not only overworks the pancreas, it also eventually leads to insulin resistance and diabetes. When this occurs, despite having high sugar levels in your blood, the sugar can't get into your cells to be used as fuel, starving your organs, tissues, hormones, bones, nerves, and muscles. Your body needs high-quality carbohydrates such as vegetables, brown rice, beans, and legumes that promote the steady, low release of insulin and are packed with vitamins, minerals, and fiber. Eating lean protein, healthy fats, and high-quality carbohydrates keeps your insulin and glucagon levels normalized, stabilizing your blood sugar and eliminating sugar cravings and addictions!

All the recipes in this cookbook have been carefully created to include low-glycemic carbohydrates for maintaining balanced blood sugar levels, along with lean proteins and healthy sources of fat. Further, the recipes all contain whole foods, which means they have not been processed or refined, are free of additives such as colorings and preservatives, and are as close as possible to their original or natural state prior to preparing or cooking them.

Many of the recipes are also gluten-free, using whole grains that don't have gluten protein. For many people, especially those with hidden wheat allergies, these offer fantastic health benefits, ease of preparation, and healing properties. Some of the grains may be new taste treats for you, such as amaranth, buckwheat, and quinoa. We also include soy foods such as tempeh and tofu that may be unfamiliar. Include them in one new recipe each week, or more often if you're feeling adventurous. Experiment by combining recipes to create complete meals, always including some protein, fat, and low-glycemic carbohydrate on your plate every time you eat—then watch how much better you feel and how your health improves.

NUTRITIONAL BASICS TO HELP YOU BEAT SUGAR ADDICTION

It's very important to listen to your body as you try these new recipes, paying close attention to how you feel in order to find the best balance of macronutrients and micronutrients. Let's take a closer look at protein, fat, carbohydrates, enzymes, antioxidants, and fiber and the role they play in keeping your blood sugar in check.

Protein for Long-Lasting Energy

Protein stimulates the release of glucagon, a fat-burning hormone that maintains stable blood glucose levels and releases stored fat so it can be burned for energy. This makes protein one of your primary weapons in the battle against sugar addiction.

Protein foods primarily come from animal sources, but they can also come from grains and legumes (beans, lentils, etc.). The quality of a protein food is determined by two factors: the amino acid balance it contains and its digestibility. A complete protein contains all the essential amino acids in relatively the same amount as humans require. High-quality protein sources should also be easy to digest and low in fat.

As you digest proteins, their long peptide chains begin to break down into amino acids, enter the bloodstream, and are rearranged into more than 50,000 new body proteins that make up, build, and repair the human body on a continuous basis. If you consume adequate amounts of quality protein at every meal, a continuous supply of amino acids is available to build and repair your body. Proteins also are digested slowly and steadily, so they don't cause high and low blood sugar swings. By keeping your blood sugar level stable, protein markedly decreases your sugar cravings and your risk of insulin resistance.

Best High-Quality Protein Sources

- Cottage cheese, Greek yogurt, and other dairy products (low-fat and nonfat)
- Chicken and turkey (skinless)
- Eggs and egg whites
- Fish
- Lean meats
- Low-fat tofu and tempeh (fermented soy products)
- Whey protein powder (90 percent pure)

What Are Your Protein Requirements?

Your gender, size, and activity level determine how much protein you require. However, as a general guideline, you should get at least 15 to 30 percent of your daily dietary calories from protein, or at least 1 gram of protein for every 3 pounds (1360.8 g) of body weight per day. Including protein every time you eat will ensure you're getting enough.

Fat: Your Secret Weapon Against Sugar

There's lots of confusion surrounding fat—whether it is good or bad, and how much and what types our bodies need. The most important point to remember is that consuming the right types of fat is essential to good health and to helping you keep your sugar intake in check. Fats are made up of essential fatty acids, which play a critical role in energy production, balancing hormones, controlling hunger, and stabilizing blood sugar. Eating fat in a meal slows digestion, ensuring a steady release of energy into the bloodstream and keeping blood glucose levels normal.

Your best bet is to choose foods that contain monounsaturated fats and omega 3, 6, and 9 fatty acids. Unprocessed and naturally occurring, these "good" fats provide other health benefits besides balancing blood sugar. Aim for getting 20 to 30 percent of your daily calories from these healthful fats.

Best-High Quality Fat Sources

- Olives and olive oil
- Other vegetable oils (such as safflower or canola)
- Avocados
- Nuts, such as almonds, walnuts, macadamia nuts, and pecans
- Seeds, such as sunflower, pumpkin, sesame, flaxseed
- Fish and fish oils (especially from wild-caught coldwater fish such as salmon, tuna, sardines, herrings, and mackerel)

Fats to Avoid

You may have heard about trans fats, found in vegetable oils that have had hydrogen added (a process called hydrogenation) to make them shelf-stable. Trans fats are toxic to cells and cause oxidation, leading to rapid aging, inflammation, low energy, and fatigue—which in turn can cause you to crave sugar for a quick energy hit. Nutrition facts labels now specify how many grams of trans fats a product contains, but thanks to a tricky loophole, if the amount is less than 0.5 grams per serving, manufacturers are allowed to round down and claim that the product contains 0 grams. Those small amounts can add up quickly, however, so the surest path to avoiding trans fats is to read ingredients labels and shun products made with partially hydrogenated oils.

Carbohydrates: Choose Wisely to Avoid Sugar Shock

Carbohydrates are macronutrients found in virtually all plant foods. Their primary role is to supply energy to the body, especially the brain. All carbohydrates, whether simple or complex, eventually convert into the same thing—blood sugar, or glucose. If you eat a meal that is primarily made of refined carbohydrates, such as a bowl of cereal, fruit juice, or toast made with white flour, the level of glucose in your body rises swiftly. When large amounts of glucose enter the bloodstream at one time, your body releases excessive insulin to lower your blood sugar. These elevated insulin levels then cause your blood sugar to plummet, leading to severe sugar cravings. Even worse, having repeatedly elevated insulin levels causes insulin resistance, meaning that your body converts excess carbohydrates into fat, and resulting in weight gain you can't lose until you stop overdosing on sugar.

Problems can also occur for some people if they don't eat enough carbohydrates (for example, eating a breakfast of only eggs and bacon). High-protein, high-fat, low-carbohydrate diets can leave susceptible people feeling sluggish or even depressed. So listen to your body to see what feels best to you!

You should get about 40 to 50 percent of your daily calories from carbohydrates. The best sources are whole and whole-grain foods high in fiber, low in starch, and low in sugar. Fiber helps your body digest foods more slowly, providing a steady stream of glucose that won't trigger insulin spikes and blood sugar crashes.

Best High-Quality Carbohydrate Sources

- Whole Fruits: Apples, oranges, grapefruit, strawberries, pears, peaches, and plums. Avoid juices and canned fruit.
- Vegetables: Broccoli, asparagus, green beans, cauliflower, zucchini, and spinach
- Grains: Barley, oatmeal, rye, brown and wild rice, and whole wheat
- Legumes: Black beans, white beans, garbanzo beans, kidney beans, and lentils

Enzymes Feed Your Body's "Energy Factories"

Enzymes are large proteins that support life. Enzymes are particularly effective in providing energy to cells because they speed up the breakdown of food into fuel and accelerate your metabolism in general. Without them, we easily become fatigued and run-down—and crave sugar for an energy boost.

Many of my patients have found that adding more raw foods to their diets ensures that they get a variety of enzymes that give them natural energy, which ultimately helps them stabilize their blood sugar levels and beat sugar addiction. A simple way to do this is to eat raw fruits and vegetables (such as in a green salad) every day.

Good Info to Know!

If you have indigestion (one of the many problems aggravated by sugar addiction), it may be because of a lack of enzymes in your food. Naturally occurring enzymes that ripen foods are also needed for digestion. Food processors have learned that they can prolong a food's shelf life by destroying its enzymes. Unfortunately, this can make the food hard to digest, causing indigestion. To restore healthy digestion, I recommend taking two capsules of a plant-based digestive enzyme (for example, Complete-Gest by Enzymatic Therapy) with each meal.

Antioxidants

Antioxidants are natural compounds that help protect the body from harmful free radicals, unstable molecules that steal electrons from healthy cells—a process called oxidization. In one way or another, free radicals are involved in the progression of almost every ailment because of the oxidative stress and inflammation that they cause. The common denominator in the process of aging and its associated diseases is oxidative damage. Consuming too many empty calories in the form of sugar leads to antioxidant deficiencies—one reason sugar is a major contributor to illness and premature aging.

Diet can have a profound effect on antioxidant levels in the human body, providing essential antioxidant vitamins such as A, C, and E, and the precursor of vitamin A, beta-carotene. Beta-carotene is found in red/orange/yellow vegetables and fruits. Vitamin C is also abundant in vegetables and fruits eaten raw, but heat rapidly destroys it. Vitamin E is found in "seed" foods including nuts, seeds, and their oils; vegetables such as peas, broad beans, and corn; and whole grains. The more colorful a fruit or vegetable, the higher its antioxidant levels.

Fiber Keeps Blood Sugar Balanced

Fiber, or "roughage," is found almost exclusively in plant foods—vegetables, fruits, legumes, whole grains, nuts, and seeds. Diets high in vegetable fiber are also high in magnesium, which reduces your risk of diabetes by 47 percent. While there are many other aspects of health and metabolism that contribute to healthy blood sugar function, research shows that diets high in fiber, low in sugar, and high in magnesium markedly decrease the risk of developing diabetes, a key measure of blood sugar health. Aim for at least 40 to 50 grams of fiber per day.

Good Info to Know!

Avoid overcooking vegetables and fruit, which destroys much of their nutritional content. Instead, lightly cook or steam foods until they are crisp-tender (never mushy).

Best High-Quality Fiber Sources

Each of the following food items contains 10 grams of dietary fiber:

Vegetables
- ½ cup (96 g) mixed beans, lentils
- ½ cup (75 g) peas
- 1 cup (145 g) peanuts

- 2 cups (515 g) soybeans
- 2 cups (360 g) steamed vegetables
- 4 servings mixed salad
- 4 carrots

Fruits

- 3 pears
- 3 bananas
- 4 peaches
- 4 ounces blueberries
- 5 apples
- 6 oranges
- 6 dried pear halves
- 10 dried figs
- 20 prunes
- 20 dried apricots

Grains

- ½ cup (30 g) All-Bran cereal
- 1 cup (80 g) rolled oats
- 1 cup (30 g) whole-grain cereal
- 2 cobs sweet corn
- 3 slices whole rye bread
- 3 cups (35 g) puffed wheat
- 4-ounce (115 g) bag popcorn

CHAPTER 3

How to Use This Cookbook to Beat Sugar Addiction Now!

To make it easier to choose the recipes that will best help you kick the sugar habit, we've included a rating for each recipe that takes into account the six health facilitators covered in Chapter 2. These ratings give you a quick and easy guideline for planning nutritious meals that keep blood sugar levels stable and balanced and help you beat sugar cravings. The more nutrient-dense a meal is, by way of both macro- and micronutrients, the more stable and balanced your blood sugar levels will become, and the faster you will recover from your sugar addiction!

HOW THE RATING SYSTEM WORKS

Every recipe contains an easy-to-read chart (see example on page 35) rating each of the health facilitators, which we've combined to give an overall rating of that particular recipe's ability to balance your blood sugar. A recipe's **Blood Sugar Balance Rating** will be labeled None, Low, Medium, High, or Very High, depending on that recipe's macronutrients and fiber content.

None—no useful quantity present in the recipe

Low—small amounts present

Medium—provides average levels

High—provides better-than-average levels

Very High—provides optimum levels

For example, a leafy green salad contains enzymes, antioxidants, fiber, carbohydrate, and protein, all in varying amounts. By including some avocado, tuna, olive oil, walnuts, and sunflower seeds, you raise both the fat and the protein content, which also raises its blood sugar balance rating.

By understanding the health facilitator categories and nutrient density of the foods in each recipe, you will be able to use your own creativity by adding and deleting ingredients until you optimally balance your blood sugar. In a short time, by working with these recipes and following the principles outlined above, you will become an expert at "listening to your body" and fine-tuning these and other recipes to your particular health needs. For more information, see the Glycemic Index in Appendix B.

Now, it's time to learn about the recipes for your unique sugar addiction type(s). If you are not sure which type you are, take the quiz at the beginning of each chapter. Then you can follow the recommendations and use the recipes for that specific type, along with the recipes for all types to help you squash your sugar habit for good. Let's get started!

TUNA SALAD

For Salad

4 cups (80 g) mixed leafy salad greens
8 ounces (225 g) water-packed tuna, flaked
1 avocado, cubed
½ cup (70 g) diced cucumber
½ cup (50 g) sliced radishes
½ cup (60 g) diced celery
½ cup (60 g) grated carrots
½ cup (45 g) thinly sliced fennel
½ cup (110 g) raw sunflower seeds
½ cup (60 g) chopped raw walnuts

For Dressing

¼ cup (60 ml) extra-virgin olive oil
2 tablespoons (30 ml) flaxseed oil
1 lemon, squeezed
1 clove garlic, pressed
Dash of cayenne

To make the salad: In a large bowl, toss together all salad ingredients.

To make the dressing: Combine dressing ingredients in a small bowl or lidded jar. Whisk in bowl or shake jar vigorously to combine.

Pour dressing over salad and toss gently. Serve immediately.

YIELD: 4 SERVINGS

EACH WITH: Calories 444.35; Fat 36.42 g; Cholesterol 17.01 mg; Total Carbohydrates 12.76 g; Fiber 6.06 g; Protein 20.11 g

BLOOD SUGAR BALANCE RATING: Very High

Health Facilitators	Nutrient Density Rating
Protein	High
Fat	High
Carbohydrate	High
Enzymes	High
Antioxidants	Very High
Fiber	High

You can also modify a recipe to adjust the health facilitators and raise its blood sugar–balancing effects. Here are some suggestions, using this tuna salad as an example:

- To increase the protein, add a hard-boiled egg, extra tuna (or swap in salmon or chicken), or feta cheese.
- To increase the fatty acid levels, add black olives or feta.
- Adding grains and legumes like brown rice, lentils, garbanzo beans, and quinoa will increase the protein, carbohydrate, and fiber levels.
- To increase enzymes, simply add raw vegetables.
- For more antioxidants and fiber, add more vegetables (any of the ones listed, or other non-starchy picks).

CHAPTER 4

Type 1 Sugar Addiction

The Energy Loan Shark: Chronically exhausted and hooked on quick hits of caffeine and sugar

ARE YOU A TYPE 1 SUGAR ADDICT?

Your total score will tell you whether you fit the Type 1 profile.

____Do you feel tired much of the time? (20 points)

____Do you need coffee to get jumpstarted in the morning? (10 points)

____Do you experience a mid-afternoon slump? (10 points)

____Do you have occasional insomnia? (20 points)

____Do you have indigestion? (15 points)

____Do you feel achy? (15 points)

____Do you have frequent headaches? (15 points)

____Are you gaining weight? Or have trouble losing weight? (Score 1 point for every two pounds gained over the past three years.)

____What is the average number of ounces of nondiet soda or caffeinated coffee you drink daily? (Score 2 points for each ounce.)

____What is the average number of ounces of "energy drinks" containing sugar or caffeine that you drink daily? (Score 6 points for each ounce.)

____Do you repeatedly crave sweets or caffeine to give you the energy to get through the day? (25 points)

____Are you working more than forty hours a week? (Score 2 points for each hour over forty.)

____Your total score

Score

0–40: No problem. Skip to the quiz at the beginning of the next chapter.

41–70: The recipes in this chapter will help restore your blood sugar balance and optimize energy production.

Over 70: Type 1 sugar addiction is a major issue for you. Enjoy these recipes!

THE TYPE 1 SUGAR ADDICT

If you are a Type 1 Sugar Addict, it's likely that you are a type-A personality who strives for perfection and is constantly on the go, go, go. Twenty-four hours is just not enough time to get your to-do list done! Rather than rely on a well-balanced diet (regular exercise also takes a back seat) to give you the energy you need, you eat on the run and turn to the quick fix of energy drinks like Red Bull, coffee, and soda. Energy drinks temporarily boost energy with sugar and caffeine, but the energy boost is artificial. The empty calories these loan sharks provide don't help your body produce energy at all, so you end up spending energy you don't have. Just a few hours later you are in worse shape than when you started. That's because that quick hit of sugar causes your insulin to spike as it tries to get your blood sugar levels under control, and the resulting steep drop in blood sugar leaves you feeling even more fatigued than before and craving more sugar. Eventually, you become a Type 1 Sugar Addict.

Energy Drinks: the Good, the Bad, and the Ugly

So-called energy drinks have resulted in an energy crisis worldwide. Most of them are simply a nickel's worth of sugar, caffeine, and water. The other components on the label, such as vitamins and nutrients, are usually present in such low doses that they are unlikely to have any effect. Furthermore, researchers at Henry Ford Hospital in Detroit found that energy drinks with caffeine can increase heart rates and blood pressure levels, which is especially a concern for people with cardiovascular problems due to diabetes or other conditions related to poor blood sugar control.

Energy drinks that are safe should be sugar-free, contain less than 60 to 75 mg caffeine, and include significant levels of nutrients such as B vitamins, magnesium, ribose, amino acids, and other nutrients. A healthy energy drink might include:

Key Components		Optional Add-Ins	
Ribose	1,000–1,500 mg	Taurine	500 mg
Magnesium	100–200 mg	Tyrosine	500 mg
B1, B2, B3, B5, B6	5–20 mg each	Folate	100–200 mcg
		Vitamin C	50–80 mg
Caffeine	40–60 mg OR guarana 37.5–75 mg OR green tea base	Vitamin D	100–200 IU
		CoQ10	20 mg
		Rhodiola	400
Iodine	200 mcg	Acetyl-l-Carnitine	100–300 mg
B12	100–1,000 mcg		

Type 1 Sugar Addiction Takes a Toll on Your Health

Not only do Type 1 addicts need to continually get a "fix" of sugar and caffeine all day long, using sweets and energy drinks repeatedly to artificially boost energy can also lead to all sorts of health problems, including a weakened immune system, poor sleep, headaches, high blood pressure, and, when severe, even chronic fatigue syndrome (CFS) and fibromyalgia. Over the past 10 years, the incidence of CFS and fibromyalgia has exploded by more than 400 percent, with over 12 million Americans (three-quarters of them female) being affected! Meanwhile more than 30 percent of adults are chronically fatigued, and most people feel like they simply don't have enough energy.

Sugar Impairs Your Immune System

The biggest overarching problem sugar addicts face is a weakened immune system. The amount of sugar in one can of an energy drink or soda has been shown to suppress your immune system by 30 percent over three hours!

In addition, when you repeatedly pump the empty calories from sugar into your body, you're less likely to consume enough of essential nutrients like zinc that we need for proper immune function.

Sugar suppresses your immune system in a host of ways beyond nutritional deficiencies as well. For example, being on the sugar roller coaster for an extended time can wear out your adrenal glands (see Chapter 6 for more information about sugar and adrenal health). Your adrenals play a key role in regulating your immune system, so when sugar sends them off-balance, weakened immunity leaves you more susceptible to frequent infections and autoimmune illnesses.

Excess sugar can also lead to an overgrowth of the yeast candida (see Chapter 8 for more information about candida). These organisms, which thrive on sugar, exhaust your immune system in two key ways. One is by their sheer size, being thousands of times larger than a virus. In addition, they cause breaks in the intestinal lining (called "leaky gut"), which results in partially digested food particles being absorbed into the blood. Your immune system has to treat these as invaders (just like fighting an infection), and can get exhausted by breaking them down.

You can tell if your immune function is impaired if you seem to always have a cold, the flu, or a sore throat. In more severe cases, immune dysfunction can lead to short-term infections becoming chronic, such as chronic Epstein-Barr virus and chronic Lyme disease. Most importantly, sugar can also trigger infections, including candida, which will leave you tired and reaching for more sugar. Once you get your sugar intake under control and get proper nutritional support, you may be pleasantly surprised at how few infections you do get and how quickly they go away!

High Sugar Intake Leads to Insomnia, Weight Gain, and Diabetes

Insomnia is a common problem for Type 1 addicts because it actually takes energy for the hypothalamic sleep center to work properly, and if your main source of energy is caffeine and sugar, that's not exactly going to help you fall or stay asleep. Sleep is critical for many functions. It recharges your batteries (so you don't rely on sugar for energy), helps tissues repair, and enables you to produce growth hormone. Without enough growth hormone, you will gain weight (from fat) and lose muscle mass. Sleep also regulates the production of ghrelin and leptin, our appetite-controlling hormones. When ghrelin and leptin are out of balance, it's much harder to resist cravings, especially for high-calorie foods such as sweets. In fact, research shows that getting less than 7 hours of sleep a night increases the risk of obesity by as much as 30 percent, and sleep-deprived folks weigh an extra 5½ pounds (2.5 kg), on average, than their well-rested peers.

Carrying excess weight (especially as fat) increases your risk of insulin resistance. Insulin resistance means insulin cannot get sugar out of your bloodstream and into your cells where it is needed as fuel. That leaves you endlessly craving sugar, overweight, exhausted, and, if the insulin resistance gets severe enough, even diabetic.

EATING TO BALANCE BLOOD SUGAR

To stop the destruction that sugar leaves in its wake, it's time to go back to basics. The first step? No more quick fixes from "loan shark" sweets and energy drinks loaded with sugar and caffeine. From now on, you'll be choosing foods that keep your blood sugar balanced throughout the day, slash sugar cravings, support your immune system, and replenish vital nutrients such as B vitamins, zinc, and magnesium. When you change the way you eat, you'll dramatically improve your energy and no longer need to rely on sugar and unhealthy energy drinks, ending the cycle of addiction.

Have an Energizing Cup of Tea

For a safe, energizing drink, brew some green tea. It's packed with theanine, an amino acid that boosts energy while leaving your mind calm, clear, and relaxed. You can have your regular cup of coffee in morning, but switch to green tea for the rest of day. To avoid caffeine withdrawal headaches, reduce the amount of coffee you drink by half every week or two until you get down to one cup (8 ounces [235 ml]) a day.

Top Nutrients for Type 1 Sugar Addicts

The recipes in this section provide nutrients that reduce your risk of insulin resistance by stabilizing your blood sugar, produce natural energy, combat stress, support immune function, and help you stay sharp and alert. Here are some of the standout nutrients.

B-complex Vitamins Keep You Energized but Calm

Often called your stress vitamins because they increase energy and help you stay cool under pressure, the B vitamins work together to encourage cell growth and division, help your immune system and nervous system work properly, boost metabolism, keep your skin and muscles healthy, and support your health in a variety of other ways. Their specific sugar-busting benefits are listed below.

Brewer's yeast is one of the best sources of B vitamins. Other food sources include leafy green vegetables, nuts, legumes, eggs, organ meats, chicken, and fish such as salmon and tuna. Most of the recipes in this cookbook include one or more of the B vitamins. Even though you can get the recommended daily allowance through these recipes, because the B vitamins are critical for energy production, I recommend supplementing with a multivitamin that contains at least 50 mg each of vitamins B1, B2, B3, B5, and B6, plus 250 mcg of B12 and 400 mcg of folate. Here's a breakdown of how B vitamins help Type 1 sugar addicts:

Thiamine (B1) In addition to helping your cells produce energy, vitamin B1 is critical for proper brain functioning, making it especially important for Type 1 sugar addicts who have "brain fog." Research shows that supplementation with vitamin B1 improves mood, possibly by increasing synthesis of acetylcholine, a neurotransmitter associated with memory, along with making you more clearheaded, composed, and energetic.

Riboflavin (B2) This B vitamin is especially critical for energy production. In addition, research shows that higher doses (75–400 mg/day) of B2 decrease migraine frequency (a common problem in sugar addicts) by 67 percent after six to twelve weeks.

Niacin (B3) Niacin is a key part of the energy molecule NADH (which also helps make the mood-boosting neurotransmitter dopamine).

Pantothenic acid (B5) This B vitamin helps your adrenal glands function optimally to produce hormones such as adrenaline and cortisol.

Pyridoxine (B6) Vitamin B6 enhances immune function. Type 1 sugar addicts often experience fluid retention, and supplementing with B6 at higher doses (50 to 200 mg a day) can help with this.

Cobalamin (B12) Vitamin B12 is another key nutrient in energy production and brain function.

Folic acid/Folate Some studies show that supplementing with 800 mcg of folate a day can help memory and improve cognitive function, mimicking some of the effects of caffeine but without being addictive. Other research suggests limiting your supplemental dose to 400 mcg a day is best, so that's what I recommend.

Magnesium Regulates Insulin and Metabolism

Magnesium deficiency may contribute to obesity by increasing the risk of insulin resistance. In fact, one 15-year study found that people with high magnesium intakes had a 31 percent lower chance of developing "metabolic syndrome," a common form of insulin resistance flared by excess sugar intake, a major cause of heart attacks.

Magnesium is directly involved in the metabolism of proteins, fats, and carbohydrates, and it helps your muscles and cells store adequate amounts of fuels for long-lasting energy. Consuming magnesium-rich foods will help you to beat sugar addiction by keeping you calm in times of stress.

Good sources of magnesium include broccoli, spinach, Swiss chard, kale, green beans, celery, turnip and mustard greens, squash, blackstrap molasses, halibut, and a variety of seeds, including sunflower, sesame, and flaxseed. You will find sources of magnesium in many of the recipes that follow. In addition, I suggest supplementing with 150–400 mg/day (your daily multi might contain enough).

Zinc Strengthens Immunity

Zinc is highly beneficial for helping to balance and support the immune system. Recurrent infections caused by yeast, such as sinusitis and spastic colon, are often treated with antibiotics and can also make you deficient in zinc. Unfortunately, antibiotics allow yeast to thrive, which causes big-time sugar cravings. Getting enough zinc through diet and in your daily multi will help ward off infections and prevent you from spiraling into a yeast-induced sugar addiction. Foods containing zinc include sea vegetables, spinach, mushrooms, asparagus, collard and mustard greens, squash, chard, broccoli, peas, shrimp, beef, lamb, chicken liver, pumpkin seeds, sesame seeds, venison, and maple syrup.

Ribose: The Amazing Sugar-Free Sugar

Ribose, a special type of sugar, does not raise blood sugar or feed yeast overgrowth, but because it looks and tastes like sugar, you can use it as a sugar substitute. It actually has a negative glycemic index and will tend to lower blood sugar in diabetics, and it may even contribute to weight loss as well.

Ribose is also an excellent nutrient for energy production. A recent study I led of 257 chronic fatigue syndrome and fibromyalgia patients at 53 medical centers found that taking ribose daily boosted energy by an average 61 percent after three weeks! It also was quite effective in helping mental clarity, sleep, and overall well-being while decreasing pain. In addition to its role in making DNA and RNA, ribose is the key building block for generating energy. In fact, the main energy molecules in your body are made of ribose plus B vitamins or phosphate. Ribose may well be the ultimate energy nutrient!

Start with a (5 g) scoop of ribose three times a day for three to six weeks, then decrease to one scoop once or twice a day, but lower the dose if you get hyper from being too energized. Try it for a month to see if it works for you. Find it at www.vitality101.com or in most health food stores under the brand name Corvalen.

Using Low-Glycemic Foods to Balance Blood Sugar

The recipes in this cookbook also incorporate foods that are low on the glycemic index. (See sidebar on page 46 and the glycemic index in Appendix B to guide you to make healthy choices). When you eat these foods, they raise blood sugar slowly and gradually, preventing blood sugar spikes and sugar cravings.

One of the most important low-glycemic, blood sugar–balancing nutrients is fiber. Fiber prevents the sugar in foods from being absorbed quickly and causing blood sugar to spike. You'll find fiber-rich ingredients such as quinoa, whole wheat flour, and brown rice are the focus of many of the recipes here. We also direct you to vegetables that are high in fiber and low on the glycemic index. Since fruits tend to be high in sugar and have a high glycemic index, we'll show you how to use them to satisfy your sugar cravings in a way that is healthy.

You'll also find recipes for chicken, meat, eggs, and fish—high-protein foods with a zero glycemic index, which raise blood sugar only slightly.

What Is the Glycemic Index?

The glycemic index (GI) gives us an idea of which foods raise blood glucose fastest and highest. Pure glucose is given a GI score of 100; all other foods are then measured in relation to glucose. A food with a glycemic index over 85 raises blood sugar almost as much as pure glucose, but a food with a glycemic index under 30 does not raise blood sugar much at all. See Appendix B for the glycemic index scores of many common foods.

Start with Breakfast

When it comes to controlling blood sugar, breakfast is the most important meal of the day for Type 1 sugar addicts. Unfortunately, for always-on-the-go Type 1s, breakfast is also the one meal you are most likely to skip. This is a mistake because it depletes your energy reserves and makes you hungry throughout the day. It also means that you are more likely to reach for a quick fix of caffeine and sugar. When you eat a proper breakfast, it allows you to restock the energy stores that have been depleted overnight and begin the day with a tank full of the right fuel.

The breakfast (and lunch and dinner) recipes you'll find here contain all three of the macronutrients—lean protein, healthy fats, and low-glycemic carbohydrates—you need most. Starting with breakfast, consuming regular meals throughout the day will keep your blood sugar levels balanced and allow you to function at your best. So, it's very important that you not skip any meals, and you may find you need to add in a snack or two. You'll know when your blood sugar levels have become too low if you:

- feel hungry or have "hunger pains."
- feel shaky or start to tremble.
- feel drowsy, fatigued, or dizzy and need to sit down.
- feel confused or have brain fog.
- notice your heart rate increases rapidly.
- get headaches or migraines.
- feel moody, irritable, or cranky.
- have blurred or double vision.
- have seizures or convulsions.
- lose consciousness (pass out).

The SHINE Protocol

Diet and nutrition are one element of a comprehensive recovery plan for Type 1 Sugar Addiction that I call the SHINE protocol. I have used this highly effective, holistic treatment plan to help tens of thousands of my patients recover from chronic fatigue and fibromyalgia. Here's an overview.

SHINE stands for:

*S*leep. You'll learn how to sleep better and treat sleep disorders.

*H*ormonal support. You'll learn if you need hormonal support, for example, if you have hypothyroidism.

*I*nfections. You'll learn how to boost your immune system, making you more resistant to cold and flu.

Nutritional support. You'll learn which vitamins and minerals can give you energy naturally.

Exercise. You'll learn how to move for health.

You can learn more about the SHINE Protocol by reading *Beat Sugar Addiction Now!* and by visiting www.beatsugaraddictionnow.com. In addition, you can use a free online symptom analysis program at www.Vitality101.com that helps determine the cause of your fatigue, CFS, or fibromyalgia, and tailors a treatment protocol for you.

For now, let's focus on recipes that will help heal your sugar addiction.

CHAPTER 5

Recipes for Type 1 Sugar Addiction

These recipes are easy to prepare, which is a big plus in your on-the-go lifestyle. Over time, you will find that you actually prefer eating this way because it just tastes better! You're not looking to deny yourself pleasure. In fact, pleasure is good! You are simply learning healthier ways to enjoy your food. That makes this healthy form of eating easy to sustain, because it becomes a habit over the long term. Remember, the best approach is to simply listen to your body by noticing what foods and combinations leave you feeling the best. Let's get cookin'!

GROUNDING GRAINS WITH BERRIES, NUTS, AND SEEDS

This is one of the most nutrient-dense, fiber-filled breakfasts you can eat to both balance blood sugar and give you energy. This balanced meal of plant proteins, healthy fats, and low-GI carbohydrates also contains raw foods to help digestion. Flaxseeds are high in filling fiber and omega-3s, which help fight inflammation. Almonds are probably the best all-around nut for protein, with 6 grams of protein per ounce. They are also high in antioxidant vitamin E, energy-producing B vitamins, and calcium.

Other noteworthy ingredients include pumpkin seeds, a great source of immunity-strengthening zinc. Research published in the *Journal of Agriculture and Food Chemistry* in 2005 showed that they also are high in phytosterols, a plant compound shown to lower bad cholesterol levels. Sunflower seeds also contain high amounts of phytosterols and boost energy.

1 tablespoon (9 g) raw almonds
1 tablespoon (14 g) raw sunflower seeds
1 tablespoon (14 g) raw pumpkin seeds
2 tablespoons (20 g) flaxseeds
½ to 1 cup (120 to 240 ml) almond, rice, or cow's milk
½ to 1 cup (80 to 165 g) cooked whole-grain brown rice (optional)
½ to 1 cup (120 to 240 ml) goat's milk or cow's milk yogurt
½ to 1 cup (75 to 200 g) fresh fruit (such as berries, peaches, pears, or banana)
1 tablespoon (15 ml) flaxseed oil

Soak the almonds, sunflower, and pumpkin seeds in purified water overnight to enhance digestibility and increase enzymes. Place soaked nut/seed mixture and flaxseeds in a coffee grinder or food processor and blend into a meal. Place in a bowl and add rice (if using, almond or rice milk, yogurt, fruit, and flaxseed oil coarse). Serve immediately.

YIELD: 1 SERVING

EACH WITH: Calories 666.11; Calories from Fat 336.94; Total Fat 38.54 g; Cholesterol 16.68 mg; Sodium 149.26 mg; Potassium 646.5 mg; Total Carbohydrates 63.7 g; Fiber 10.74 g; Sugar 10.5 g; Protein 22.62 g

BLOOD SUGAR BALANCE RATING: Very High

Health Facilitators	Nutrient Density Rating
Protein	High
Fat	Medium
Carbohydrate	High
Enzymes	Very High
Antioxidants	High
Fiber	Very High

FATIGUE-FIGHTING FETA FRITTATA

2 teaspoons (10 ml) unsalted butter, extra-virgin olive oil, or coconut oil
½ red or brown onion, chopped
½ cup (60 g) zucchini, chopped
3 whole eggs, well beaten
1 cup (67 g) kale, chopped
¼ cup (15 g) parsley, chopped
2 tablespoons (20 g) crumbled sheep's milk feta

Preheat broiler. Heat the butter or oil in a small ovenproof skillet over medium-high heat. Sauté onions and zucchini until onions are translucent, about 5 minutes. Add the eggs, kale, parsley, and feta, and cook without stirring, tilting the skillet while lifting the edge of the cooked egg with a spatula, allowing uncooked egg to flow underneath. When no more uncooked egg will flow, place skillet under the broiler and broil until top begins to brown, 1 to 2 minutes.

YIELD: 3 TO 4 SERVINGS

EACH WITH: Calories 101.29; Calories From Fat 60.83; Total Fat 6.83 g; Cholesterol 167.88 mg; Sodium 116.54 mg; Potassium 212.29 mg; Total Carbohydrates 4.34 g; Fiber 0.89 g; Sugar 1.43 g; Protein 6.42 g

BLOOD SUGAR BALANCE RATING: Very High

Health Facilitators	Nutrient Density Rating
Protein	Very High
Fat	Medium
Carbohydrate	High
Enzymes	Medium
Antioxidants	High
Fiber	High

Hail to kale because it rules for Type 1 sugar addicts when it comes to health benefits and nutrients. In fact, the USDA ranks kale as one of the best antioxidant sources. It's loaded with vitamins C, A, and K, which are excellent immune boosters for Type 1s. Parsley also contains these vitamins, plus energy-boosting magnesium and iron. Add in zucchini and onions (which provide zinc; magnesium; calcium; iron; vitamins C, A, K, B6, B1, and folate; and dietary fiber), and this frittata offers all the nourishment you need to help you balance blood sugar and feel energized for hours. Fiber, protein, and good fats round out the tastes, textures, and nutritional benefits.

PROTEIN POWER SMOOTHIE

A smoothie for breakfast is quick and easy to prepare and to take with you on the run—something Type 1s love because of their busy lifestyles. This smoothie is nutrient-dense, with plenty of protein and healthy fats to give you long-lasting energy. Nutritional yeast is packed full of B vitamins and minerals, while the nuts and seeds add protein, good fats, and fiber, plus tons of vitamins and minerals. The milk and yogurt provide calcium to strengthen bones and magnesium to relax your nervous system. This means you'll have more energy throughout the day.

1 cup (240 ml) cow's or goat's milk
½ cup (120 ml) plain yogurt
½ cup (120 ml) coconut milk
½ cup (75 to 100 g) fresh fruit (such as berries or peaches)
2 tablespoons (16 g) or 1 large scoop of rice, egg, or whey protein powder
1 teaspoon to 1 tablespoon (7 to 12 g) nutritional yeast (optional)
2 tablespoons (18 g) raw almonds, walnuts, sesame seeds, pumpkin seeds, and/or sunflower seeds
2 tablespoons (20 g) flaxseeds, freshly ground

Combine all ingredients in a blender. Blend well, and serve immediately.

YIELD: 3 TO 4 SERVINGS

EACH WITH: Calories 190.85; Calories From Fat 98.94; Total Fat 11.77 g; Cholesterol 6.37 mg; Sodium 66.96 mg; Potassium 297.77 mg; Total Carbohydrates 12.05 g; Fiber 2.81 g; Sugar 7.35 g; Protein 12.9 g

BLOOD SUGAR BALANCE RATING: Very High

NOTE: If you have milk allergies, avoid the whey protein powder and substitute coconut milk, almond milk, or water for the milk and yogurt.

Health Facilitators	Nutrient Density Rating
Protein	High
Fat	High
Carbohydrate	Medium
Enzymes	High
Antioxidants	High
Fiber	High

STRESS-SQUASHING MUSHROOM AND ASPARAGUS OMELET

1⅓ teaspoons unsalted butter or coconut oil
⅔ cup (47 g) shiitake or white mushrooms, sliced
2 tablespoons (20 g) diced red or brown onion
4 large eggs
½ cup (67 g) asparagus tips, steamed until tender
¼ cup (15 g) parsley, chopped
2 tablespoons (20 g) feta or Parmesan cheese
2 tablespoons (30 ml) purified water
Salt and freshly ground black pepper to taste

Heat the butter or oil in a medium skillet over moderate heat. Add mushrooms and onions and sauté for 4 minutes. Remove pan from heat then add cheese and water. In a small bowl, combine eggs and beat with a fork or hand mixer. Add cooked mushrooms, onions, and asparagus tips. Spray the skillet with nonstick cooking spray and return to moderate heat. Pour egg mixture into the pan and allow it to cook, undisturbed, until the eggs are mostly set. If necessary, gently lift the edges of the cooked egg and allow the uncooked portion to run underneath to cook. Once the omelet is slightly browned, use a wide spatula to lift and turn the omelet over quickly. Cook on the second side until golden brown. Slide the omelet out of the skillet onto a serving plate. Season with salt and pepper to taste. Slice and serve hot.

YIELD: 2 TO 3 SERVINGS

EACH WITH: Calories 139.27; Calories From Fat 84.43; Total Fat 9.45 g; Cholesterol 289.45 mg; Sodium 220.67 mg; Potassium 248.23 mg; Total Carbohydrates 3.33 g; Fiber 1.03 g; Sugar 1.52 g; Protein 11.11 g

BLOOD SUGAR BALANCE RATING: Very High

Health Facilitators	Nutrient Density Rating
Protein	High
Fat	High
Carbohydrate	High
Enzymes	High
Antioxidants	High
Fiber	High

This omelet will keep your blood sugar levels stable for hours and help you stay calm and balanced. Eggs are an excellent source of protein, choline, selenium, vitamin D, and B vitamins for fighting stress. Feta is chock full of protein, calcium, and tryptophan for enhancing your mood and keeping you calm. Parsley contains tons of vitamins C, A, and K, plus magnesium and iron for boosting your immune system. Shiitake mushrooms provide plant protein, more B vitamins, and minerals, and also boost immunity. And asparagus offers more vitamins and minerals and is a great source of fiber to help you feel full longer.

CRAVING-CONQUERING COCONUT VEGGIE MUFFINS

Coconuts are rich in protein, healthy fats (research published in the *American Journal of Clinical Nutrition* showed coconut oil may help prevent heart disease, atherosclerosis, and colon cancer), and low-glycemic carbohydrates, making them the ideal food to keep your blood sugar levels perfectly balanced. Not only that, they taste delicious! If you have never tried coconut flour, you're in for an added treat. These muffins work well for breakfast, lunch, a light dinner, or as a snack. The addition of kale and spinach (which are packed with potent antioxidants) and pumpkin seeds (which are chock full of zinc) not only boosts your immune function but makes the muffins even more delicious.

1 tablespoon (15 ml) extra-virgin olive oil or coconut oil
2 cups (250 g) coconut flour
½ cup (30 g) finely chopped fresh parsley
Pinch of sea salt
2 eggs, beaten
1 cup (130 g) grated or finely chopped vegetables (try squash, kale, spinach, and/or crimini mushrooms)
1 tablespoon (14 g) pumpkin seeds, roughly chopped
1 cup (240 ml) coconut, rice, or almond milk
1 avocado, cut into quarters
Freshly ground black pepper

Preheat oven to 325°F (170°C, or gas mark 3). Lightly oil a muffin pan with coconut oil. Mix flour, parsley, and salt in a bowl. Add eggs, vegetables, and pumpkin seeds, and mix lightly. Gradually stir in milk. Batter will be lumpy. Pour batter into prepared muffin pan and bake for 12 to 15 minutes. Remove from oven and let cool for 10 minutes before serving. Serve with an avocado wedge and sprinkle with pepper to taste.

YIELD: 4 SERVINGS
EACH WITH: Calories 492.6; Calories From Fat 237.68; Total Fat 27.92 g; Cholesterol 105.75 mg; Sodium 127.6 mg; Potassium 568.43 mg; Total Carbohydrates 52.51 g; Fiber 27.94 g; Sugar 1.16g; Protein 13.74 g
BLOOD SUGAR BALANCE RATING: Very High

Health Facilitators	Nutrient Density Rating
Protein	High
Fat	Moderate
Carbohydrate	High
Enzymes	Very High
Antioxidants	High
Fiber	Very High

TRYPTOPHAN-RICH TURKEY MEATLOAF MEDLEY

1 tablespoon (15 ml) extra-virgin olive oil or coconut oil
20 ounces (570 g) lean ground turkey, beef, or chicken
2 large eggs
½ cup (40 g) rolled oats
⅔ cup (110 g) chopped onion
½ cup (120 ml) tomato sauce, divided
1 tablespoon (4 g) fresh parsley, chopped
2 tablespoons (8 g) fresh cilantro, chopped
1 clove fresh garlic, chopped finely or minced
1 tablespoon (15 ml) Bragg's liquid amino acid or tamari sauce (wheat-free)
Salt and pepper to taste

Preheat oven to 350°F (180°C, or gas mark 4). Lightly coat the bottom of a shallow baking pan with the olive oil or coconut oil. Combine ground turkey, eggs, rolled oats, and onion in a medium bowl and mix thoroughly. Mix in ¼ cup (60 ml) of the tomato sauce, parsley, cilantro, garlic, and liquid amino acids or tamari. Add salt and pepper to taste. Shape the mixture into an oval loaf and place in prepared baking dish. Pour the remaining ¼ cup (60 ml) of tomato sauce over the meatloaf, cover with foil, and bake for 45 minutes, removing the foil for the last 10 minutes of baking. Remove the meatloaf from the pan immediately. Slice and serve with a green salad or steamed vegetables.

YIELD: 6 TO 8 SERVINGS

EACH WITH: Calories 218.61; Calories From Fat 101.05; Total Fat 11.25 g; Cholesterol 142.46 mg; Sodium 497.89 mg; Potassium 436.22 mg; Total Carbohydrates 5.8 g; Fiber 1.34 g; Sugar 1.36 g; Protein 22.71 g

BLOOD SUGAR BALANCE RATING: Very High

Health Facilitators	Nutrient Density Rating
Protein	Very High
Fat	Medium
Carbohydrate	Medium
Enzymes	Low
Antioxidants	High
Fiber	Medium

Turkey contains high amounts of tryptophan, a powerful amino acid that converts to serotonin, a "feel good" neurotransmitter that gives you a natural lift, making it less likely that you'll reach for an energy drink to do the job. You can also substitute beef and chicken, which contain tryptophan as well. Garlic adds delicious flavor and is antiviral, antimicrobial, and immune-protective. Served with steamed veggies or a spinach salad, this dish is wonderful eaten hot or cold.

VERSATILE PURE PROTEIN SALAD

This delicious, nutritious dish is bound to become a blood sugar–balancing staple. You can change the variety of the protein, from tuna to chicken to turkey or eggs, as it suits your taste buds or the occasion. Place your protein salad on top of greens or herbs like parsley and basil, or on a piece of whole-grain pita bread with lettuce and tomato, or on half red bell pepper or avocado. Simple, easy, quick: this one's great for any occasion and ideal for Type 1s who are on the go.

3 to 4 ounces (85 to 115 g) of protein (tuna, chicken breast, or roasted turkey) or 3 hard-boiled eggs
1 to 2 teaspoons mayonnaise (choose a brand that does not contain sugar)
1 teaspoon mustard
2 teaspoons mashed avocado
2 teaspoons of any two or three of the following, chopped: red onion, scallions, parsley, pine nuts, red bell pepper

Chop your protein of choice into bite-sized pieces and place in a small bowl. Add mayonnaise, mustard, avocado, and remaining ingredients and stir to combine.

YIELD: 1 SERVING

EACH WITH: Calories 166.86; Calories From Fat 70.35; Total Fat 7.88 g; Cholesterol 37.39 mg; Sodium 403.68 mg; Potassium 276.5 mg; Total Carbohydrates 2.34 g; Fiber 1.04 g; Sugar 0.64 g; Protein 20.64 g

Try these substitutions for variety:
Sheep's milk feta, walnuts, and organic canned cannellini beans
Garbanzo beans, goat cheese, mint, and pine nuts
White beans, sage, goat cheese, Gouda, and roasted peppers

BLOOD SUGAR BALANCE RATING: Very High

Health Facilitators	Nutrient Density Rating
Protein	High
Fat	Medium
Carbohydrate	High
Enzymes	High
Antioxidants	High
Fiber	High

HIGH-ENERGY BANGKOK COCONUT CHICKEN STIR FRY

2 teaspoons (10 ml) extra-virgin olive oil or coconut oil

4 garlic cloves, minced

4 green onions, chopped

½ cup (130 g) smooth almond butter

1 cup (240 ml) light coconut milk

2 tablespoons (30 ml) fresh lemon juice

2 tablespoons (30 ml) tamari sauce (wheat-free)

1 tablespoon (15 ml) fish sauce

½ cup (30 g) fresh parsley, chopped

½ cup (120 ml) purified water

1½ pounds (680 g) boneless, skinless organic chicken breasts, cubed

2 heads of broccoli, including the stalk, chopped

¼ cup (38 g) dried cranberries

¼ cup (30 g) sliced almonds, toasted

1 cup (170 g) quinoa, cooked (or any other grain, such as brown rice)

Heat the oil in a saucepan over medium-high heat. Sauté the garlic and onions until softened and slightly brown. In a blender, combine cooked garlic and onions with almond butter, coconut milk, lemon juice, tamari, fish sauce, parsley, and water. Blend until smooth. In a large skillet, combine blended sauce, chicken, and broccoli. Cover and cook until chicken is cooked through, about 15 minutes. Before serving, add cranberries and almonds. Serve with quinoa.

YIELD: 6 SERVINGS

EACH WITH: Calories 398.17; Calories From Fat 175.95; Total Fat 20.35 g; Cholesterol 22.67 mg; Sodium 726.81 mg; Potassium 586.16 mg; Total Carbohydrates 39.87 g; Fiber 4.95 g; Sugar 1.97 g; Protein 17.73 g

BLOOD SUGAR BALANCE RATING: Very High

Health Facilitators	Nutrient Density Rating
Protein	Very high
Fat	High
Carbohydrate	High
Enzymes	High
Antioxidants	High
Fiber	High

Coconut is an excellent source of plant-based protein and healthy fat, especially for vegetarians. It also gives this recipe a special kick! Coconut supports balanced blood sugar levels, and it provides thirst-quenching sodium, potassium, and calcium, which help keep blood sugar stable. Water also helps increase stamina and sustained energy. The almonds in this recipe may help you maintain a healthy weight, according to several studies. We suggest protein-rich quinoa here, but you can serve this rich and hearty dish with just about any whole grain, such as brown rice, buckwheat, or amaranth.

GET-UP-AND-GO GARBANZO BURGERS

Garbanzos, or chickpeas, contain a whopping 12.5 grams of insoluble fiber per cup, which is great for your digestive health and excellent for stabilizing your blood sugar levels. Packed with energizing protein, iron, folate, magnesium, and tryptophan, it's no wonder that these delicious legumes are popular around the world.

2 tablespoons (30 ml) extra-virgin olive oil or coconut oil, divided
1½ cups (240 g) chopped or minced brown or red onion
3 cloves fresh garlic, chopped
1 teaspoon ground cumin
1 cup (130 g) finely chopped carrot
1¾ cups (425 g, or one 15-ounce can) cooked garbanzo beans, drained
1½ tablespoons (22 ml) tahini (sesame paste)
¼ cup (15 g) fresh parsley, chopped
Dash of cayenne
1⅓ cups (165 g) chickpea flour
½ teaspoon baking soda
1 teaspoon salt
Juice of half a medium lemon
2 to 4 cups (40 to 80 g) mixed lettuce greens or spinach (optional)

Heat 1 tablespoon (15 ml) oil in a large skillet over medium heat; sauté onions until soft. Add garlic, cumin, and carrot. Sauté for 2 more minutes. Transfer to a large bowl. Add drained garbanzo beans; mash by hand or in food processor until the mixture is thick and moist. Add tahini, parsley, and cayenne. In a smaller bowl, combine chickpea flour, baking soda, and salt. Add to mashed chickpea mixture in large bowl, and mix well. With floured hands, form 4 patties and lightly dust with remaining chickpea flour. Heat remaining 1 tablespoon (15 ml) oil in a large skillet over medium heat. Add patties to skillet. After 1 minute, or when browning begins, flip the patties. Cook for about 2 minutes before flipping again. Keep cooking, turning every minute or two until patties are golden brown on both sides. Squeeze fresh lemon juice on top. Serve immediately over a bed of lettuce greens or spinach.

YIELD: 4 SERVINGS
EACH WITH: Calories 385.91; Calories From Fat 112.55; Total Fat 13.09 g; Cholesterol 0 mg; Sodium 1113.49 mg; Potassium 755.36 mg; Total Carbohydrates 54.95 g; Fiber 11.54 g; Sugar 7.46 g; Protein 14.94 g
BLOOD SUGAR BALANCE RATING: Very High

Health Facilitators	Nutrient Density Rating
Protein	High
Fat	Medium
Carbohydrate	High
Enzymes	High
Antioxidants	High
Fiber	Very High

SUPERCHARGED SPICY SALMON

1 tablespoon (15 ml) extra-virgin olive oil or coconut oil

1 medium red onion, chopped

2 garlic cloves, chopped or pressed

1 can (14 ounces, or 425 ml) light coconut milk, unsweetened

1 cup (240 ml) chicken stock

½ to 1 tablespoon (7 to 15 ml) red curry paste, depending on desired spiciness

2 medium carrots, julienned

1 medium zucchini, julienned

Four 5-ounce (140-g) salmon fillets

Salt and pepper to taste

4 scallions, thinly sliced

Preheat broiler. Heat oil in a medium saucepan over medium heat. Add onions and garlic, sautéing until onion is translucent. Mix in coconut milk and stock. Add curry paste, and then bring to a boil. Reduce heat and cook until liquid becomes slightly creamy, about 20 minutes. Add carrots and zucchini to coconut milk mixture and cook until crisp-tender, about 5 minutes. Meanwhile, place salmon on baking sheet greased with olive or coconut oil. Season with salt and pepper to taste, then broil until fish turns opaque, about 10 minutes. Place salmon on serving plates and spoon sauce over fish. Top with scallions.

YIELD: 4 SERVINGS

EACH WITH: Calories 435.41; Calories From Fat 233.84; Total Fat 26.17 g; Cholesterol 89.3 mg; Sodium 426.05 mg; Potassium 909.64 mg; Total Carbohydrates 15.01 g; Fiber 3.92 g; Sugar 3.49 g; Protein 34.36 g

BLOOD SUGAR BALANCE RATING: Very High

Health Facilitators	Nutrient Density Rating
Protein	Very High
Fat	High
Carbohydrate	High
Enzymes	Medium
Antioxidants	High
Fiber	Medium

Salmon is a super fish. High in protein and loaded with omega-3 essential fatty acids, salmon helps regulate blood sugar levels, quiets inflammation, improves circulation, and boosts brain health by feeding necessary neurotransmitters. Together with coconut, the combination works powerfully to keep blood sugar stable. The zucchini, carrots, and red onions in this dish are high in key vitamins C, A, B6, B1, and folate, as well as zinc, calcium, magnesium, and tryptophan; plus dietary fiber that all support metabolism, energy production, and overall health. Serve with a side salad, steamed veggies, or over a bed of steamed brown rice for extra fiber, protein, and nutrients.

PROTEIN-PACKED CUMIN QUINOA

Quinoa is a perfect plant-based protein, which makes it ideal to help balance blood sugar levels. It's rich in essential nutrients, including calcium, phosphorus, magnesium, potassium, copper, manganese, zinc, and iron, plus it's high in fiber and easy to prepare. Quinoa complements many different vegetables, so feel free to improvise based on what is in your refrigerator. Add some turkey, chicken, or a can of tuna to the mix for extra flavor or higher protein content.

⅓ cup (57 g) quinoa
⅔ cup plus ½ cup (160 ml plus 120 ml) purified water, divided
½ teaspoon salt, divided
1 tablespoon (15 ml) extra-virgin olive oil or coconut oil
¼ teaspoon mustard seeds
½ teaspoon cumin seeds
1 medium red or brown onion, chopped
4 large kale leaves, chopped
2 large carrots, chopped
2 cups (140 g) chopped broccoli (heads and stem),
3 tablespoons (11 g) parsley, chopped
1 teaspoon (5 ml) sesame oil
Dash of sea salt, Bragg's liquid amino acids, or tamari sauce (wheat-free)
¼ cup chopped almonds

Rinse quinoa well. In a small saucepan, bring quinoa, ⅔ cup (160 ml) water, and ⅛ teaspoon salt to a boil. Cover, reduce heat to medium, and simmer for 15 minutes. In a deep, large pan over medium heat, heat oil and sauté mustard and cumin seeds until mustard seeds pop. Add onions and sauté on low heat until onions soften. Immediately add kale, carrots, broccoli, and ½ cup (120 ml) filtered water. Sauté 3 to 5 minutes on low to medium heat, until the vegetables are crisp-tender. Add remaining ingredients and stir well; combine in a large bowl with cooked quinoa. Serve warm or cool.

YIELD: 2 SERVINGS
EACH WITH: Calories 367.59; Calories From Fat 178.18; Total Fat 20.67 g; Cholesterol 0 mg; Sodium 810 mg; Potassium 830.53 mg; Total Carbohydrates 38.63 g; Fiber 7.6 g; Sugar 4.77 g; Protein 11.74 g
BLOOD SUGAR BALANCE RATING: Very High

Health Facilitators	Nutrient Density Rating
Protein	High
Fat	Medium
Carbohydrate	High
Enzymes	Medium
Antioxidants	High
Fiber	Very High

BLOOD SUGAR–BALANCING BARLEY WITH MUSHROOMS

3 tablespoons (42 g or 45 ml) unsalted butter or olive or coconut oil
1 small red or brown onion, chopped
2 cloves garlic, chopped
2 cups (140 g) sliced brown, white, or shiitake mushrooms
1 cup (200 g) pearl barley, rinsed and drained
3 cups (710 ml) vegetable stock or purified water
3 scallions, chopped
½ cup (70 g) peas, fresh or frozen and thawed
½ cup (30 g) fresh parsley, chopped
Freshly ground black pepper
Dash of cayenne

In a large saucepan with a tight-fitting lid, melt butter or oil over medium-high heat. Add onion and garlic and sauté until softened, about 5 minutes. Add mushrooms and barley and sauté 5 minutes. Add stock or water, bring to a boil, cover, and reduce heat to low. Simmer about 45 to 60 minutes, or until all liquid has been absorbed and barley is tender. Add the peas, scallions, and parsley. Season to taste with black pepper and a dash of cayenne.

YIELD: 4 SERVINGS
EACH WITH: Calories 403.57; Calories From Fat 104.06; Total Fat 11.77 g; Cholesterol 28.3 mg; Sodium 292.73 mg; Potassium 715.31 mg; Total Carbohydrates 65.48 g; Fiber 11.71 g; Sugar 4.97 g; Protein 13.1 g
BLOOD SUGAR BALANCE RATING: Very High

Health Facilitators	Nutrient Density Rating
Protein	Medium
Fat	Medium
Carbohydrate	High
Enzymes	Low
Antioxidants	Very High
Fiber	Very High

Enjoy the nutlike flavor and the appealing chewy, pasta-like consistency of this high-fiber cereal grain. Barley is high in tryptophan, making it a wonderful choice for calming your mind, boosting your mood, and balancing your blood sugar levels. This dish also offers antioxidant selenium, which boosts energy and metabolism. Mushrooms contain a powerful antioxidant called L-ergothioneine that zaps cell-damaging free radicals. Use shiitake mushrooms, and you'll stimulate your immune system into action. The high-nutrient veggies add savory appeal to this delicious dish.

HEARTY RICE AND LENTIL LOAF WITH GREEN SAUCE

Lentils are an excellent source of soluble fiber (1 cup, or 200 g, contains 16 grams of fiber!), which helps control blood sugar by slowing down the digestion and absorption of foods. These legumes are also an excellent source of immune-boosting B vitamins such as folate and B1, potassium, iron, copper, and tryptophan. Brown rice is also high in fiber, contains some protein, is high in tryptophan, selenium, and manganese, all of which support healthy blood sugar levels and efficient metabolism. Feel free to add your favorite in-season vegetables. The green sauce with sesame oil and garlic (a potent antioxidant) add a delicious flavor. Serve this dish with any meat, vegetable, or salad, or on its own.

Health Facilitators	Nutrient Density Rating
Protein	Medium
Fat	Medium
Carbohydrate	High
Enzymes	High
Antioxidants	High
Fiber	Very High

2 tablespoons (30 ml) sesame oil
1 red onion, finely chopped
1 carrot, finely chopped
1 celery stalk, finely chopped
2 cloves garlic, chopped
1 tablespoon (1.7 g) rosemary
½ tablespoon (1.2 g) sage
2 cups (330 g) cooked brown rice
2 cups (400 g) cooked lentils or lentil soup
2 tablespoons (30 ml) tamari sauce (wheat-free)

Preheat oven to 350°F (180°C, or gas mark 4). In a large skillet, heat sesame oil over medium-high heat. Sauté onion, carrot, celery, and garlic until onion is limp and transparent, then add rosemary and sage and sauté a few minutes longer. Add rice, lentils, and tamari and mix well. Place mixture into an oiled loaf pan and bake, covered with foil, for 20 minutes. Remove foil and bake for another 10 minutes. Let sit for a few minutes before slicing.

YIELD: 6 TO 8 SERVINGS
EACH WITH: Calories 202.83; Calories From Fat 72.18; Total Fat 8.34 g; Cholesterol 0 mg; Sodium 772.73 mg; Potassium 293.64 mg; Total Carbohydrates 25.49 g; Fiber 6.18 g; Sugar 2.07 g; Protein 8.12 g
BLOOD SUGAR BALANCE RATING: Very High

For Green Sauce
2 cups (480 ml) purified water
1 tablespoon (15 ml) toasted sesame oil
¼ cup (60 ml) tamari sauce (wheat-free), or to taste
1 tablespoon (8 g) kudzu, diluted in ¼ cup (60 ml) cold water
¼ cup (15 g) parsley, finely minced

In a medium saucepan, bring water and oil to a boil. Add tamari. Stir in diluted kudzu and simmer until thickened. Stir in parsley. Serve over lentil loaf.

YIELD: ½ cup
EACH WITH: Calories 360.12; Calories From Fat 281.35; Total Fat 32.86 g; Cholesterol 0 mg; Sodium 4045.13 mg; Potassium 369.47 mg; Total Carbohydrates 8.97 g; Fiber 3.03 g; Sugar 2.11 g; Protein 12.47 g
NOTE: Kudzu is a thickener and is available in most well-stocked supermarkets. If you are unable to find it, substitute corn or rice starch.

LOW-GLYCEMIC GREEK GREEN BEANS

1 pound (455 g) fresh green beans, ends trimmed, sliced diagonally into
   1-inch (2.5-cm) pieces and steamed until tender
½ red onion, thinly sliced
⅔ cup (90 g) kalamata olives, pitted and diced
⅔ cup (100 g) feta cheese, crumbled
¼ cup (10 g) slivered fresh basil, or 2 teaspoons (1.4 g) dried basil
3 tablespoons (45 ml) apple cider vinegar
1 tablespoon (15 ml) Dijon mustard
2 cloves fresh garlic, minced
Freshly ground black pepper
3 tablespoons (45 ml) extra-virgin olive oil

Combine green beans, onion, olives, feta, and basil in a large bowl. In a
small bowl, using a fork, combine vinegar, mustard, garlic, and black pepper
to taste. Slowly drizzle in olive oil, whisking until smooth and well blended.
Taste, and adjust seasonings.

YIELD: 4 SERVINGS
EACH WITH: Calories 234.79; Calories From Fat 166.15; Total Fat 18.78 g; Cholesterol 22.25 mg;
Sodium 513.13 mg; Potassium 295.69 mg; Total Carbohydrates 12.28 g; Fiber 4.52 g;
Sugar 2.68 g; Protein 6.14 g
BLOOD SUGAR BALANCE RATING: Very High

Health Facilitators	Nutrient Density Rating
Protein	High
Fat	Medium
Carbohydrate	High
Enzymes	High
Antioxidants	High
Fiber	High

In addition to antioxidant nutrients like vitamin C and beta-carotene, green beans contain healthy amounts of the antioxidant mineral manganese. Antioxidants support healthy blood sugar metabolism because they protect our cells against disease, thereby giving us greater energy. Green beans are also high in fiber and contain small amounts of omega-3 essential fatty acids, both of which support healthy glucose metabolism. Green beans also contain calcium, potassium, tryptophan, and protein. Olives are high in omega-6s, which boost brain function and healthy hormone production. Olives also contain polyphenols, plant compounds that are anti-inflammatory and improve immune function. Feta cheese is an excellent source of both protein and healthy fat.

SUGAR-BUSTING MEXICAN GREENS

Avocadoes have gotten a bad rap as a high-fat vegetable. In fact, most of the fat is monounsaturated, which lowers cholesterol and has been shown to lower the risk of cancer and diabetes by balancing blood sugar levels. This creamy green vegetable is also high in antioxidants, minerals, fiber, and essential fatty acids including omega-9s. The onion, lemon juice, and fresh cilantro here provide more antioxidants and will please your taste buds. Eat this spread with rice crackers, rice and beans, or corn-free burrito wraps. Your biggest problem? When to stop eating!

3 ripe avocados
2 tablespoons (30 ml) lemon or lime juice
2 cloves garlic, finely chopped
½ to 1 small red onion, chopped (optional)
Sea salt
Freshly ground black pepper
Dash of cayenne (optional)
2 to 3 tablespoons (8 to 12 g) minced fresh cilantro (optional)
1 teaspoon tamari sauce (wheat-free) or liquid amino acids (optional; if using, reduce or exclude sea salt)
2 cups (40 g) mixed salad greens
2 cups (40 g) spinach greens

Mash avocados with lemon or lime juice. Add remaining ingredients and mix well. Let sit for 30 minutes or more to allow the flavors to meld. Serve the guacamole on top of the greens.

YIELD: 4 SERVINGS

EACH WITH: Calories 231.06; Calories From Fat 168.57; Total Fat 20.1 g; Cholesterol 0 mg; Sodium 108.07 mg; Potassium 772.99 mg; Total Carbohydrates 14.3 g; Fiber 9.55 g; Sugar 0.68 g; Protein 3.46 g

BLOOD SUGAR BALANCE RATING: Very High

Health Facilitators	Nutrient Density Rating
Protein	Low
Fat	High
Carbohydrate	High
Enzymes	High
Antioxidants	Very High
Fiber	High

SIMPLY SESAME BROCCOLI

2 teaspoons (5 g) raw sesame seeds
2 bunches broccoli, cut into bite-sized florets
1 tablespoon (15 ml) cold-pressed sesame oil
1 tablespoon (15 ml) extra-virgin olive oil
2 cups (480 ml) water
1 tablespoon (15 ml) rice wine vinegar or lemon juice
2 teaspoons (10 ml) low-sodium tamari sauce (wheat-free), or liquid amino
   acids
Freshly ground black pepper

Put sesame seeds in an ungreased skillet over medium-high heat. Stir seeds or shake pan almost constantly until seeds are evenly browned and toasted and begin to pop. Remove from pan immediately and set aside. In a large saucepan, bring water to boil. Add broccoli florets and cook until barely tender, about 5 to 7 minutes. Drain and set aside. In a small bowl, using a fork, mix sesame oil, olive oil, rice wine vinegar, tamari, and black pepper. Toss gently with steamed broccoli. Taste and adjust seasonings. Sprinkle with sesame seeds before serving.

YIELD: 4 SERVINGS
EACH WITH: Calories 90.89; Calories From Fat 61.95; Total Fat 7.5 g; Cholesterol 0 mg; Sodium 190.96 mg; Potassium 309.43 mg; Total Carbohydrates 6.4 g; Fiber 0.12 g; Sugar 0.05 g; Protein 3 g
BLOOD SUGAR BALANCE RATING: High

Health Facilitators	Nutrient Density Rating
Protein	Low
Fat	Low
Carbohydrate	High
Enzymes	High
Antioxidants	High
Fiber	Very high

The high fiber content of antioxidant-rich broccoli makes it an all-star player when it comes to balancing your blood sugar levels. Broccoli also contains anti-cancer phytochemicals, potassium, vitamin C, folate, magnesium, phosphorus, beta-carotene, and vitamin A. Combine it with calcium-rich sesame seeds, and you have one nutritional powerhouse.

HEARTY GINGERED HALIBUT

Heart-healthy halibut is loaded omega-3s that help reduce inflammation, while the shiitake mushrooms help strengthen your immune system. The ginger helps with insulin production—it increases sensitivity to insulin and can mimic its effects. Ginger also keeps your blood sugar balanced by stimulating and regulating your digestive system. This dish will keep your blood sugar stable and you satisfied for hours.

¼ cup (60 ml) vegetable stock
1 tablespoon (15 ml) tamari sauce (wheat-free) or Bragg's liquid amino acids
1 tablespoon (6 g) fresh ginger, finely chopped or minced
3 cloves fresh garlic, finely chopped
1 to 2 tablespoons (15 to 30 ml) fresh lemon or lime juice
1 cup (100 g) scallions, coarsely chopped
2 cups (140 g) shiitake mushrooms, sliced ¼-inch (0.6-cm) thick
2 halibut steaks, ¼ to ½ pound (115 to 225 g) each
Salt and freshly ground black pepper
2 cups (135 g) kale, chopped
1 cup (165 g) cooked brown rice, optional

In a medium skillet, heat the vegetable stock and the tamari or Bragg's liquid amino acids. Add the ginger, garlic, lemon or lime juice, scallions, and mushrooms and cook for several minutes over a high heat. Place the halibut steaks on top, reduce heat to low, and cover. Cook until fish flakes easily with a fork, approximately 5 minutes depending on thickness. Season with salt and pepper. Meanwhile, steam the kale and divide among plates. Place steaks on top of the kale and spoon scallion and mushroom broth over the fish. Serve immediately with brown rice, if desired.

YIELD: 2 SERVINGS
EACH WITH: Calories 737.47; Calories From Fat 103.88; Total Fat 11.68 g; Cholesterol 131.28 mg; Sodium 812.78 mg; Potassium 2911.94 mg; Total Carbohydrates 64.25 g; Fiber 9.04 g; Sugar 3.37 g; Protein 96.02 g
BLOOD SUGAR BALANCE RATING: Very High

Health Facilitators	Nutrient Density Rating
Protein	Very High
Fat	Medium
Carbohydrate	Medium
Enzymes	Low
Antioxidants	High
Fiber	Medium

SPEEDY STIR-FRY 101

2 tablespoons (30 ml) extra-virgin olive oil
2 cloves garlic, minced or finely chopped
1 medium red onion, chopped
1 cup (115 g) sliced zucchini
3 cups sliced or chopped carrots
8 cremini mushrooms, chopped
1 large green pepper, chopped
⅓ cup (20 g) fresh parsley, chopped
2 tablespoons (30 ml) tamari sauce (wheat-free) or Bragg's liquid amino
  acids
Sea salt and black pepper to taste
Dash red pepper flakes or cayenne (optional)
2 tablespoons (8 g) cilantro (optional)
1 can (8 ounces, or 225 g) water-packed tuna
½ avocado, cubed
1 cup (165 g or 185 g) cooked brown rice or quinoa (optional)

Heat oil in a large skillet over medium-high heat; sauté garlic and onion until softened. Add zucchini, carrots, mushrooms, green pepper, parsley, tamari, salt and pepper, red pepper flakes or cayenne, and cilantro; cook, stirring often, until vegetables are crisp-tender. Add the canned tuna with the water and stir to combine. Top with avocado and serve over a bed of steamed brown rice or quinoa, if desired.

YIELD: 4 SERVINGS

EACH WITH: Calories 285.06; Calories From Fat 107.48; Total Fat 12.36 g; Cholesterol 18.06 mg; Sodium 746.51 mg; Potassium 854.91 mg; Total Carbohydrates 30 g; Fiber 7.12 g; Sugar 6.97 g; Protein 15.67 g

BLOOD SUGAR BALANCE RATING: Very High

Health Facilitators	Nutrient Density Rating
Protein	Low
Fat	Low
Carbohydrate	High
Enzymes	Low
Antioxidants	Very High
Fiber	Very High

If you feel like experimenting with the foods in your refrigerator and your pantry, this is a great place to start. In fact, you may make it a point to have these ingredients available so you can make it any time. The veggies here are only suggestions; feel free to substitute your favorites or what you have on hand. The main goal is to use a variety of vegetables so that their fiber content will slow blood sugar absorption while nourishing the body with a wide range of nutrients.

MOOD-BOOSTING TURKEY MEATLOAF

Turkey is a feel-good food because it contains tryptrophan, a precursor to serotonin, the "happiness" molecule. Eating turkey not only nourishes your body, it calms your nervous system and lifts your mood, restoring a sense of well-being. Add fresh herbs and antioxidant-laden veggies, and you have an easy and delicious dish. Serve it with steamed vegetables for additional fiber or over a bed of mixed salad greens.

1 pound (455 g) ground organic turkey
½ cup (80 g) finely chopped red onion
1 large carrot, grated
½ cup (30 g) finely chopped fresh parsley or cilantro
½ cup (55 g) finely chopped celery
¼ cup (60 ml) chicken or vegetable stock
1 egg
2 tablespoons (28 g) pumpkin seeds or sunflower seeds
½ to 1½ teaspoons onion powder
½ to 1½ teaspoons fresh garlic, minced or finely chopped
½ to 1½ teaspoons dried oregano
½ to 1½ dried sage
½ teaspoon salt
¼ teaspoon black pepper
Dash of cayenne (optional)

Preheat oven to 350°F (180°C, or gas mark 4). Combine all ingredients in a bowl, mixing well with your hands. Pat mixture into a greased 9 × 5-inch (23 × 13-cm) loaf pan. Bake for 1 hour. Drain juices and serve by the slice.

YIELD: 4 SERVINGS
EACH WITH: Calories 1287.84; Calories From Fat 471.95; Total Fat 54.71 g; Cholesterol 774.54 mg; Sodium 1870.98 mg; Potassium 2739.21 mg; Total Carbohydrates 297.97 g; Fiber 8.11 g; Sugar 11.06 g; Protein 144.76 g
BLOOD SUGAR BALANCE RATING: Very High

Health Facilitators	Nutrient Density Rating
Protein	Very High
Fat	Medium
Carbohydrate	Medium
Enzymes	Low
Antioxidants	High
Fiber	High

STRESS-LESS LENTIL NUT LOAF

1 cup (225 g) dried lentils
1 tablespoon (15 ml) extra-virgin olive oil
8 garlic cloves, chopped
1 large red onion, chopped
2 cups (250 g) ground walnuts
2 cups (330 g) cooked brown rice
2 tablespoons (30 ml) tamari sauce (wheat-free), or liquid amino acids
2 teaspoons oregano
3 tablespoons (12 g) fresh parsley, chopped
2 organic eggs
½ banana, mashed
Sea salt to taste
Black pepper to taste
Dash of cayenne pepper (optional)

Soak lentils for at least 3 hours; discard soaking water. Place lentils in a medium saucepan with 2 cups (480 ml) water over medium-high heat. Simmer for 20 minutes or until softened. Preheat oven to 350°F (180°C, or gas mark 4). Heat oil in a small skillet over medium heat. Sauté garlic and onions for 3 to 5 minutes. Combine lentils, garlic, onions, and remaining ingredients and press into a greased 9 × 5-inch (23 × 13-cm) loaf pan. Bake for 1 hour or until cooked through.

YIELD: 6 SERVINGS

EACH WITH: Calories 437.31; Calories From Fat 255.49; Total Fat 30.29 g; Cholesterol 70.5 mg; Sodium 365.78 mg; Potassium 399.55 mg; Total Carbohydrates 33.06 g; Fiber 7.55 g; Sugar 3.46 g; Protein 14 g

BLOOD SUGAR BALANCE RATING: Very High

Health Facilitators	Nutrient Density Rating
Protein	High
Fat	Low
Carbohydrate	High
Enzymes	Low
Antioxidants	Medium
Fiber	Very High

The tiny, mighty lentil contains plenty of fiber to help regulate blood glucose and keep you off of the sugar roller coaster. The nutrients in lentils—such as folate, vitamin B1, and potassium—strengthen kidneys and adrenal glands, which in turn helps with the stress response, cellular renewal and regeneration, and sex hormone production. The mixture of delicious flavors and textures makes this a tasty dish that will leave you satisfied, calm, and full of energy.

RESTORATIVE RISOTTO

The fiber, selenium, and tryptophan in this dish support your adrenal (stress handler) glands, balancing your blood sugar and making you ready to handle whatever life sends your way. This recipe is well-suited for Type 1s because it is so nutrient-dense. The rice provides protein and essential amino acids; the feta contains blood sugar–stabilizing fat, protein, and calcium; and other ingredients supply calcium, magnesium, B vitamins, tryptophan, potassium, and fiber. For extra protein, add tempeh or tofu.

3 tablespoons (45 ml) extra-virgin olive oil (or oil from sun-dried tomatoes)
2 fresh garlic cloves, minced
1 small red or brown onion, diced
½ cup (55 g) oil-packed sun-dried tomatoes, strained and slivered
1½ cups (285 g) brown rice, rinsed and drained
4 cups (960 ml) vegetable stock or purified water, simmering hot
½ pound (225 g) asparagus, cut into ½-inch (1.3-cm) pieces
¼ cup (10 g) shredded fresh basil, or 2 teaspoons (1.4 g) dried basil
1 cup (150 g) crumbled goat's milk feta cheese
1 tablespoon (15 ml) lemon juice
2 teaspoons (3.5 g) grated lemon zest
Freshly ground black pepper
4 cups (80 g) fresh mixed lettuce greens or raw spinach

In a large saucepan, heat oil over medium-high heat. Add garlic and onion and sauté until softened, about 5 minutes. Add sun-dried tomatoes and brown rice. Stir gently, thoroughly coating grains with oil. Ladle 1 cup (240 ml) of simmering hot stock into rice and cook over medium heat, uncovered, stirring constantly until all liquid is absorbed. Continue adding 1 cup (240 ml) of stock at a time, stirring constantly until stock has been absorbed between each addition. Cook until rice is tender, about 15 to 20 minutes.

Meanwhile, in a separate saucepan, bring 4 cups (960 ml) water to boil. Cook asparagus in boiling water until just barely tender, about 3 to 6 minutes. Drain, rinse under cold water, and drain again.

After all stock has been added and rice is cooked, add asparagus, basil, feta, lemon juice, lemon zest, and black pepper. Taste and adjust seasonings. Serve risotto over a bed of mixed lettuce greens or raw spinach.

YIELD: 4 SERVINGS
EACH WITH: Calories 592.16; Calories From Fat 222.94; Total Fat 25.4 g; Cholesterol 40.58 mg; Sodium 806.02 mg; Potassium 725.2 mg; Total Carbohydrates 79.98 g; Fiber 8.17 g; Sugar 6.46 g; Protein 18.91 g
BLOOD SUGAR BALANCE RATING: Very High

Health Facilitators	Nutrient Density Rating
Protein	High
Fat	Medium
Carbohydrate	Very High
Enzymes	Low
Antioxidants	Medium
Fiber	Very High

BLOOD SUGAR–STABILIZING STUFFED SALMON

1 medium butternut squash, sliced
1 tablespoon (15 ml) extra-virgin olive oil
Sea salt and black pepper
6 fillets of salmon (or whole fish, 3 to 4 pounds [1.37 to 1.82 kg] total)
4 stalks celery, finely chopped
1 red or brown onion, diced
1 clove garlic, finely chopped
1 medium carrot, grated
1 bay leaf
2 tablespoons (8 g) fresh parsley, chopped
1 tablespoon (3 g) dried thyme
1 tablespoon (3 g) dried oregano

Preheat oven to 325°F (170°C, or gas mark 3). In a glass baking pan, make a layer of squash slices. Sprinkle squash with olive oil and salt. Rub fish fillets with salt and pepper and place celery, minced onion, garlic, grated carrot, bay leaf, parsley, and half of the thyme and oregano on top. Roll fillets up to enclose the filling and secure with a toothpick. Place fillets in the baking dish, sprinkle with the rest of the thyme and oregano, salt, and pepper. Cover with foil and bake for about 30 minutes.

YIELD: 6 SERVINGS

EACH WITH: Calories 365.21; Calories From Fat 182.41; Total Fat 20.31 g; Cholesterol 92.23 mg; Sodium 111.07 mg; Potassium 1003.94 mg; Total Carbohydrates 15.35 g; Fiber 3.36 g; Sugar 3.77 g; Protein 32.15 g

BLOOD SUGAR BALANCE RATING: Very High

NOTE: To make this dish using a whole fish (I recommend snapper), stuff it with the herbs and vegetables and place it belly down in a baking dish the same size as the fish. Cover with foil and bake for about 45 minutes.

Health Facilitators	Nutrient Density Rating
Protein	Very High
Fat	High
Carbohydrate	Low
Enzymes	Low
Antioxidants	High
Fiber	Low

High in tryptophan, vitamin D, selenium, B vitamins, magnesium, and omega-3s, is it any wonder why salmon is considered one of the healthiest fish around? Salmon is not only beneficial for your heart and brain, its protein and omega 3s help balance blood sugar. Choose wild salmon if you can; it contains more omega 3s than farmed varieties. This delicious dish is also easy to prepare, making it likely to become a regular in your recipe rotation.

INDIAN CHICKEN SMOTHERED IN VEGETABLES

This meal is guaranteed to delight more than your taste buds—the protein keeps your blood sugar stable, while antioxidant-rich spices like turmeric and coriander strengthen your immune system. Serve with rice or spinach.

1 cup (240 ml) whole milk yogurt
2 garlic cloves, finely chopped
1 teaspoon curry powder
½ teaspoon sea salt
½ teaspoon pepper
1 tablespoon (6 g) coriander
½ teaspoon turmeric
1 tablespoon (6 g) fresh ginger, chopped
1¼ pounds (570 g) boneless, skinless chicken breasts and thighs, cubed
1⅓ teaspoons (7 ml) extra-virgin olive oil or coconut oil
½ cup (80 g) chopped red or brown onion
1 cup (180 g) chopped fresh tomato
1 bay leaf

Combine yogurt, garlic, curry powder, salt, pepper, coriander, turmeric, and ginger in a large bowl. Add chicken, stirring to thoroughly coat. Let stand for at least 30 minutes at room temperature. Heat the oil in a large skillet; add onion and sauté until tender. Add tomatoes and bay leaf and simmer for 5 minutes. Add chicken and yogurt mixture, stir to combine, and bring to a boil. Reduce heat, cover, and simmer for 15 to 20 minutes, turning chicken once or twice. Remove bay leaf before serving. Serve over a bed of rice or steamed spinach.

YIELD: 4 SERVINGS
EACH WITH: Calories 101.88; Calories From Fat 38.08; Total Fat 4.14 g; Cholesterol 21.27 mg; Sodium 282.57 mg; Potassium 298.88 mg; Total Carbohydrates 8.42 g; Fiber 1.75 g; Sugar 4.95 g; Protein 8.4 g
BLOOD SUGAR BALANCE RATING: Very High

Health Facilitators	Nutrient Density Rating
Protein	High
Fat	Medium
Carbohydrate	Low
Enzymes	Low
Antioxidants	Medium
Fiber	Low

NOURISHING NUT MILK SMOOTHIE

¼ to ½ cup (40 to 75 g) raw nuts, preferably unsalted, or fresh coconut
pieces or shreds
¾ to 1½ cups (180 to 360 ml) purified water
1 to 2 teaspoons (5 to 10 ml) pure maple syrup, or 2 pitted fresh dates
½ teaspoon vanilla extract (optional)
1 to 2 pinches sea salt
1 cup (140 g) fresh or frozen berries or cherries

Put half of the nuts and half of the water in a blender and blend on high.
When this is liquefied, blend with half of the maple syrup or dates, vanilla (if
using), and salt. Strain the liquid into a bowl and transfer to a storage jar or
airtight container. Repeat with the remaining nuts, water, maple syrup, and
salt. You may vary the proportions according to taste. Reserve the nut pulp
for another use. Pour the nut milk back into the blender and add the berries
or cherries. Blend and serve immediately.

YIELD: 2 SERVINGS

EACH WITH: Calories 139.08; Calories From Fat 78.18; Total Fat 9.35 g; Cholesterol 0 mg;
Sodium 145 mg; Potassium 254.25 mg; Total Carbohydrates 11.55 g; Fiber 3.56 g; Sugar 6.69 g;
Protein 4.32 g

BLOOD SUGAR BALANCE RATING: Very High

NOTE: Instead of using the nut milk to make a smoothie, you can refrigerate and serve as a drink
or on cereal. Nut milk lasts several days refrigerated (use coconut milk within 24 hours).
The leftover nut pulp can be used in cooking, such as in grain/vegetable dishes, or in baking.

Health Facilitators	Nutrient Density Rating
Protein	Medium
Fat	High
Carbohydrate	High
Enzymes	High
Antioxidants	High
Fiber	Medium

Make this dairy-free, nutrient-rich beverage treat in a blender with a variety of nuts, a touch of maple syrup or fresh dates for sweetness, and sea salt to highlight the flavors. Use almonds, Brazil nuts, cashews, or coconut—all are high in healthy fats and contain protein as well as minerals and enzymes. This drink is great for keeping blood sugar levels stable and makes a delicious dessert, breakfast, or snack. Sweet!

REFRESHING RHUBARB AND STRAWBERRY PUDDING

Try this delicious combination of antioxidant-rich fruits on a hot summer afternoon. Walnuts and almonds balance out the flavors and textures of the pudding while keeping blood sugar levels stable. Rhubarb and strawberries are both high in vitamin C, fiber, and calcium, and walnuts are loaded with omega 3 essential fatty acids—important nutrients to keep you off the sugar roller coaster. This delicious dessert tastes just as yummy at breakfast.

4 cups (680 g) sliced strawberries
2 cups (245 g) diced rhubarb
3 tablespoons (45 ml) maple syrup, or to taste
1 teaspoon grated lemon zest
2 tablespoons agar-agar flakes
1 tablespoon kudzu, diluted in 2 tablespoons (30 ml) cold water
1 cup (240 ml) yogurt
½ cup (60 g) almonds, chopped
¼ cup (30 g) walnuts, chopped

Combine strawberries, rhubarb, maple syrup, and lemon rind in a saucepan and bring to a boil. Sprinkle in agar-agar flakes and simmer until all flakes are dissolved (about 7 to10 minutes). Add dissolved kudzu and stir until mixture thickens. Transfer to a bowl or individual cups and refrigerate until set. Serve with yogurt and chopped nuts on top. Garnish with strawberry slices and a sprig of mint, if desired.

YIELD: 4 SERVINGS
EACH WITH: Calories 290.23; Calories From Fat 129.47; Total Fat 15.44 g; Cholesterol 3.68 mg; Sodium 48.53 mg; Potassium 743.9 mg; Total Carbohydrates 33.23 g; Fiber 6.72 g; Sugar 22.4 g; Protein 9.71 g
BLOOD SUGAR BALANCE RATING: High
NOTE: Kudzu is a thickener and is available in well-stocked supermarkets. If you can't find it, substitute corn or rice starch.

Health Facilitators	Nutrient Density Rating
Protein	Low
Fat	Low
Carbohydrate	High
Enzymes	High
Antioxidants	High
Fiber	High

CHAPTER 6

Type 2 Sugar Addiction

"Feed Me Now or I'll Kill You": When life's stress has exhausted your adrenal glands

ARE YOU A TYPE 2 SUGAR ADDICT?

Your total score will tell you whether you fit the Type 2 profile.

____Do you find that you are often thirsty and have to urinate frequently? (10 points)

____Do you get recurrent sore throats and swollen glands? (10 points)

____Is life a crisis to you? (15 points)

____Do you enjoy the rush of energy you feel when you are in a crisis? (15 points)

____When you are stressed out, does your energy take a nosedive? (15 points)

____Do you sometimes get dizzy when you stand? (15 points)

____Do you have chronic severe exhaustion, chronic fatigue syndrome, or fibromyalgia, which followed an acute infection, pregnancy, or incident of extreme stress? (25 points)

____Are you very irritable when hungry? Do you get a "feed me *now* or I'll kill you" feeling? (35 points)

____Your total score

Score

0–24: You are probably a type B "low-key" person with healthy adrenals.

25–49: You are developing early stages of adrenal fatigue.

50–75: This suggests moderate adrenal exhaustion, and your body is crying out for help.

Over 75: You are suffering from severe adrenal exhaustion, and likely are feeling awful overall.

THE TYPE 2 SUGAR ADDICT

If you are a Type 2 sugar addict, life is an ongoing crisis. Like an air traffic controller, you are always scanning your environment for the next big problem. Although some of your problems are real, many of your crises are self-made because you are anxious and overreact to what is really happening. Most Type 2 sugar addicts are women, which means you may also be juggling the stress of work along with the already heavy demands of being a wife and mother. All this taxes your adrenal, or "stress handler," glands.

How the Adrenal Glands Work

You've probably heard of the fight or flight response. When you are stressed out or perceive danger, your pituitary gland tells your adrenal glands to release adrenaline, or epinephrine, so that your heart rate and pulse increase to prepare you for action. The adrenal glands are also responsible for maintaining stable blood sugar levels when you are stressed out. They do this by producing cortisol, which raises blood sugar slowly and steadily.

In prehistoric times, this response was only triggered occasionally; for example, when a saber-toothed tiger was running after you. But today, when everything seems like a crisis, you are repeatedly reacting to stimuli, even the cell phone ringing, the e-mail dinging, and the car horn honking. For some time, the adrenal glands can keep you going, giving you an adrenaline high that feels good, like Superwoman! But pretty soon your glands begin to get stressed out and tired and don't give you the "kick" that you need. That's when you reach for sugar and caffeine to give them a boost.

When the sugar hits your system, your blood sugar skyrockets, dramatically increasing insulin production to process the sugar out of your bloodstream. This reaction results in a steep drop in blood sugar levels known as hypoglycemia. This can make you irritable and hungry and feel like you need to eat right *now*!

To make matters worse, caffeine amplifies your body's irritable and anxious reaction to low blood sugar. So, you reach for more sugar. This helps you feel better temporarily as your blood sugar rises, but when your blood sugar drops again, the adrenals have to kick into gear and stimulate more cortisol to keep blood sugar stable. Every time you eat sweets you put your body under stress and drive your sugar addiction. You also are likely gaining weight because the sugar triggers an excess of insulin, which packs on fat. When severe to the point of triggering chronic fatigue or fibromyalgia, adrenal fatigue is associated with an average weight gain of 32.5 pounds.

Good Info to Know!

Did you know that the adrenal glands also help maintain normal energy levels, regulate immunity, maintain blood pressure, and produce several different hormones? Besides cortisol and adrenaline, your adrenals also create dehydroepiandrosterone (DHEA, also called the fountain-of-youth hormone, which can help you feel more energetic), aldosterone (which maintains salt and water at proper levels in the body), and even part of your estrogen and testosterone.

The Effect of Sugar on Your Adrenal Glands over Time

When you repeatedly "use" sugar for an energy boost, you experience subsequently more severe dips in blood sugar, which drive the adrenals even harder. Ultimately, if you stay in this pattern your adrenals can become exhausted. With adrenal fatigue, you may find it difficult to get out of bed in the morning. You may have chronic sore throats and recurrent swollen glands in your neck. You might get sick more often and have difficulty recovering. You may have low blood pressure and feel dizzy upon standing. All these are symptoms of underproduction of cortisol, which happens when we are excessively stressed out and the adrenals get exhausted and produce too little cortisol. The most overt symptom besides the fatigue is irritability when you're hungry, leaving anyone standing between you and a sugar snack in mortal danger!

If left untreated, adrenal fatigue can lead to chronic fatigue syndrome and fibromyalgia. These conditions are characterized by insomnia despite exhaustion, as your adrenal glands lose their ability for self-regulation. Cortisol levels are too low during the day, causing fatigue, irritability, and muscle spasms, and at night, as cortisol levels go too high, insomnia occurs. Low blood sugar can also throw your muscles into spasm, causing chronic pain.

Because of its effects on the immune system, adrenal exhaustion can also lead to autoimmune diseases (e.g., lupus). Excess cortisol elevates blood sugar, increasing your risk of diabetes. It directly raises blood pressure (hypertension), can cause loss of bone strength (osteoporosis), and can trigger sometimes massive weight gain from the elevated insulin levels. Many people who have adrenal problems also have hypothyroidism, or low thyroid function, the symptoms of which may include fatigue, aches and pains, weight gain, cold intolerance, and elevated cholesterol levels.

Treating Adrenal Exhaustion

Supporting your adrenal glands increases their effectiveness at balancing production of cortisol, the primary stress hormone that keeps your blood sugar stable. This will help stop sugar cravings, ending the cycle of addiction. For many people, dietary and lifestyle changes are enough to help heal their adrenal glands. Adding natural support with adrenal glandulars, licorice, vitamins C and B5, and other nutrients (such as in the Adrenal Stress-End supplement by Enzymatic Therapy) can resolve adrenal fatigue for most people.

In severe cases, holistic physicians can prescribe bioidentical cortisol in tiny (physiological) amounts. Studies and decades of clinical experience show that cortisol, or hydrocortisone (called Cortef by prescription), in these tiny amounts is very safe, even if used long term. Higher doses (over 20 mg/day of Cortef, or 4 to 5 mg of prednisone), however, can be very toxic. A holistic practitioner will know how to interpret your symptoms and lab tests and give you the dose you need to feel better. For more information, see *Beat Sugar Addiction Now!*

HEAL YOUR ADRENAL GLANDS BY EATING TO BALANCE BLOOD SUGAR

It's time to get off of the sugar addiction roller coaster. The first step is ending the high caused by that adrenaline rush and the low that follows, hypoglycemia. To do this, you will need to learn new ways to eat, regarding both *what* you put into your mouth and how often you do so. While healing your adrenal glands, you'll be choosing foods that will keep your blood sugar balanced throughout the day.

Stabilize Blood Sugar with Protein

Protein is a Type 2 sugar addict's best defense against sugar addiction. Because you digest protein slowly and steadily, it gives you long-lasting energy without causing blood sugar swings. And by keeping your blood-sugar level stable, protein markedly decreases your sugar cravings.

A healthy diet should include at least 15 to 30 percent of daily calories from protein, or at least 1 gram of protein for every 3 pounds of body weight. For most people, 50 grams of protein a day is adequate, although when you are trying to break a sugar addiction, you might find that you need more to manage cravings. You'll find that protein is the main element in the recipes that follow, and they provide more than enough protein to help you feel better. You can then use these recipes as a model for meals you may want to create on your own or eat in a restaurant.

Good high-protein foods include lean meats, such as beef, chicken, and turkey, as well as fish, eggs, beans, nuts and seeds, cheese and low-fat dairy, tofu, and eggs. Try to include protein in all your meals and snacks for the best blood-sugar balance.

Other Critical Sugar-Busting Strategies

Along with eating more protein, Type 2s need to decrease carbohydrates from refined grains (like white flour and white rice) because they raise your blood sugar too quickly. Instead, choose whole grains (in moderation) and other high-fiber foods. Other good choices include fruits and vegetables that are low on the glycemic index, such as berries, apples, peaches, broccoli, red cabbage, chard, asparagus, green beans, and cauliflower. Add variety with seasonings like cinnamon and other spices, lemon, butter, avocado, and extra-virgin olive oil. All of these foods will raise your blood sugar slowly, helping you avoid the sugar roller coaster.

Another benefit to eating fruits and vegetables is that they are rich in vitamin C. Vitamin C boosts your adrenal gland function by helping balance cortisol levels, which in turn keeps your blood-sugar levels stable and decreases the symptoms of low blood sugar and associated sugar cravings. It also allows your body to use fat as fuel, which provides long-lasting energy and fights fatigue. And because vitamin C boosts immune function, it may alleviate the sore throats and respiratory infections that Type 2s are prone to as well.

Although all B vitamins are important for health and stress management, pantothenic acid (vitamin B5) is critical for optimal adrenal function. Like vitamin C, pantothenic acid helps the adrenal glands produce cortisol to keep blood sugar stable. And when you don't get enough pantothenic acid, your adrenal glands may actually shrink.

Chromium, a mineral found in tiny amounts in the human body, is an especially critical nutrient for people with reactive hypoglycemia (low blood sugar during stress). Research in the *Journal of the American College of Nutrition* found that taking chromium can decrease the symptoms of low blood sugar and help battle insulin resistance. In addition to eating chromium-containing foods, you may want to supplement it with 200 mcg a day, an amount found in many multivitamins.

Most of the recipes in this section contain ample amounts of vitamin C, along with B vitamins and minerals like chromium that help strengthen your adrenal glands and fight stress, thereby warding off your tendency to reach for high-glycemic carbohydrate foods.

Good Info to Know!

If you have atypical depression, which is characterized by episodes of severe anxiety (and has symptoms similar to adrenal exhaustion), research has shown that a 600 mcg dose of the mineral chromium may be more effective than Prozac. Egg yolks, beef, cheese, and wine are good chromium sources. Never stop taking prescribed medication without your doctor's approval, but you may want to talk to your holistic doctor about adding chromium to your treatment plan. It is very safe, and it can be found in most health food stores.

What Is the Glycemic Index?

The glycemic index (GI) rates foods in terms of which ones will raise your blood sugar (glucose) fastest and highest. Pure glucose gets a GI score of 100. All other foods are measured relative to this. So if you eat a food with glycemic index over 85, it raises blood sugar almost as much as pure glucose, but a food with a glycemic index under 30 does not raise blood sugar much at all. You also need to keep in mind how much you are eating (portion size). See Appendix B for more information about the index.

Eat More Often for Better Blood Sugar Control

For Type 2s to maintain stable blood sugar, it's also important not to get too hungry. Be sure to include protein with breakfast—it's your first chance to fuel your tank and kick-start your metabolism after fasting the night before. Skipping breakfast yields a stress response that depletes your energy reserves and makes you overly hungry and more likely to reach for sweets and stimulants like caffeine. The best breakfast choices for Type 2 include eggs, high-protein smoothies, fish, lean meats, or a tofu scramble. Try to eat at least 25 percent of your day's food intake at breakfast to give yourself a solid foundation for the rest of the day.

Instead of consuming three large meals, eating small, high-protein, low-sugar meals every few hours (known as "grazing") can keep blood sugar levels balanced by preventing big spikes after eating and steep drops in the long lulls between meals. This can make a huge difference in the way you feel. Of course, you'll have to downsize your meals in order to avoid gaining weight. Determine the number of calories you normally consume and divide them among five smaller meals.

Another way to space out your food intake is to have three smaller meals plus two snacks per day. High-protein snack options include mixed nuts and an apple, hard-boiled eggs, cheese, no-sugar-added nut butter and celery, a protein smoothie, and coconut milk. Try eating a snack about two to three hours after breakfast or lunch, or if your blood sugar feels like it is starting to drop (e.g., if you feel irritable or shaky).

If you have adrenal fatigue, at night you may experience a drop in blood sugar that causes you to wake up suddenly (usually wide awake and sometimes in a sweat). If low blood sugar is the cause, a high-protein bedtime snack will keep your blood sugar from dropping while you sleep. To combat this, eat one to two ounces of turkey, an egg, or a bit of cheese at bedtime.

Nuts: A Sugar-Busting Snack

Besides containing enough fat and protein to keep you from reaching for a sweet pick-me-up, nuts have an interesting side benefit. Research shows that eating ½ cup of walnuts a day tends to lower your cholesterol level, without causing weight gain. This may be because nuts are high in an essential fatty acid called alpha-linolenic acid, which seems to increase your metabolism.

You Don't Have to Swear Off Sweets Entirely

Remember that the eating plan for Type 2 does not say you can never have any sweets. Simply save them for when they will give you the most pleasure and have them in very small amounts. For example, if you are out for dinner with friends and you see a dessert to die for, have one or two bites and share the rest. Eighty percent of the pleasure comes from the first bite or two. It's eating the rest that puts you on the sugar roller coaster!

Rather than reaching for cookies or a candy bar, eat ½ to 1 ounce of antioxidant-rich dark chocolate instead. Choose the best quality chocolate you can afford, and savor every bite! You might pair your daily chocolate allowance with other healthful indulgences like a hot bath or a glass of wine so it feels like more of a splurge. In addition, you can "have your cake and eat it too" by occasionally eating sugar-free chocolate. Our favorites are the ones made by Russell Stover and Godiva. For a real treat, try the sugar-free line from Abdallah Candies (www.abdallahcandies.com).

If you need a "sugar fix," you may also eat one or two pieces of a low-glycemic whole fruit, such as cherries, grapefruit, apples, pears, plums, peaches, strawberries, oranges, grapes, and kiwi. Whole fruits contain dietary fiber, which slows down the rate at which your insulin levels spike. Higher-glycemic fruits such as mangoes, apricots, and pineapple are okay in moderation.

Dr. T's Tip: A Healthy Energy Boost

If you need a caffeine "kick" in the morning to get jump started, limit yourself to one 8-ounce cup of coffee, or better yet, drink a cup of regular tea in the morning. Then switch to caffeine free or herbal teas for the rest of the day. Green tea (regular or decaf) is a good choice because it contains theanine, which provides energy but helps you stay calm and focused. Licorice tea is another good choice. Not only is it naturally sweet, it also helps improve your adrenal function (and, thus, your ability to handle stress) thanks to a compound called glycyrrhizin. Don't drink more than one cup a day, and don't drink licorice tea if you have high blood pressure.

Stop Hypoglycemia in Its Tracks

When your blood sugar is dropping and you get irritable and shaky, like you're going to pass out, place a few Tic Tacs (not the sugar-free ones), or one packet or ½ to 1 teaspoon (2 to 4 g) of sugar, or a half a Lifesaver under your tongue so that the sugar can be absorbed immediately into your bloodstream. This brings your blood sugar levels back to normal and stops the low blood sugar symptoms in seconds, without putting you on the sugar roller coaster. Follow up with a high-protein snack to keep your blood sugar steady.

Drink More Water and Enjoy Your Salt Shaker to Support Your Adrenal Glands

Your adrenal glands help your body handle stressful periods by maintaining blood sugar, blood volume, and blood pressure. But low adrenal function also makes it hard to hold on to the salt and water needed to maintain proper blood pressure. That means Type 2s, who generally have some degree of adrenal exhaustion, are frequently dehydrated and often have low blood pressure. The solution is to drink more water and eat more salt (salt acts like a sponge that keeps water in your body). If your mouth and lips feel dry, drink up!

When you have underactive adrenal glands, you will often have salt cravings as well—this is your body's way of telling you that it needs sodium. If you have low blood pressure, get lightheaded occasionally when you stand up, or sweat a lot, especially during the summertime, you probably need to consume more salt. However, if you have high blood pressure or congestive heart failure, it is usually best not to increase your salt intake unless directed by your health practitioner.

Support the Adrenals with Supplements

In addition to following a high-protein, low-carb diet with frequent small meals, and optimizing water and salt intake, you can also take supplements to support and help heal your adrenal glands directly. These include adrenal glandulars, licorice, vitamin C, pantothenic acid, tyrosine, and glutathione. To simplify things, the first five supplements below can all be found in a combination product called *Adrenal Stress-End from Enzymatic Therapy*. You'll find more information about this in Appendix A.

Adrenal glandulars Basically ground-up adrenal glands from animals, these have the exact nutrients that your own adrenals need and are a rich source of nutritional support. Choose a brand that ensures that the animal sources are not at risk of having worrisome infections.

Licorice Licorice slows the breakdown of the adrenal hormones in your body. Take 200–400 mg a day of an extract standardized to contain 5 percent of the active agent glycyrrhizin.

Vitamin C Vitamin C helps balance the production of cortisol, which regulates blood sugar. It also improves immune function. Take 300–1,000 mg daily.

Vitamin B5 (Pantothenic Acid) Vitamin B5 is also necessary to produce cortisol, which regulates blood sugar. Take 100–300 mg daily.

Tyrosine An amino acid and building block for adrenal hormones, tyrosine decreases sugar cravings. Take 500–1,000 mg daily.

Glutathione (GSH) A mix of three amino acids, glutathione helps insulin function, stabilizing blood sugar and helping to decrease sugar cravings. Take 250-600 mg N-Acetyl Cysteine (NAC) a day, 500–1,000 mg glutamine a day, and 500–1,000 mg glycine a day. These, along with most other key nutrients, can be found in the Energy Revitalization System multivitamin powder from Enzymatic Therapy.

These supplements are discussed in depth in *Beat Sugar Addiction Now!* I recommend working with a holistic physician. You can find more than 1,400 board-certified holistic physicians at www.holisticboard.org. An accredited naturopathic doctor (ND) can also be very helpful. Search for one at www.naturopathic.org, the website of the American Association of Naturopathic Physicians. If you also have severe fatigue, CFS, or fibromyalgia, you can find a physician at a Fibromyalgia and Fatigue Center near you (www.fibroandfatigue.com).

Make Stress Relief a Part of Your Day

Besides giving your body and adrenal glands the nutritional and supplemental support they need, it's also important to find ways to release stress. Many kinds of yoga, meditation, and tai chi are wonderful adrenal healers! So is the relaxation response, created by Herbert Benson, M.D., Associate Professor of Medicine at Harvard Medical School and founder of the Mind Body Medical Institute in Chestnut Hill, Massachusetts. The relaxation response refers to a physical state of deep rest that changes your physical and emotional responses to stress. Visit www.relaxationresponse.org for more information. You may also activate the relaxation response by practicing Yoga Nidra, or yogic sleep. To learn more, visit www.sacredfireyoga.com. Transcendental meditation is another excellent and easy-to-learn yoga technique that research has shown to be helpful for stress relief (I recommend the book *Transcedence* by Norman Rosenthal, M.D., or see www.TM.org).

CHAPTER 7

Recipes for Type 2 Sugar Addiction

The ingredients in these recipes have been specifically chosen to help nourish your adrenal glands and balance your blood sugar levels. For the best blood sugar control, try eating at least three meals a day, or five smaller meals per day, each with 20 to 30 grams or more of protein. Over the course of a day you should also eat at least four cups of low-GI vegetables, one or two fruits, and several tablespoons of healthy fat. These recipes provide easy, delicious ways to meet those goals. Let's get cookin'!

SATIATING SEAFOOD SCRAMBLE

Enjoy the delicious flavor of this wholesome seafood and egg dish rich in omega-3s—it's sure to satisfy and to keep blood sugar levels balanced for hours. Omega-3s satiate hunger, curbing your appetite for long periods in between meals, and these healthy fats score a zero on the glycemic index. (An added bonus: Omega-3s decrease inflammation and improve brain function.) This recipe also contains ingredients high in vitamin C to support your adrenal glands, antioxidant vitamin E, and blood sugar–balancing minerals.

1 teaspoon butter or coconut oil
2 trout or salmon fillets (4 ounces, or 115 g each)
1 tablespoon (15 ml) apple cider vinegar
4 organic eggs
4 to 6 romaine lettuce leaves, or 2 cups (40 g) raw spinach
¼ cup (15 g) chopped fresh parsley
¼ cup (15 g) chopped fresh cilantro
2 tablespoons (10 g) grated Parmesan cheese

Preheat grill or grill pan over medium heat. Melt butter or coconut oil in a small bowl over hot water; baste the trout with the butter or coconut oil before lightly grilling over medium heat. Grill until fish flakes easily, about 20 to 25 minutes.

In a deep medium skillet, bring 2 inches (5 cm) of water and the vinegar to a boil over high heat. Reduce heat to simmer. Crack an egg into a small bowl and tip gently into boiling water-vinegar mixture. Repeat with remaining eggs. Cover skillet and cook 3 minutes for soft yolks, or 5 minutes for firmer yolks. Using a slotted spoon, remove the eggs and drain thoroughly.

Divide the lettuce or spinach between two plates. Place the fish on top of the lettuce, and sprinkle with half the parsley and cilantro. Top fish with the poached eggs, then sprinkle with Parmesan cheese and the remaining parsley and cilantro. Serve immediately.

YIELD: 2 SERVINGS
EACH WITH: Calories 426.33; Calories From Fat 246.93; Total Fat 27.48 g; Cholesterol 503.93 mg; Sodium 324.87 mg; Potassium 784.38 mg; Total Carbohydrates 2.67 g; Fiber 0.96 g; Sugar 0.99 g; Protein 40.58 g
NOTE: Choose wild Alaskan salmon if you can; farm-raised salmon has less omega-3s, more inflammatory fats, and 16 times the toxic PCBs (polychlorinated biphenyls).
BLOOD SUGAR BALANCE RATING: Very High

Health Facilitators	Nutrient Density Rating
Protein	High
Fat	Moderate
Carbohydrate	Moderate
Enzymes	High
Antioxidants	High
Fiber	High

GET-UP-AND-GO HUEVOS RANCHEROS

2 large eggs
1⅓ teaspoons extra-virgin olive oil
1 small tomato, chopped
1¼ cups (125 g) scallions, chopped
¼ cup (37 g) green pepper, chopped
¼ cup (36 g) salsa or green chile peppers
½ teaspoon chili powder
¼ teaspoon cilantro, chopped
2 ounces (55 g) shredded low-fat cheddar cheese
Two 6-inch (15-cm) corn tortillas
1 ripe avocado, sliced
⅓ cup (80 ml) sour cream
4 sprigs fresh cilantro
½ cup (120 ml) salsa

Combine the eggs in a mixing bowl and beat with a fork. Heat the oil in a medium nonstick skillet over moderately high heat. Cook the eggs, undisturbed, for 2 to 3 minutes. Meanwhile, in a bowl, combine the tomato, scallions, green pepper, salsa or chiles, chili powder, and cilantro. Add the tomato mixture to the eggs, and scramble with a fork. Reduce heat if necessary, and continue to cook until eggs are set. Remove pan from heat, sprinkle shredded cheese on top of eggs, cover, and let stand for 2 to 3 minutes, or until cheese is melted.

Place tortillas on plates and divide egg mixture between them. Top with avocado slices, sour cream, and cilantro sprigs. Serve with salsa on the side.

YIELD: 2 SERVINGS
EACH WITH: Calories 747.65: Calories From Fat 379.18; Total Fat 43.58 g; Cholesterol 451.76 mg; Sodium 1340.01 mg; Potassium 1903.58 mg; Total Carbohydrates 60.37 g; Fiber 16.71 g; Sugar 12.8 g; Protein 38.28 g
BLOOD SUGAR BALANCE RATING: Very High

Health Facilitators	Nutrient Density Rating
Protein	High
Fat	High
Carbohydrate	Medium
Enzymes	Medium
Antioxidants	High
Fiber	Medium

This perfectly balanced breakfast of protein, healthy fat, and carbohydrate supports your adrenals, which helps balance your blood sugar levels and keep your metabolism running smoothly. Corn tortillas are not only more nutritious than those made from refined white flour (they contain vitamin C, which supports adrenal gland function), they are tastier too. Fresh herbs, avocado, salsa, and cheddar cheese add flavor and stimulate your energy levels and your metabolism.

STRENGTHENING SALMON OMELET WITH FRESH DILL

This is great for a hearty breakfast, a light lunch, or a snack. Salmon is high in vitamins A, B, C, D, and E, and calcium, potassium, zinc, and iron—a veritable multivitamin! Combined with eggs, this delicious dish is true brain food to keep you focused and your blood sugar stable for hours. Serve with a mixed green salad topped with avocado, and you will be more than satisfied.

1 can (7.5 ounces, or 210 g) salmon, packed with spring water
¼ teaspoon salt
2 teaspoons (10 ml) lemon or lime juice
Dash of cayenne (optional)
1 tablespoon (4 g) chopped fresh dill, or 1 teaspoon (1 g) dried oregano
　　or basil
Freshly ground black pepper
2 organic eggs
1 teaspoon unsalted or clarified butter (ghee) or extra-virgin olive oil
2 cups (40 g) mixed salad greens or spinach
½ avocado, sliced

Drain the liquid from the can of salmon and place the fish in a mixing bowl. With a fork, mash the salmon well to break up all the pieces, skin, and bones. Add the salt, lemon juice, cayenne, and dill, and mix well with a fork. Season with pepper to taste. Add the eggs to the salmon mixture and mix in thoroughly. Heat the butter or oil in a 9-inch (23-cm) skillet. Pour in the salmon-egg mixture and smooth out with a fork or spatula. Cook over very low heat for 5 to 6 minutes, or until set. The whole omelet should slide around when you shake the pan. Turn omelet over and cook another 3 minutes; or finish under the broiler. Serve with salad greens and avocado slices.

YIELD: 2 SERVINGS
EACH WITH: Calories 317.8; Calories From Fat 168.08; Total Fat 19.17 g; Cholesterol 298.68 mg; Sodium 812.5 mg; Potassium 799.6 mg; Total Carbohydrates 5.98 g; Fiber 3.76 g; Sugar 0.77 g; Protein 32.62 g
BLOOD SUGAR BALANCE RATING: Very High

Health Facilitators	Nutrient Density Rating
Protein	High
Fat	High
Carbohydrate	Medium
Enzymes	Low
Antioxidants	High
Fiber	Medium

FATIGUE-FIGHTING FLOURLESS CHICKEN FLAPJACKS

1 cooked chicken breast
3 eggs
Dash of cayenne (optional)
Nonstick cooking spray
2 cups (40 g) salad greens or spinach
½ avocado, sliced
2 tablespoons (30 ml) fresh lemon or lime juice

Blend chicken, eggs, and cayenne, if using, in a food processor until completely smooth. (Mixture will look just like thick pancake batter.) Spray a skillet with nonstick cooking spray and heat over medium-high heat. Pour ¼ cup (60 ml) of the chicken mixture into the skillet. You may need to spread the batter a bit so that it is not too thick. Cook for 1 to 2 minutes on each side (these pancakes cook much faster than regular flour pancakes, so watch them closely).

Serve over a bed of fresh salad greens or spinach and top with avocado slices. Sprinkle with lemon or lime juice.

YIELD: 4 TO 5 PANCAKES

EACH WITH: Calories 651.5; Calories From Fat 290.17; Total Fat 30.59 g; Cholesterol 776.02 mg; Sodium 424.9 mg; Potassium 1292.59 mg; Total Carbohydrates 13.54 g; Fiber 7.37 g; Sugar 2.63 g; Protein 78.61 g

BLOOD SUGAR BALANCE RATING: Very High

Health Facilitators	Nutrient Density Rating
Protein	High
Fat	High
Carbohydrate	Medium
Enzymes	High
Antioxidants	High
Fiber	High

These nutrient-dense flourless chicken pancakes are not only delicious, they balance blood sugar too. Free from white flour, which is quickly converted to sugar in the body, this low-carb dish gets you off of the sugar roller coaster and leaves you satisfied.

STIMULATING SNOW PEAS SAUTÉED WITH CHICKEN

Naturally sweet and succulent, snow peas are full of vital nutrients, including vitamin C to nourish your adrenal glands and folate for strengthening your heart (especially important for people with blood sugar disorders like insulin resistance or diabetes). Enjoy the flavors and textures of this energizing dish.

3 tablespoons (45 ml) natural peanut butter
2 tablespoons (30 ml) tamari sauce (wheat-free), or liquid amino acids
2 tablespoons (30 ml) apple cider vinegar
1½ teaspoons (3 g) fresh ginger, minced, or ¼ teaspoon ground ginger
1 clove garlic, minced
⅛ teaspoon cayenne, or to taste
1 pound (455 g) boneless, skinless chicken breasts
1 cup (160 g) chopped red or brown onions,
½ cup (50 g) sliced radishes
¾ cup (115 g) water chestnuts
2 cups (125 g) fresh snow peas, ends trimmed
2 tablespoons (30 ml) extra-virgin olive oil or coconut oil
2 tablespoons (12 g) sliced scallions

Place the first six ingredients (peanut butter through cayenne) in a large mixing bowl and whisk until well blended. Cut the chicken breast into thin strips and toss to coat with peanut butter mixture. Add onions, radishes, and water chestnuts; toss lightly and set aside.

Place the snow peas into a steaming basket inside a medium saucepan with 2 inches (5 cm) of hot water, cover, and place over high heat. Bring water to a boil and steam for 3 to 4 minutes, until peas are crisp-tender. Drain and arrange on a serving platter. Meanwhile, heat oil in a skillet over medium-high heat. Sauté the chicken mixture until meat is cooked through and vegetables are crisp-tender, about 10 minutes. Spoon chicken over snow peas and sprinkle with scallions. Serve immediately.

YIELD: 4 TO 6 SERVINGS
EACH WITH: Calories 213.51; Calories From Fat 87.97; Total Fat 9.38 g; Cholesterol 45.33 mg; Sodium 431.5 mg; Potassium 276.23 mg; Total Carbohydrates 9.39 g; Fiber 2.48 g; Sugar 2.91 g; Protein 22.14 g
BLOOD SUGAR BALANCE RATING: Very High

Health Facilitators	Nutrient Density Rating
Protein	High
Fat	High
Carbohydrate	High
Enzymes	Medium
Antioxidants	High
Fiber	High

BLOOD SUGAR–STABILIZING SEAFOOD SALAD

1 pound (455 g) seafood, such as shrimp, scallops, lobster, crabmeat, or a flaky white fish like flounder (your choice)

1 large head romaine lettuce, gently torn into small pieces

2 large tomatoes, chopped

1 large green bell pepper, chopped

2 celery stalks, chopped

1 carrot, chopped

1 large red onion, chopped

1 cucumber, peeled and chopped

1 avocado, peeled and sliced

1 cup (70 g) broccoli florets, chopped

½ cup (50 g) chopped green olives with pimentos

½ cup (16 g) alfalfa sprouts

4 large garlic cloves, chopped

2 teaspoons fresh basil, chopped

1 teaspoon fresh oregano, chopped

Salt and black pepper

½ lemon

2 tablespoons (30 ml) extra-virgin olive oil

Grill, steam, sauté, or pan-fry the seafood until it is cooked to your liking. Combine seafood and next 14 ingredients (through oregano) into a large salad bowl and toss. Season with salt and pepper to taste, and squeeze lemon over salad. Lightly toss. Drizzle oil over salad, toss lightly again, and serve.

YIELD: 4 SERVINGS

EACH WITH: Amount Per Serving; Calories 343.62; Calories From Fat 147.36; Total Fat 17.07 g; Cholesterol 37.8 mg; Sodium 398.16 mg; Potassium 1159.45 mg; Total Carbohydrates 26.9 g; Fiber 11.04 g; Sugar 7.68 g; Protein 24.87 g

BLOOD SUGAR BALANCE RATING: Very High

Health Facilitators	Nutrient Density Rating
Protein	High
Fat	Medium
Carbohydrate	High
Enzymes	High
Antioxidants	High
Fiber	High

This delicious blend of tasty seafood, extra-virgin olive oil, and nutritious veggies is chock full of omega-3 fatty acids that help balance blood sugar levels. It's also packed with vitamins and minerals, including adrenal-supporting vitamins C, D, E, A, and B; calcium; potassium; magnesium; and zinc; along with immune-boosting, antibacterial, and antiviral garlic.

MOOD-BOOSTING CURRIED QUINOA SALAD WITH TURKEY

This meal is high in both plant and animal protein, which stabilizes blood sugar and ignites neurotransmitters like tryptophan to lift your mood. Are you a vegetarian? No problem. Just take out the turkey and increase the quinoa. You can also substitute lentils or whole grain brown rice. The curry in this recipe adds exotic flavor, and the turmeric it contains is one of the most healthful of spices, improving brain function, speeding wound healing, and even fighting cancer.

½ cup (85 g) quinoa
1 cup (240 ml) purified water
¾ pound (340 g) cooked turkey breast
¼ cup (25 g) chopped scallions
1 tablespoon (15 ml) extra-virgin olive oil
¼ cup (60 ml) lemon juice
Fresh basil, chopped
Curry powder to taste
4 large romaine lettuce leaves

Rinse quinoa well, and drain. Combine quinoa and water in a 2-quart (1.9-L) saucepan, bring to boil, then simmer uncovered for 15 to 20 minutes, or until all the water is absorbed. Fluff quinoa with a fork and let cool slightly. Place quinoa in a large bowl and add the turkey breast, scallions, olive oil, and lemon juice. Add basil and curry powder to taste. Refrigerate for 1 to 2 hours to allow flavors to blend. When ready to serve, divide mixture among lettuce leaves.

YIELD: 3 SERVINGS

EACH WITH: Calories 272; Calories From Fat 72.68; Total Fat 8.16 g; Cholesterol 48.76 mg; Sodium 1157.49 mg; Potassium 583.97 mg; Total Carbohydrates 25.76 g; Fiber 3.13 g; Sugar 4.82 g; Protein 23.75 g

BLOOD SUGAR BALANCE RATING: Very High

Health Facilitators	Nutrient Density Rating
Protein	Very High
Fat	Medium
Carbohydrate	High
Enzymes	Low
Antioxidants	High
Fiber	Very High

STRENGTHENING SALMON LOAF

1 to 1½ cups (225 to 335 g) canned salmon (drained and cleaned)
1 cup (175 g) steel-cut oats
1 teaspoon salt
1 teaspoon black pepper
1 cup (240 ml) rice or almond milk
2 organic eggs, lightly beaten
2 tablespoons (30 ml) ghee, butter, or extra-virgin olive oil
½ cup (75 g) green pepper, diced
½ cup (80 g) red or brown onion, diced

Preheat oven to 350°F (180°C, or gas mark 4). Mix the salmon, oats, salt, pepper, rice or almond milk, and eggs in a bowl and set aside. Heat ghee, butter, or oil in a small skillet over medium-high heat; sauté green pepper and onion until tender, about 7 to 10 minutes. Stir vegetables into salmon mixture. Coat an 8-inch (20-cm) loaf pan with nonstick cooking spray. Spread salmon mixture into pan and bake 30 minutes, or until golden brown.

YIELD: 4 TO 5 SERVINGS

EACH WITH: Calories 276.2; Calories From Fat 101.28; Total Fat 11.51 g; Cholesterol 133.55 mg; Sodium 674.16 mg; Potassium 332.8 mg; Total Carbohydrates 25.19 g; Fiber 3.93 g; Sugar 0.52 g; Protein 18.94 g

BLOOD SUGAR BALANCE RATING: Very High

Health Facilitators	Nutrient Density Rating
Protein	High
Fat	High
Carbohydrate	Medium
Enzymes	Low
Antioxidants	High
Fiber	High

Ghee (clarified butter) increases digestive function and metabolism and is a healthier choice than regular butter because it strengthens rather than clogs the liver and is considered a "pure" fat. It's good for people who are lactose intolerant and provides zero-glycemic fat to keep your blood sugar stable and immune-strengthening vitamins A and D. Ghee also contains butyric acid, which has antiviral and anticancer benefits. The salmon and eggs in this dish provide plenty of healthy lean protein, while the vegetables and oats add a nice balance of low-glycemic carbohydrates. Feel free to add your own favorite herbs and spice it up even more. Serve with a large green salad or other green vegetables.

TOFU EGG SALAD SUPREME

If you are a vegetarian looking for a rich source of protein, make tofu part of your meal plan! Eggs boost the protein content and increase the nutrient density of this delicious dish even more. The raw spinach, avocado, and scallions add plenty of vitamin C and essential minerals that will feed your adrenals while keeping your blood sugar stable. Vary the spices according to your taste and serve as a hearty snack or light meal. Add a whole-grain mini pita if desired.

1 pound (455 g) non-GMO firm tofu
1 to 2 eggs, hard-boiled and chopped
1 tablespoon (9 g) dry mustard powder
¼ teaspoon turmeric
½ teaspoon salt
¼ teaspoon black pepper
1 cup (120 g) diced celery
¼ cup (25 g) minced scallions
3 tablespoons (45 ml) reduced-fat mayonnaise
½ avocado
2 cups (40 g) mixed salad greens or spinach

Crumble tofu and place in a large bowl. Add the eggs, mustard, turmeric, salt, black pepper, celery, scallions, and mayonnaise, and mix well. Serve with avocado and spinach or mixed salad greens.

YIELD: 2 SERVINGS
EACH WITH: Calories 425.97; Calories From Fat 288.86; Total Fat 32.37 g; Cholesterol 113.25 mg; Sodium 976.6 mg; Potassium 1071.82 mg; Total Carbohydrates 13.93 g; Fiber 5.5 g; Sugar 4.8 g; Protein 21.53 g
BLOOD SUGAR BALANCE RATING: Very High

Health Facilitators	Nutrient Density Rating
Protein	High
Fat	Medium
Carbohydrate	Medium
Enzymes	High
Antioxidants	High
Fiber	High

ENERGY-BOOSTING BLACK BEAN CHILI

1 pound (455 g) black beans, picked over and rinsed and soaked overnight
7 cups (1.68 L) purified water
2 tablespoons (30 ml) extra-virgin olive oil
1 medium red or brown onion, chopped
2 cloves garlic, minced
1 small jalapeno pepper, diced
1 green bell pepper, chopped
2 teaspoons (5 g) ground cumin
2 teaspoons (2 g) dried oregano
1 teaspoon dried chili powder
½ teaspoon cayenne
2 bay leaves
½ teaspoon red pepper flakes
28 ounces (785 ml) canned whole tomatoes, chopped (reserve the liquid)
2 tablespoons (8 g) fresh cilantro, chopped
Freshly ground black pepper
1 tablespoon (15 ml) fresh lime juice
2 cups (220 g) grated Gouda or Parmesan cheese
1 cup (240 ml) sour cream

In a heavy-bottomed soup pot, cover drained beans with water and bring to a boil. Reduce heat to medium and cook, uncovered, until beans are tender, about 45 minutes to 1 hour, skimming off any foam that may collect on the surface. In a large nonstick skillet, heat oil over medium-high heat. Sauté onion, garlic, jalapeno pepper, bell pepper, cumin, oregano, and chili powder until vegetables are softened and tender, about 10 minutes. Add to cooked beans the sautéed vegetables, cayenne, bay leaves, red pepper flakes, tomatoes and their juices, cilantro, and black pepper. Cook over low heat for 30 minutes. Add lime juice. Taste and adjust seasonings. Ladle into bowls and top with grated cheese and a spoonful of sour cream.

YIELD: 8 SERVINGS
EACH WITH: Calories 264.06; Calories From Fat (15%) 38.44; Total Fat 4.4 g; Cholesterol 0 mg; Sodium 236.76 mg; Potassium 1131.46 mg; Total Carbohydrates 45.4 g; Fiber 16.17 g; Sugar 5.38 g; Protein 13.57 g
BLOOD SUGAR BALANCE RATING: Very High

If you're wondering how to replace red meat in your diet, try rich-tasting black beans. They are high in fiber and low on the glycemic index, which means they prevent blood sugar levels from rising too rapidly— making them an excellent choice for Type 2s and people with hypoglycemia or diabetes. Chili powder, cumin, tomatoes, lime, garlic, and onions pack this dish with vitamins A, C, B6, and folate; chromium; potassium, tryptophan, and fiber to support healthy adrenal glands as well as an efficient metabolism.

Health Facilitators	Nutrient Density Rating
Protein	High
Fat	Medium
Carbohydrate	High
Enzymes	Medium
Antioxidants	High
Fiber	Very High

SUSTAINING SALMON-AVOCADO SALAD

On the run? Try this salad when you want a balanced, nutritious, tasty lunch and don't have much time for preparation. Avocadoes are high in fiber, which helps stabilize blood sugar levels. Omega-3–rich salmon gives you energy for hours. And the onions and lime juice add vitamin C for adrenal support and a zesty flavor too.

1 ripe medium avocado
1 teaspoon lemon or lime juice
1 can (6 ounces, or 170 g) salmon or light tuna, packed in water
3 black olives
1 tablespoon (6 g) chopped scallions
½ teaspoon sea salt (optional)
¼ teaspoon black pepper
1 cup (20 g) mixed salad greens or spinach

Mash avocado and add lemon or lime juice. Add salmon or tuna, olives, scallions, salt, and pepper. Mix together, and serve on salad greens.

YIELD: 1 SERVING
EACH WITH: Calories 546.86; Calories From Fat 310.62; Total Fat 36.4 g; Cholesterol 139.48 mg; Sodium 1772.56 mg; Potassium 1604.04 mg; Total Carbohydrates 18.07 g; Fiber 13.16 g; Sugar 0.91 g; Protein 43.78 g
BLOOD SUGAR BALANCE RATING: Very High

Health Facilitators	Nutrient Density Rating
Protein	High
Fat	High
Carbohydrate	High
Enzymes	High
Antioxidants	High
Fiber	High

LESS-STRESS SHIITAKE CREAMED SPINACH

3 to 4 cups (60 to 80 g) spinach, rinsed, well-drained, and chopped
2 tablespoons (28 g or 30 ml) unsalted butter, ghee, or extra-virgin olive oil, divided
2 tablespoons (20 g) chopped red onion
2 cups (140 g) shiitake mushrooms, thinly sliced
1 teaspoon lemon zest
Freshly ground black pepper
1 teaspoon Dijon mustard
½ cup (120 ml) heavy cream, heated to simmering
1 clove garlic, chopped

Wash spinach well, removing stems. With water still clinging to leaves, place in a medium saucepan with a tight-fitting lid. Turn heat to medium-high and steam until leaves are wilted, about 2 to 3 minutes. Drain in a colander, pressing out all liquid with the back of a wooden spoon. Chop finely and set aside. In a large nonstick skillet, melt 1 tablespoon (14 g or 15 ml) butter, ghee, or oil over medium-high heat. Sauté onion and mushrooms until softened, about 5 minutes. Add lemon zest and season to taste with black pepper. Remove from pan and set aside. Melt remaining 1 tablespoon (14 g or 15 ml) butter or oil in same skillet. Add mustard and cook 2 minutes over medium heat, sitting constantly. Whisk in the hot cream and stir until smooth and thickened. Add chopped spinach, onion mixture, and garlic, and stir well. Cook until heated through. Taste and adjust seasonings.

YIELD: 4 SERVINGS
EACH WITH: Calories 301.82; Calories From Fat 153.17; Total Fat 17.45 g; Cholesterol 56.02 mg; Sodium 40.17 mg; Potassium 346.17 mg; Total Carbohydrates 33.5 g; Fiber 2.25 g; Sugar 0.46 g; Protein 5.77 g
BLOOD SUGAR BALANCE RATING: High

Health Facilitators	Nutrient Density Rating
Protein	Medium
Fat	Medium
Carbohydrate	High
Enzymes	Medium
Antioxidants	High
Fiber	High

Shiitake mushrooms have more flavor than other mushrooms, and they are highly medicinal and are high in blood sugar–stabilizing protein as well. In addition, they are loaded with B vitamins to fight stress, calcium to strengthen bones, and magnesium for soothing the nerves, and they are known for immune-boosting properties that help fight against invading viruses and bacteria. Spinach provides vitamin C and minerals to support adrenal health.

LOW-GLYCEMIC GREEN BEANS IN PUNCHY PEANUT SAUCE

Green beans are an excellent source of protein, fiber, and low-glycemic carbohydrates. They also offer folic acid and vitamin C and contain significant amounts of magnesium, iron, potassium, and phosphorus, all of which support a healthy metabolism. Peanut butter, fresh ginger, garlic, and herbs help support adrenal glands and heal Type 2 sugar addiction.

1 pound (455 g) fresh green beans, ends trimmed, and sliced diagonally into 1-inch (2.5-cm) pieces
3 tablespoons (45 ml) organic natural peanut butter, smooth or chunky
1 cup (240 ml) vegetable stock or purified water
1 clove garlic, minced
2 teaspoons (4 g) fresh ginger, peeled and finely minced
1 tablespoon (15 ml) fresh lime juice
¼ teaspoon cayenne
1 tablespoon (15 ml) low-sodium tamari sauce (wheat-free)
1 tablespoon (4 g) fresh cilantro, minced

Cook green beans in boiling water until just tender, about 5 minutes or more. Drain and set aside. In a small saucepan, bring peanut butter, stock or water, garlic, ginger, lime juice, cayenne, and tamari to a boil. Reduce heat and simmer 5 minutes. Taste and adjust seasonings. Pour sauce over green beans. Sprinkle with cilantro and serve immediately.

YIELD: 4 SERVINGS
EACH WITH: Calories 135.12; Calories From Fat 59.08; Total Fat 6.99 g; Cholesterol 1.8 mg; Sodium 324.11 mg; Potassium 398.51 mg; Total Carbohydrates 13.68 g; Fiber 4.7 g; Sugar 3.75 g; Protein 7.23 g
BLOOD SUGAR BALANCE RATING: High

Health Facilitators	Nutrient Density Rating
Protein	Medium
Fat	Medium
Carbohydrate	High
Enzymes	High
Antioxidants	Very High
Fiber	Very High

REVITALIZING VEGETABLE STIR-FRY

2 tablespoons (30 ml) peanut oil
2 teaspoons (4 g) fresh ginger, peeled and finely minced
2 cloves garlic, minced
1 cup (130 g) thinly slivered carrots
1 cup (120 g) thinly slivered zucchini
1 green or red bell pepper, thinly sliced
2 cups (140 g) thinly sliced shiitake or cremini mushrooms
1 tablespoon (15 ml) low-sodium tamari sauce (wheat-free)
½ cup (120 ml) vegetable stock
2 teaspoons (10 ml) sesame oil
1 tablespoon (6 g) chopped scallions

In a wok or a large nonstick skillet, heat oil over medium-high heat. When oil is hot, add ginger and garlic and stir-fry for 30 seconds. Add carrots, zucchini, and bell pepper and stir-fry 2 minutes. Add mushrooms and stir-fry 2 minutes more. Sprinkle with tamari and stir-fry until well-blended. Add stock or water and turn heat to high. Cover and cook about 2 minutes, or until vegetables are tender. Sprinkle with sesame oil and scallions.

YIELD: 4 SERVINGS
EACH WITH: Calories 287.24; Calories From Fat 108.11; Total Fat 12.18 g; Cholesterol 0.9 mg; Sodium 245.97 mg; Potassium 679.07 mg; Total Carbohydrates 36.2 g; Fiber 5.01 g; Sugar 3.87 g; Protein 9.24 g
BLOOD SUGAR BALANCE RATING: High

Health Facilitators	Nutrient Density Rating
Protein	Medium
Fat	Low
Carbohydrate	High
Enzymes	Medium
Antioxidants	High
Fiber	High

The combination of delicious vegetables in this dish is flavor-filled and nutrient-dense, and it promotes balanced blood sugar levels. It's loaded with vitamin C and lutein, both of which are good for eyes as well as adrenal glands, and shiitake mushrooms provide energizing protein that will strengthen your immune system. Serve alongside fish or chicken or over a bed of steamed rice, quinoa, or a raw salad. Your body will thank you!

COMFORTING CAULIFLOWER SALAD

Choose this wonderful winter salad when temperatures drop and you want to feel cozy. The sweet, aromatic, aniselike flavor of fennel perfectly balances the milder but distinctive taste of cauliflower, an excellent source of vitamins C and K, fiber, potassium, and the B complex (stress-busting) vitamins. Fennel is loaded with vitamin C and filling fiber, and the Parmesan cheese and olive oil round out the flavor and add a serving of healthy, hunger-quelling fat.

1 large head of cauliflower
1 pound (455 g) fennel stalks, coarsely chopped
⅓ cup (80 ml) extra-virgin olive oil
2 tablespoons (30 ml) balsamic vinegar
Salt and freshly ground black pepper
2 tablespoons (10 g) grated Parmesan

Break the cauliflower into florets and steam it until just tender, about 10 minutes. Cool it in ice water immediately after cooking. Put the florets in a salad bowl and add the chopped fennel. In a small bowl, mix together the olive oil and balsamic vinegar. Add salt and pepper to taste. Pour the dressing over the cauliflower and fennel, toss, and serve with grated Parmesan.

YIELD: 6 SERVINGS
EACH WITH: Calories 176.29; Calories From Fat 112.63; Total Fat 12.76 g; Cholesterol 1.47 mg; Sodium 108.26 mg; Potassium 745.36 mg; Total Carbohydrates 13.91 g; Fiber 5.84 g; Sugar 4.17 g; Protein 4.38 g
BLOOD SUGAR BALANCE RATING: High

Health Facilitators	Nutrient Density Rating
Protein	Low
Fat	Low
Carbohydrate	Very high
Enzymes	Very high
Antioxidants	Very High
Fiber	Very High

SATISFYING SPAGHETTI SQUASH WITH PINE NUTS

½ cup (70 g) pine nuts
2 medium spaghetti squash
2 tablespoons (28 g or 30 ml) unsalted butter or ghee (clarified butter)
½ cup (30 g) chopped fresh basil or parsley
1 teaspoon salt
1 teaspoon freshly ground black pepper

Preheat oven to 350°F (180°C, or gas mark 4). Spread the pine nuts on a baking sheet and toast them until lightly browned, 1 to 2 minutes, watching carefully to be sure they do not burn. Remove them from the oven and set aside to cool. Liberally prick the spaghetti squash with a fork to prevent them from bursting when baking. Place them on a baking sheet and bake 45 minutes to 1 hour. Remove from the oven and set aside to cool. Cut the squash in half lengthwise, then scoop out and discard the seeds. With a fork, comb strands of squash flesh from each half. Discard remaining squash skin. In a large skillet, melt the butter over low heat, add the squash strands, and toss until squash is heated through. Stir in the pine nuts, basil or parsley, salt, and pepper. Serve hot.

YIELD: 4 TO 6 SERVINGS

EACH WITH: Calories 125.31; Calories From Fat 99.56; Total Fat 11.7 g; Cholesterol 10.18 mg; Sodium 519.85 mg; Potassium 143.66 mg; Total Carbohydrates 5.13 g; Fiber 1.29 g; Sugar 1.73 g; Protein 2.07 g

BLOOD SUGAR BALANCE RATING: High

Health Facilitators	Nutrient Density Rating
Protein	Medium
Fat	Medium
Carbohydrate	High
Enzymes	Low
Antioxidants	High
Fiber	Very High

Protein-rich pine nuts are high in fiber; vitamins C, A, E, and B6; and zinc; magnesium; and calcium—a micronutrient combo that contributes to keeping your blood sugar balanced. Spaghetti squash is fun to prepare and even more fun to eat. The flavor of basil and crunch of toasted pine nuts are the perfect partners for this mild-mannered squash.

TIJUANA TROUT WITH CORN SALSA

This light and zesty salsa is especially good with such oily fish as trout, halibut, and salmon. Corn is a good source of B vitamins (for fighting stress and keeping you calm) and vitamin C (friend to the adrenal glands, antioxidant, and immune booster). It's also filled with fiber to slow nutrient absorption and prevent spikes in blood sugar, making this a perfect dish for Type 2s. Serve it with crackers for a delicious snack. Keep the salsa for up to a week in the refrigerator.

1 cup (165 g) corn kernels, fresh or frozen and thawed
¼ green pepper, seeded and diced
¼ red pepper, seeded and diced
½ medium red or brown onion, diced
⅔ cup (160 ml) freshly squeezed lemon juice
⅔ cup (160 ml) freshly squeezed lime juice
2 teaspoons seeded, diced chiles
Four 6-ounce (170-g) trout fillets
6 sprigs fresh cilantro, finely chopped
1 avocado, sliced into 4 sections

In a small glass bowl, combine the corn, green and red peppers, onions, lemon juice, lime juice, and chiles. Stir well and chill for at least 1 to 2 hours. Preheat broiler. Broil trout fillets for 5 to 7 minutes, or until they flake easily with a fork. Garnish each serving with corn salsa, cilantro, and a slice of avocado.

YIELD: 4 SERVINGS
EACH WITH: Calories 420.38; Calories From Fat 169.89; Total Fat 19.29 g; Cholesterol 115.67 mg; Sodium 183.96 mg; Potassium 1224.52 mg; Total Carbohydrates 19.95 g; Fiber 4.84 g; Sugar 4.03 g; Protein 43.79 g
BLOOD SUGAR BALANCE RATING: Very High

Health Facilitators	Nutrient Density Rating
Protein	High
Fat	Medium
Carbohydrate	Low
Enzymes	Medium
Antioxidants	High
Fiber	Medium

NOURISHING LENTIL AND BROWN RICE CASSEROLE

1 cup (190 g) brown rice
6 cups (1.44 L) vegetable stock
2 cloves garlic, peeled and minced
1 tablespoon (3 g) freshly chopped basil
2 tablespoons (30 ml) extra-virgin olive oil
2 cups (450 g) lentils
6 carrots, sliced into small chunks
2 cups (240 g) diced celery
1 small red or brown onion, diced
Salt and freshly ground black pepper

Place the rice, vegetable stock, garlic, basil, and olive oil in a large pot. Rinse and pick over the lentils. Add the lentils, carrots, celery, and onion to the pot. Bring to a boil, stir once, cover, reduce heat to simmer, and cook for 45 minutes or until liquid is absorbed and the vegetables are tender. Season with salt and pepper to taste.

YIELD: 8 SERVINGS
EACH WITH: Calories 382.47; Calories From Fat 62.41; Total Fat 7.01 g; Cholesterol 5.4 mg; Sodium 326.54 mg; Potassium 923.52 mg; Total Carbohydrates 62.72 g; Fiber 18.46 g; Sugar 7.25 g; Protein 19.33 g
BLOOD SUGAR BALANCE RATING: Very High

Health Facilitators	Nutrient Density Rating
Protein	High
Fat	Low
Carbohydrate	Very High
Enzymes	Medium
Antioxidants	High
Fiber	Very High

The combination of lentils and brown rice makes this dish a complete protein, an ample main course, and a balanced meal, especially when topped with your favorite vegetables. This tasty casserole contains plant protein and loads of fiber for balancing blood sugar levels. Top it with a stir-fry of cauliflower, yellow squash, and red peppers. It keeps in the refrigerator for several days and freezes well.

SUPERCHARGED CHICKEN VEGGIE STIR-FRY

Bell peppers are packed with nutrients and antioxidants like vitamin C to support adrenal function and B vitamins for managing stress. Chicken provides plenty of healthy protein for balancing your blood sugar levels, while being a rich source of many mood-boosting and calming nutrients, such as vitamin C, B6, folate, chromium, potassium, manganese, tryptophan, and fiber.

1 pound (455 g) boneless, skinless chicken breasts
2 tablespoons (30 ml) liquid amino acids
2 tablespoons (30 ml) extra-virgin olive oil
3 large tomatoes, cut into chunks
1 green bell pepper, cut into large chunks
1 cup (70 g) shiitake mushrooms, chopped (optional)
1 medium red or brown onion, thinly sliced
1 to 2 garlic cloves, minced
½ cup (120 ml) purified water

Cut chicken breast into 1-inch (2.5-cm) cubes. Place chicken in a small bowl and add the liquid amino acids. Heat the oil in a large skillet over medium heat. Add the tomato, green pepper, mushrooms (if using), onion, and garlic and stir-fry for 2 minutes. Add the chicken mixture to the skillet, add the water, and stir-fry until chicken is cooked through, about 7 to 10 minutes. Serve hot.

YIELD: 2 TO 3 SERVINGS

EACH WITH: Calories 464.36; Calories From Fat 112.67; Total Fat 11.25 g; Cholesterol 144.22 mg; Sodium 524.45 mg; Potassium 1054.31 mg; Total Carbohydrates 24.13 g; Fiber 5.71 g; Sugar 7.54 g; Protein 63.48 g

BLOOD SUGAR BALANCE RATING: Very High

Health Facilitators	Nutrient Density Rating
Protein	Very High
Fat	Low
Carbohydrate	Medium
Enzymes	Low
Antioxidants	High
Fiber	Medium

SALMON WITH JAMMIN' GINGER SALSA

For Salmon

⅓-pound (150-g) salmon fillet, cut into two pieces
2 teaspoons (10 ml) lemon juice
Sea salt and black pepper

For Salsa

1 ripe tomato, diced
½ cup (50 g) minced scallions, plus additional for gainish
1 teaspoon ginger, minced
2 teaspoons (4 g) fresh mint, minced
1 teaspoon lime juice
Sea salt and black pepper
Extra-virgin olive oil (optional)

To make the salmon: Preheat broiler and place an oven-safe stainless steel skillet or cast iron pan under the heat for about 10 minutes to get it very hot. The pan should be 5 to 7 inches from the heat source. Rub salmon with lemon juice, salt and pepper. Carefully remove preheated pan from oven and place salmon on hot pan, skin-side down. Return to broiler and cook for about 7 minutes, or until salmon flakes easily.

To make the salsa: Combine all salsa ingredients. Spoon over salmon. Garnish with additional mint and a drizzle of extra-virgin olive oil, if desired.

YIELD: 2 SERVINGS

EACH WITH: Calories 182.16; Calories From Fat 86.26; Total Fat 9.57 g; Cholesterol 47.58 mg; Sodium 55.32 mg; Potassium 562.74 mg; Total Carbohydrates 6.1 g; Fiber 1.94 g; Sugar 2.54 g; Protein 17.99 g

BLOOD SUGAR BALANCE RATING: Very High

Health Facilitators	Nutrient Density Rating
Protein	High
Fat	Low
Carbohydrate	Low
Enzymes	Medium
Antioxidants	High
Fiber	Low

Type 2s derive enormous nutritional benefits from this flavorful combination of tangy salsa and salmon. In addition to providing omega-3 fatty acids, which support blood sugar and neurotransmitter function, it's also loaded with vitamin C and minerals to support healthy adrenals and metabolism. Even better? You can prepare it in just minutes.

PROTEIN-PACKED CAJUN BEANS WITH TURKEY OR CHICKEN

Beans contain the most fiber of any vegetable, making them ideal for Type 2s to keep blood sugar levels well balanced. High in plant protein, beans are an ideal choice for both vegetarians and meat-eaters alike. Combine them with turkey or chicken and Cajun spices to make a delicious dish that you can eat for lunch or dinner—it's even wonderful for breakfast!

2 teaspoons (10 ml) extra-virgin olive oil, coconut oil, or ghee
1 cup (120 g) celery, diced
¼ cup (40 g) red or brown onion, chopped
½ cup (75 g) green pepper, chopped
1 can (15 ounces, or 425 g) kidney beans
1 can (15 ounces, or 425 g) pinto beans
1 can (15 ounces, or 425 g) black beans
8 ounces (225 g) cooked turkey or chicken breast
1 to 2 cloves garlic, chopped
1 cup (240 ml) purified water
1 bay leaf
1 teaspoon chili powder
1 teaspoon Cajun spices

Pour the oil into a 2-quart (1.9-L) saucepan over medium-high heat; when hot, add the celery, onions, and green pepper and cook, stirring until brown, about 5 to 7 minutes. Add the kidney, pinto, and black beans, chicken or turkey, garlic, water, bay leaf, chili powder, and Cajun spices to the saucepan. Bring to a boil, and then simmer at low heat for 20 minutes. Serve hot.

YIELD: 6 SERVINGS

EACH WITH: Calories 279.09; Calories From Fat 36.25; Total Fat 4.14 g; Cholesterol 32.13 mg; Sodium 604.74 mg; Potassium 735.54 mg; Total Carbohydrates 37.13 g; Fiber 12.65 g; Sugar 2.45 g; Protein 24.13 g

BLOOD SUGAR BALANCE RATING: Very High

Health Facilitators	Nutrient Density Rating
Protein	Very High
Fat	Medium
Carbohydrate	Very High
Enzymes	Low
Antioxidants	High
Fiber	Very High

QUICK CHICKEN CURRY

1 tablespoon (15 ml) extra-virgin olive oil, divided
3 to 4 garlic cloves, minced
1 large red or brown onion, chopped
5 to 6 medium carrots, sliced into sticks
1½ pounds (680 g) boneless, skinless organic chicken breast, cubed
1½ cups (360 ml) chicken stock or broth
1 can (13.5 ounces, or 410 ml) coconut milk
1 cup (130 g) peas, fresh or frozen and thawed
2 to 4 teaspoons (4 to 8 g) curry powder
1 to 2 teaspoons (2 to 4 g) ground ginger

Heat half the oil in a large saucepan over medium heat; sauté garlic and onions about 5 to 10 minutes. Add carrots and continue sautéing several more minutes. Heat remaining oil in a medium saucepan over medium-high heat, and sauté chicken until cooked through. To the onion-carrot mixture, add chicken broth, coconut milk, peas, and cooked chicken. Add curry powder and ginger to taste. Continue to cook until flavors meld and sauce is heated through, about 10 minutes.

YIELD: 5 SERVINGS

EACH WITH: Calories 480.91; Calories From Fat 207.59; Total Fat 24.24 g; Cholesterol 115.67 mg; Sodium 427.92 mg; Potassium 896.83 mg; Total Carbohydrates 18.73 g; Fiber 3.9 g; Sugar 5.61 g; Protein 47.52 g

BLOOD SUGAR BALANCE RATING: Very High

NOTE: You can add any vegetables you like to this versatile recipe. Broccoli and cauliflower are always good additions to curries.

Health Facilitators	Nutrient Density Rating
Protein	High
Fat	High
Carbohydrate	High
Enzymes	Low
Antioxidants	High
Fiber	High

This is comfort food that leaves you balanced and satisfied. It's perfect for those busy nights when you don't want to spend much time in the kitchen. To make the job even quicker, chop the vegetables ahead of time. Coconut milk is a tasty and healthy fat that helps stabilize blood sugar. Peas add a fiber and flavor. Boost the protein by serving over a whole grain such as quinoa or brown rice.

HEALING HALIBUT WITH MEDITERRANEAN TOMATOES

The delicately sweet flavor of halibut pairs well will the herbed tomatoes and makes this dish a nutritional powerhouse. With plenty of protein and fiber; vitamins C, B3 (niacin), B6, B12; antioxidant selenium; magnesium; potassium; chromium; mood-boosting tryptophan; and omega-3s, this dinner will keep your blood sugar levels stable for hours and help restore your adrenal glands. Eat up!

1 tablespoon (15 ml) extra-virgin olive oil
½ cup (120 ml) chicken or vegetable broth, divided
2 medium red or brown onions, cut into medium slices
3 medium cloves garlic, chopped
1 can (15 ounces, or 420 g) diced tomatoes
2 tablespoons (30 ml) fresh lemon juice
½ cup (20 g) chopped fresh basil
2 teaspoons (1.5 g) chopped fresh rosemary
2 teaspoons (1.5 g) chopped fresh thyme
2 pounds (910 g) halibut fillets, cut into 2-inch (5-cm) pieces
Salt and cracked black pepper
Red pepper flakes

Heat oil and 1 tablespoon (15 ml) broth in a 10- to 12-inch (25- to 30-cm) stainless steel pan or skillet over medium heat. Sauté onion for about 5 minutes, until translucent. Add garlic and continue to sauté for another minute. Add remaining broth, diced tomatoes, and lemon juice. Bring to a simmer over high heat, then reduce heat to medium and simmer for about 5 minutes. Add basil, rosemary, thyme, and halibut fillets; cover and simmer for about 5 minutes, or until fish is cooked through. Season with salt, black pepper, and red pepper flakes to taste.

YIELD: 4 SERVINGS

EACH WITH: Calories 330.41; Calories From Fat 81.09; Total Fat 9.05 g; Cholesterol 72.58 mg; Sodium 372.4 mg; Potassium 1285.19 mg; Total Carbohydrates 10.82 g; Fiber 2.31 g; Sugar 2.84 g; Protein 49.63 g

BLOOD SUGAR BALANCE RATING: Very High

Health Facilitators	Nutrient Density Rating
Protein	High
Fat	Medium
Carbohydrate	Medium
Enzymes	Medium
Antioxidants	High
Fiber	High

BANANA BERRY BUZZ

½ cup (120 ml) yogurt
1 cup (170 g) sliced fresh strawberries
1 small banana, broken into pieces
1 scoop (⅓ cup, or 40 g) whey, rice, or pea protein powder
1 tablespoon (8 g) chopped walnuts
½ cup (120 ml) coconut milk
½ cup (120 ml) purified water
6 ice cubes (optional)

Combine all ingredients except ice in a blender and process on high until creamy. Add ice cubes, one at a time, and continue to blend until ice is crushed. Pour into a tall glass and serve immediately.

YIELD: 1 SERVING

EACH WITH: Calories 586.28; Calories From Fat (43%) 253.3; Total Fat 30.46 g; Cholesterol 7.35 mg; Sodium 170.71 mg; Potassium 1164.7 mg; Total Carbohydrates 55.23 g; Fiber 7.75 g; Sugar 30.44 g; Protein 37.67 g

BLOOD SUGAR BALANCE RATING: Very High

Health Facilitators	Nutrient Density Rating
Protein	High
Fat	High
Carbohydrate	High
Enzymes	High
Antioxidants	High
Fiber	High

Simple, easy, and healthfully satisfying, this smoothie is perfect as a dessert, a snack, or even breakfast! Protein, healthy fats, and low-glycemic carbohydrates will keep your blood sugar levels balanced and your adrenal glands healthy. Half of the fat in coconut milk is lauric acid, the essential fatty acid most important to building and maintaining the body's immune system. Coconut milk is also a great source of calcium. Best of all? It may actually help you lose weight.

CALMING COCONUT COOKIES

Can something that tastes this good be good for you? Yes! Not only do these cookies have great flavor, they are packed with fiber to stabilize blood sugar and full of vitamins and minerals such as zinc and calming B vitamins that Type 2 sugar addicts need. Any nut or seed, and many fruits, will work in this recipe, so don't be afraid to experiment. For example, add 2 to 3 tablespoons (15 to 23 g) of grated zucchini to the wet ingredients to add moisture and flavor. If you can't tolerate any dairy, you can swap coconut oil for the butter without changing the flavor. The only sugar in this delicious treat comes from the fruit and the honey, which is all natural. Sweet!

1 organic egg, beaten
¼ cup (60 ml) rice or coconut milk
½ cup (1 stick, or 112 g) organic butter, softened
½ cup (120 ml) coconut oil, warmed to a liquid consistency
½ cup (120 ml) honey
1 teaspoon vanilla extract
1½ cups (190 g) coconut flour
1 teaspoon baking soda
1 teaspoon cinnamon
1 teaspoon sea salt
3 cups (240 g) rolled oats
½ cup (60 g) walnut pieces
¼ cup (55 g) sunflower seeds
½ cup (75 g) minced, peeled apple

Preheat oven to 375°F (190°C, or gas mark 5). Mix together egg, rice or coconut milk, butter, coconut oil, honey, and vanilla in a large bowl. In a small bowl, mix together flour, baking soda, cinnamon, and sea salt. Slowly add dry ingredients (coconut flour, baking soda, cinnamon, sea salt) to wet ingredients, stirring constantly, until you have a smooth batter. Add oats, nut, sunflower seeds, and apple, stirring gently until the mixture is uniform. Drop by spoonfuls onto a greased cookie sheet, and bake for 9 to 12 minutes, or until golden brown around the edges.

YIELD: 25 TO 30 COOKIES
EACH WITH: Calories 133.9; Calories From Fat 65.89; Total Fat 7.63g; Cholesterol 0.03mg; Sodium 15.8mg; Potassium 49.71mg; Total Carbohydrates 15.16g; Fiber 4.58g; Sugar 4.93g; Protein 2.23g
BLOOD SUGAR BALANCE RATING: Medium

Health Facilitators	Nutrient Density Rating
Protein	Medium
Fat	High
Carbohydrate	High
Enzymes	Low
Antioxidants	High
Fiber	Very High

CHAPTER 8

Type 3 Sugar Addiction

The Happy Ho-Ho Hunter: Sugar cravings caused by yeast/candida overgrowth

ARE YOU A TYPE 3 SUGAR ADDICT?

Your total score will tell you whether you fit the Type 3 profile.

_____Do you have chronic nasal congestion or sinusitis? (50 points)

_____Do you have spastic colon or irritable bowel syndrome (gas, bloating, diarrhea and/or constipation)? (50 points)

_____Have you been treated for acne with tetracycline, erythromycin, or any other antibiotic for one month or longer? Or, have you taken antibiotics for any type of infection for more than two consecutive months, or shorter courses more than three times in a twelve-month period? (50 points)

_____Have you taken an antibiotic—even for a single course? (6 points)

_____Do you have chronic fatigue syndrome or fibromyalgia? (50 points)

_____Have you had prostatitis or chronic yeast vaginitis? (25 points)

_____Have you been pregnant? (5 points)

_____Have you taken birth control pills? (15 points)

_____Have you taken corticosteroids, such as Prednisone, for over a month? (15 points)

_____When you are exposed to perfumes, insecticides, or other odors or chemicals, do you develop wheezing, burning eyes, or any other distress? (10 points)

_____Are your symptoms worse on damp or humid days or in moldy places? (10 points)

_____Have you had a fungal infection, such as jock itch, athlete's foot, or a nail or skin infection, that was difficult to treat? (20 points)

_____Do you have postnasal drip or clear your throat a lot? (20 points)

_____Do you crave sugar or breads? (20 points)

_____Do you have food allergies? (20 points)

_____Your total score

Score

If your total is 70 or higher, you likely have yeast/candida overgrowth and should follow the recommendations in this chapter.

THE TYPE 3 SUGAR ADDICT

If you are a Type 3 sugar addict, your life revolves around sugar. You need a sugar fix for breakfast, lunch, dinner, and for all the snacks in between. But it's really not your fault. Inside your body are tricky intestinal microbes known as *Candida albicans*, a yeast that grows in your digestive system by fermenting sugar and carbohydrates, and it is likely that it actually releases a chemical that triggers cravings for sugar. You might as well be saying, "My yeast will have a candy bar, please!"

Yeast is great for bread making because it gobbles up the sugar or honey that is added to it, making a big, puffy, gassy dough that gets bigger as flour is added in. And that's exactly how a person who has a Type 3 sugar addiction feels: bloated, gassy, and distended.

How Yeast Contributes to Sugar Addiction

Yeast wouldn't be a terrible problem if it would stay inside the gut where it belongs without overgrowing. But often it transforms into threads called mycelia that grow into the intestinal wall, which makes the problem of sugar craving worse. The intestinal wall is the main barrier, along with your skin, that determines what stays outside your body and what gets in. To function properly, the lining of your intestines needs to be intact and whole. But when mycelia start permeating the gut, you can get what is known as "leaky gut syndrome." When you have leaky gut syndrome, instead of absorbing your food after it's been completely digested, you absorb partially digested chunks of protein before they've been reduced to their individual amino acids. This situation causes your immune system to go on high alert because it perceives this undigested protein as an outside invader, triggering food allergies and other allergic reactions, as well as other problems.

Because a Type 3 sugar addict's immune system is in perpetual overdrive trying to finish the job of digesting food, fatigue may also drive sugar cravings. You may often feel tired; in severe cases you may even have chronic fatigue syndrome or fibromyalgia. Or in early cases, you may simply have chronic sinusitis, and often run to the doctor for antibiotics to treat what you think is a sinus infection. (Unfortunately, using antibiotics actually creates an environment where yeast flourish.) You also may have problems with your digestion, ranging from gas, bloating, and diarrhea to constipation and irritable bowel syndrome.

The Allergy–Yeast Connection

As we've seen, yeast overgrowth can cause the absorption of incompletely digested protein, triggering allergies to those foods. The more you eat of something, the more of that protein you consume, increasing the risk of developing allergies to the foods you eat most. In addition, for reasons that are not clear, people often also crave the foods they are allergic to.

The most common food allergies are to wheat, milk, chocolate, citrus, and eggs. Often, the food allergy symptoms can resolve on their own once the candida and, if present, the adrenal fatigue experienced with Type 2 sugar addiction are treated. As noted in Chapter 6, low cortisol is associated with immune problems—especially an increased sensitivity to allergens—and allergies often resolve with adrenal support.

On the other hand, if unexplained symptoms/problems persist despite being evaluated by your physician and treating your sugar addiction type, it is a good idea to consider food allergies. Blood tests to diagnose food allergies are notoriously unreliable, however. In my experience, they show that you are allergic to dozens of foods you aren't actually allergic to! Instead, I suggest using Dr. Doris Rapp's Elimination Diet, which you'll find in *Beat Sugar Addiction Now!*

Treating Food Allergies

My favorite way to eliminate food allergies and sensitivities is with a special acupressure/applied kinesiology technique called NAET. One 20-minute treatment can identify and eliminate one allergy or sensitivity. The benefits of NAET can be dramatic. I first learned about it when a practitioner knocked out my severe lifelong hay fever with a single 20-minute treatment. It was like somebody turned off the faucet in my nose. For more information, including contact information for thousands of practitioners worldwide, visit www.naet.com.

Other Contributors to the Yeast–Sugar Problem

Although the main reasons for candida overgrowth are excess sugar intake and antibiotic use, other problems also contribute. For example, frequently taking antacids can also cause yeast overgrowth and worsen sugar cravings. Antacids turn off the stomach acid that usually kills the yeast in the food we eat. Using steroids like prednisone (for asthma or other inflammation) suppresses your immune system as well, and allows the yeast to overgrow. High estrogen birth control pills, may also encourage yeast to go wild.

Another factor in yeast overgrowth and an uncontrollable sweet tooth is not getting enough sleep. Although we need eight to nine hours of sleep a night, most Americans are only getting an average of around six hours and 30 minutes. A lack of sleep makes you feel fatigued, tired, and achy, can make you gain weight, and further suppresses your immune system.

Constant stress can also fuel yeast overgrowth. Your body secretes more cortisol when you're stressed, and chronic high levels of cortisol suppresses your immune system and allows the yeast to overgrow, while also driving sugar cravings.

BREAKING THE CYCLE OF SUGAR ADDICTION

Type 3 sugar addiction is a vicious cycle that begins with the yeast in your gut, which causes sugar cravings and drives you to eat more sugar, which makes your yeast overgrow, which in turn makes you crave more sugar. When you eliminate the yeast overgrowth, your sugar cravings will often vanish and your gut can begin to heal. When it's working well again, you'll no longer be absorbing chunks of protein before they are fully digested. This will also help eliminate the drag on your immune system and many food allergies, so you'll feel less fatigued and much less likely to reach for sugar as a pick-me-up.

For more information on how to eliminate yeast overgrowth, see the recommendations in *Beat Sugar Addiction Now!* For now, let's focus on a new way of eating and how it helps heal Type 3 sugar addiction.

Cut out Sugar to End Yeast Overgrowth

To stop yeast from taking over your gut (and your life!) by fueling sugar cravings, suppressing immune function, and continuing the cycle of addition, it's essential to change the way you eat. This means cutting back on sugar and excess starches. Although some yeast experts also recommend avoiding all foods containing yeast, this is not necessary except in the small portion of people who are also allergic to the yeast. The bigger key is to stay away from sugar, which feeds the yeast!

It takes approximately four to six months to eliminate yeast overgrowth. During that time, you'll be making high protein, low-glycemic foods the foundation of your diet, adding in beans/legumes, vegetables, and greens for balance. Meat, fish, and many other high-protein foods score a zero on the glycemic index, and you can eat as much of these as you like. In addition, you'll want to add in probiotics and vitamins that support overall immune function.

What Is the Glycemic Index?

The glycemic index (GI) describes which foods raise your blood sugar the most. Here's how it works: Pure glucose is given a GI score of 100. All other foods are "rated" relative to this. The higher the number, the higher it will raise your blood sugar. For Type 3 sugar addicts, it's essential to choose foods that are low on the scale to avoid feeding the yeast. See Appendix B for more information about the glycemic index.

Strengthen Your Immune System to Defeat the Yeast-Sugar Cycle

Dietary changes to eliminate the chronic overgrowth of yeast will also help restore your immune system, which can help you break out of—and stay free from—a sugar addiction. A healthy immune system won't allow yeast to flourish and can prevent other infections that require treatment with antibiotics (which can fuel yeast overgrowth). In addition to reducing your intake of sugar and high-glycemic carbohydrates, you should increase your intake of immunity-enhancing nutrients (the recipes in this section will make that easy!). To make sure you are getting optimal levels, you'll also want to take a multivitamin daily. I recommend the Energy Revitalization System vitamin powder by Enzymatic Therapy, or a similar product that contains the amounts noted below.

Key nutrients that help your body's defenses work properly include:

Zinc This mineral may well be the single most important nutrient for maintaining optimal immune function (see sidebar). Chronic infections, including yeast overgrowth, can cause a zinc deficiency—and a self-perpetuating cycle of immune system decline. Good food sources of zinc include leafy greens, mushrooms, asparagus, squash, broccoli, peas, shrimp, red meat, chicken liver, pumpkin and sesame seeds, and maple syrup. Take 15–25 mg/day.

Vitamin A Antioxidant vitamin A is critical for mucosal immunity, which can help prevent the respiratory and bowel infections that often accompany yeast overgrowth. It also helps in healing and preventing complications from viral infections. You'll find vitamin A or its precursor, carotenoids, in eggs, milk, liver, carrots, cantaloupes, sweet potatoes, and spinach. Take 2,000–3,500 IU/day.

Vitamin C By helping the white blood cells that trigger antibody production, vitamin C actually does make you less likely to catch a cold. And, if you do catch one, C shortens its duration. Research shows that people who took 500 mg of vitamin C a day had 18 percent fewer colds than those who didn't supplement. Stellar sources include kiwi, citrus, berries, and leafy greens. Take 500–1,000 mg/day.

Vitamin D Vitamin D is especially important in regulating and supporting immune function. Vitamin D activates your immune system's "killer T cells," white blood cells that seek out and destroy both outside invaders and cancer cells. Most of our vitamin D comes from sunshine, but because of misguided medical advice to avoid the sun, vitamin D deficiency is common and contributes to cancer deaths, multiple sclerosis, and diabetes. The few foods that provide vitamin D include fatty fish, beef liver, cheese, egg yolks, and fortified foods like milk. Wise advice: Avoid sunburn, not sunshine! Take 1,000–2,000 IU/day.

Selenium An antioxidant mineral critical for optimal immune function, selenium enhances the ability of white blood cells called lymphocytes to respond to infections, and it increases the effectiveness of cancer-fighting white blood cells. Selenium also helps prevent the drop in immune function sometimes seen with aging. Take 55 mcg/day.

Zinc and Immune Function

Zinc affects multiple aspects of the immune system, partly because of its role in key functions such as DNA replication, RNA transcription, cell division, and cell activation. Zinc is crucial for normal development and function of white blood cells (like the "tanks" in your defense army) called neutrophils and natural killer cells. It also helps your white blood cells activate and produce antibodies and cytokines (immune modulators). Zinc benefits macrophages—key cells for many immune system functions—as well.

The Role of Probiotics in Beating Sugar Addiction

When you eliminate chronic yeast overgrowth in the gut, it is important to replace the yeast with healthy bacteria, or the yeast will simply grow back. Probiotics, or "friendly bacteria" such as acidophilus or milk bacteria, can help to restore the balance of good bacteria in the gut. The best probiotics are those made with a pearl coating so they pass through the stomach's acid environment and into the bowel intact—where the coating dissolves and the "good" bacteria can go to work to battle yeast. Otherwise stomach acid kills the probiotics before they can do any good.

Probiotics help restore your immune system, which in turn reduces fatigue-induced sugar cravings. A 2005 study in *Environmental Health* showed that probiotics improve immune health and reduce sick time for employees. Another study in *Clinical Nutrition* found that probiotics also shortened cold and flu time by almost two days and reduced the severity of symptoms.

While you are trying to eliminate yeast overgrowth, I suggest taking at least four to five billion probiotic bacteria (for example, *Lactobacillus acidophilus* and *Bifidobacterium longum*) a day for four to five months, and then at least one billion a day for prevention. For example, if you're using Enzymatic Therapy products, take two regular Acidophilus Pearls twice a day (or one of the Pearls Elite each day) for five months, then one a day for prevention. If you are on antibiotics, take probiotics at least three to six hours before or after the antibiotic dose. For more information on recommended brands, see the product resource guide in Appendix A.

The Impact of Yeast on Weight Loss

Following the Type 3 treatment plan may help you not only overcome your sugar addiction, but drop a few pounds as well! Research published in the medical journal *Nature* in 2006 showed that overweight people have less of the good bacteria, or probiotics, than those who are at a normal weight. (Low levels of good bacteria are often associated with excessive amounts of yeast or unhealthy bacteria.) Clinically, some of my own patients have not been able to lose weight until their excess yeast was knocked out.

"Safe" Sweets That Won't Undo Your Efforts

While you'll need to cut back significantly on your sugar intake to get rid of the yeast that's fueling your addiction, there is still some room for treats. Yes, you should avoid even "healthy" sugars, like organic honey or maple syrup. You'll also want to skip concentrated sugars like honey, maple sugar, brown sugar, dried fruits, processed sugar, high fructose corn syrup, corn syrup, jellies, pastry, cakes, and candy. Soda, fruit juice, and sugar-sweetened drinks of any kind are also off-limits.

You can, however, enjoy a few squares of good-for-you dark chocolate. Look on the label for varieties that contain at least 60 percent cocoa, which means they have less sugar and more antioxidant-rich chocolate. Savor every bite, and go for quality instead of quantity! You can also try sugar-free chocolate from Russell Stover and Godiva, which is made with a natural sugar alcohol called maltitol that yeast cannot eat and that does not wreak havoc with your blood sugar levels. For a real treat, try sugar-free chocolates from a small online company called Abdallah Candies (www.abdallahcandies.com).

You can also eat up to one to two pieces or servings of whole fruit each day. Good low-glycemic choices include cherries, grapefruit, apples, pears, plums, peaches, oranges, grapes, kiwi, and strawberries. Higher-glycemic fruits such as mangoes, apricots, and pineapple are okay in moderation.

Additional Strategies to Beat Yeast-Induced Sugar Addiction

For more information about lifestyle changes, supplements, and other steps you can take to recover from yeast overgrowth, see the chapters dedicated to Type 3 sugar addicts in *Beat Sugar Addiction Now*! There, you'll learn about a holistic approach to treating yeast overgrowth including probiotics; herbs such as oregano, uva-ursi, milk thistle and garlic; and prescription medications to treat yeast overgrowth such as Diflucan and Nystatin. The book also outlines the warning signs of yeast overgrowth, so you can keep it under control and prevent falling back into a yeast-fueled sugar addiction.

The recipes that follow will help you learn how to cook and eat differently. The ingredients they feature will strengthen your digestive tract and your immune system. They have been carefully chosen to starve the yeast, balance your blood sugar levels and your internal biochemistry, and to feed and nourish your entire body. Let's go to the kitchen and get cookin'!

CHAPTER 9

Recipes for Type 3 Sugar Addiction

Type 3 Sugar Addicts must be especially careful to shun sugar in its many forms—whether it is granulated sugar, high fructose corn syrup, honey, or white flour—to avoid feeding the yeast (candida) in the gut and encouraging an overgrowth, squeezing good bacteria out. To that end, the recipes in this chapter focus on low- or no-sugar meals.

Type 3 sugar addicts also must work to keep the immune system strong to defend against yeast and other infections that can require antibiotics, which also kill the good bacteria. In these recipes you'll find important nutrients for immune health, including zinc; vitamins A, C and D; and selenium. The most important thing, though, is that these recipes are delicious, which will keep you and your family coming back for more!

MELLOW MILLET BREAKFAST CRUNCH WITH APPLE SAUCE

1 tablespoon (15 ml) coconut oil or extra-virgin olive oil
1 cup (200 g) uncooked millet
3 cups (720 ml) unsweetened, 100 percent apple juice
¼ teaspoon salt
¾ cup (50 g) shredded coconut
1 tablespoon (15 ml) vanilla extract
⅓ cup (40 g) chopped walnuts
⅓ cup (40 g) chopped almonds
½ teaspoon cinnamon

Preheat oven to 350°F (180°C, or gas mark 4). Coat a 2-quart (1.9-L) casserole dish with the oil. Combine millet, juice, and salt in a saucepan and bring to a boil. Remove from heat and stir in coconut. Return to heat and add remaining ingredients. Simmer for a few minutes, pour into prepared casserole dish, and bake for 45 to 60 minutes, or until firm. Allow to cool before serving. Sprinkle with additional cinnamon, if desired.

YIELD: 6 SERVINGS
EACH WITH: Calories 340.97; Calories From Fat 123.42; Total Fat 14.68 g; Cholesterol 0 mg; Sodium 129.07 mg; Potassium 335.89 mg; Total Carbohydrates 46.38 g; Fiber 5.33 g; Sugar 17.74 g; Protein 6.73 g
BLOOD SUGAR BALANCE RATING: High

Health Facilitators	Nutrient Density Rating
Protein	Medium
Fat	Medium
Carbohydrate	High
Enzymes	High
Antioxidants	Medium
Fiber	High

Millet is more like a seed than a grain and is easily digestible. Millet acts as a prebiotic to help feed the good bacteria that keep the intestines healthy and the immune system primed. Prebiotics are a special form of dietary fiber that nourishes the good bacteria in your gut. Probiotics are live bacteria, available in foods such as yogurt, sauerkraut, and supplements.

Millet is an excellent source of fiber and protein, which helps keep blood sugar levels stable for hours, and is high in B complex vitamins for fighting stress and helping you stay calm. Millet is also a good source of tryptophan, a precursor to the neurotransmitter serotonin that's important for restful sleep and even moods.

HEALING HERBAL SCRAMBLER

Eggs contain choline, a nutrient important for neurotransmitter function that helps keep your mood lifted and your blood sugar levels stable and balanced for hours. If you can, choose organic, free-range eggs so you don't put the added burden of pesticides and growth hormones on your already-challenged immune system. The antibacterial, antimicrobial and antifungal properties of fresh garlic, basil, and oregano will help keep yeast in check. This trio of herbs also provides potent antioxidant activity to strengthen your immune system.

4 eggs
2 large garlic cloves, chopped
1 teaspoon chopped fresh oregano
½ teaspoon chopped fresh basil
Pinch of cayenne
Salt
2 to 3 finely chopped scallions
1 tablespoon (15 ml) extra-virgin olive oil
2 cups (40 g) mixed lettuce greens, romaine lettuce, or spinach

Whisk eggs in a medium bowl with garlic, oregano, basil, cayenne, and salt. Stir in scallions. Heat the olive oil in medium skillet over medium heat. Pour in egg mixture and scramble with spatula, cooking until eggs reach desired doneness. Serve over mixed lettuce greens, romaine lettuce, or spinach.

YIELD: 2 SERVINGS
EACH WITH: Calories 220.14; Calories From Fat 150.76; Total Fat 16.87 g; Cholesterol 423 mg; Sodium 166.91 mg; Potassium 362.76 mg; Total Carbohydrates 4.17 g; Fiber 1.34 g; Sugar 1.3 g; Protein 13.95 g
BLOOD SUGAR BALANCE RATING: Very High

Health Facilitators	Nutrient Density Rating
Protein	High
Fat	Medium
Carbohydrate	Medium
Enzymes	Medium
Antioxidants	Medium
Fiber	Medium

KEEP-YOU-GOING CAJUN FISH FILLETS

1 tablespoon (15 ml) extra-virgin olive oil or coconut oil

1¼ pounds (570 g) sole, flounder, cod, halibut, pollack, rockfish, orange roughy, or any flaky white fish

¼ cup (60 ml) fresh lemon juice with pulp

2 teaspoons (5 g) paprika

1 teaspoon sea salt

1 teaspoon garlic powder

1 teaspoon onion powder

¼ teaspoon black pepper

¼ teaspoon white pepper

¼ teaspoon dried oregano leaves

¼ teaspoon dried thyme

1 cup (20 g) mixed salad greens or spinach

Preheat oven to 325°F (170°C, or gas mark 3). Coat a nonstick baking pan with the oil. Place the fish fillets in the pan and sprinkle with the lemon juice and pulp. Combine the paprika, sea salt, garlic powder, onion powder, black pepper, white pepper, oregano, and thyme in a small bowl to create "Cajun" seasoning. Sprinkle "Cajun" seasoning to taste on the fish. Bake, uncovered, for 20 minutes. Serve over mixed salad greens or spinach.

YIELD: 4 SERVINGS

EACH WITH: Calories 193.71; Calories From Fat (40%) 77.47; Total Fat 8.67 g; Cholesterol 0 mg; Sodium 476.81 mg; Potassium 97.15 mg; Total Carbohydrates 2.99 g; Fiber 0.83 g; Sugar 0.68 g; Protein 26.96 g

BLOOD SUGAR BALANCE RATING: Very High

Health Facilitators	Nutrient Density Rating
Protein	High
Fat	High
Carbohydrate	Medium
Enzymes	Medium
Antioxidants	High
Fiber	Medium

Fish for breakfast? Absolutely! These low-fat, high-protein fillets keep yeast at bay and boost brain neurotransmitters. Rich in satiating omega-3s and high in protein, this tasty breakfast will keep your blood sugar balanced for hours.

GET-UP-AND-GO GREEK GODDESS OMELET

Nutrient-dense kale (which contains iron and vitamins A, C, and K) and spinach offer fiber, calcium, and antioxidants to stabilize hormones and blood sugar levels, strengthen bones, and protect against colon cancer. Calcium-rich feta contains conjugated linoleic acid (found in grass-fed dairy products), which helps lower your risk of developing metabolic syndrome thanks to its blood sugar—balancing effects. Combined with immune-strengthening onion and oregano and protein-packed eggs, this Greek goddess is all goodness!

4 eggs
2 tablespoons (30 ml) heavy cream or half-and-half
Freshly ground black pepper
Dash cayenne
1 cup (20 g) kale or spinach
2 tablespoons (28 g or 30 ml) butter, coconut oil, or extra-virgin olive oil, divided
3 tablespoons (30 g) chopped red onion
½ cup (75 g) crumbled feta cheese
2 teaspoons (2 g) dried oregano

In a medium bowl, whisk eggs, cream, black pepper, and cayenne. Set aside.

Rinse the kale or spinach and place in a medium saucepan with tight-fitting lid. Turn heat to medium-high and steam until leaves are wilted, about 2 to 3 minutes. Drain in a colander, pressing out all the liquid with the back of a wooden spoon. Chop finely and set aside.

In a 10-inch (25-cm) nonstick skillet, melt 1 tablespoon (14 g) butter over medium-high heat. When butter or oil is hot, add onion and sauté until softened, about 5 minutes. Remove from pan and set aside. In a small bowl, combine sautéed onion, feta, and oregano. Add to chopped kale.

In the same skillet, melt remaining 1 tablespoon (14 g) butter over medium-high heat. When butter or oil is hot and bubbly, add egg mixture, reduce heat to medium, and cook, lifting edges to allow uncooked egg to seep underneath. When bottom layer of egg is cooked but top is still moist, spread kale filling over one side of omelet. Gently fold in half. Cook 30 seconds longer. Slide omelet onto a plate and serve immediately.

YIELD: 2 SERVINGS

EACH WITH: Calories 378; Calories From Fat 281.25; Total Fat 31.73 g; Cholesterol 492.19 mg; Sodium 577.53 mg; Potassium 280.77 mg; Total Carbohydrates 5.45 g; Fiber 1.24 g; Sugar 2.46 g; Protein 19.04 g

BLOOD SUGAR BALANCE RATING: Very High

Health Facilitators	Nutrient Density Rating
Protein	High
Fat	Medium
Carbohydrate	Medium
Enzymes	Medium
Antioxidants	High
Fiber	Medium

REVIVE AND THRIVE COCONUT CURRY WITH FISH OR CHICKEN

2 tablespoons (30 ml) coconut oil or ghee

1 cup (240 ml) Thai curry paste

1 tablespoon (7 g) turmeric

1 small sweet potato, peeled and cut into 1-inch (2.5-cm) pieces

1 to 2 cloves garlic

1 carrot, sliced

1 onion, chopped

1 cup (240 ml) purified water

¼ cup (60 ml) fish sauce (optional) or salt to taste

2 tablespoons (30 ml) honey

¼ cup (60 ml) unsweetened coconut milk

8-ounce (or 225-g) fillet of fish (halibut, trout, or salmon) or one chicken breast

2 cups (140 g) broccoli florets

¼ cup (15 g) chopped cilantro

In a heavy-bottomed soup pot, heat the coconut oil or ghee over medium heat. Add the curry paste and turmeric and stir with a wooden spoon for 1 minute. Add the sweet potato, garlic, carrot, and onion. Cook for 2 minutes then add the water, fish sauce, honey, and coconut milk. Bring to a boil.

Cut the fish fillet or chicken into ½-inch (1.3-cm) pieces and add to the curry. Lower the heat and stir occasionally until cooked through, up to 30 minutes. Add the broccoli and cook for an additional 5 minutes. Adjust the seasonings and serve with cilantro.

YIELD: 2 SERVINGS

EACH WITH: Calories 712.79; Calories From Fat 229.02; Total Fat 26.47 g; Cholesterol 0 mg; Sodium 7521.9 mg; Potassium 923.9 mg; Total Carbohydrates 90.13 g; Fiber 15.68 g; Sugar 33.91 g; Protein 25.17 g

BLOOD SUGAR BALANCE RATING: Very High

Health Facilitators	Nutrient Density Rating
Protein	Very High
Fat	Medium
Carbohydrate	Medium
Enzymes	Low
Antioxidants	Medium
Fiber	Medium

This dish takes you to the irresistible East, with aromas and flavors to delight your palate and herbs that will eliminate yeast and renew and refresh your system. Curcumin, the active ingredient in turmeric, has been used for over 4,000 years for its healing properties. This powerful spice is not only protective against cancer, pain and heart disease, it is also packed with nutrients such as iron and manganese for good energy and stable blood sugar. The lauric acid and caprylic acid found in coconuts are powerful natural yeast fighters. Add in the omega-3–rich fish, and you get a triple whammy of sugar addiction-fighting deliciousness.

IMMUNE-BOOSTING LENTIL SOUP WITH BARLEY, KOMBU, AND DULSE

Sea vegetables such as seaweed and dulse contain antibiotic properties that are particularly effective against penicillin-resistant bacteria. Lentils contain iodine (for strengthening the energy-producing thyroid gland), zinc (to boost your immune system), chromium (to stabilize blood sugar levels), and vitamins E, A, C, and B12. Their high fiber content prevents blood sugar levels from rising rapidly after a meal. The whole-grain barley in this comforting soup mix adds extra fiber and minerals.

1 tablespoon (15 ml) extra-virgin olive oil
1 medium red or brown onion, chopped
1 celery stalk, chopped
2 carrots, chopped
1 cup (184 g) whole-grain barley (not pearl barley)
12 cups (2.88 L) purified water
2 bay leaves
2 cups (450 g) lentils
1 strip kombu seaweed
2 tablespoons (32 g) dark miso
Shredded dulse (optional)

In a heavy-bottomed soup pot, heat the oil over medium-high heat and sauté the onion, celery, and carrots, until onion is limp and transparent, about 5 minutes. Add barley, water, and bay leaves. Cover and simmer for 15 to 20 minutes. Add lentils and kombu, and simmer for another 30 minutes. Discard kombu and bay leaves. Place 1 cup (240 ml) of soup in a small bowl and blend with miso. Add soup-miso mixture back to pot and stir well. Serve garnished with shredded dulse, if desired.

YIELD: 6 SERVINGS
EACH WITH: Calories 396.74; Calories From Fat 32.97; Total Fat 3.76 g; Cholesterol 0 mg; Sodium 290.05 mg; Potassium 857.06 mg; Total Carbohydrates 70.95 g; Fiber 26.59 g; Sugar 4.2 g; Protein 21.01 g
BLOOD SUGAR BALANCE RATING: Very High

Health Facilitators	Nutrient Density Rating
Protein	High
Fat	Medium
Carbohydrate	High
Enzymes	Medium
Antioxidants	Medium
Fiber	High

LOW-GLYCEMIC GUACAMOLE AND SHRIMP SALAD

4 large or 8 medium shrimp, peeled and deveined
2 ripe avocados
1 to 2 tablespoons (15 to 30 ml) fresh lemon or lime juice
1 fresh large tomato, chopped and seeded
1 clove garlic, chopped or minced
1 tablespoon (10 g) chopped red onion
2 scallions, chopped finely
1 tablespoon (4 g) finely chopped cilantro
1 small jalapeno pepper, minced
Freshly ground black pepper
Dash hot pepper sauce
4 cups (80 g) mixed salad greens or spinach

Cook the shrimp as desired and set aside. Cut avocados in half. Remove pits and scoop flesh into a medium bowl. Using a fork, mash avocado with lemon juice. Gently mix in chopped tomato, garlic, onion, scallions, cilantro, jalapeno pepper, black pepper, and hot pepper sauce. Taste and adjust seasonings. Serve guacamole on a bed of mixed salad greens, top with the shrimp, and sprinkle with additional lemon or lime juice, if desired.

YIELD: 4 SERVINGS
EACH WITH: Calories 170.72; Calories From Fat 114.68; Total Fat 13.67 g; Cholesterol 9.12 mg; Sodium 44.13 mg; Potassium 743.86 mg; Total Carbohydrates 11.58 g; Fiber 7.36 g; Sugar 1.78 g; Protein 4.37 g
BLOOD SUGAR BALANCE RATING: Very High

Health Facilitators	Nutrient Density Rating
Protein	High
Fat	High
Carbohydrate	High
Enzymes	High
Antioxidants	High
Fiber	High

While shrimp may be small, they are anything but "shrimpy" in their health benefits! Shrimp are packed with protein, vitamin D, and selenium, which neutralizes the effects of free radicals and helps strengthen your immune system. Rich, creamy avocado provides blood sugar–stabilizing monounsaturated fatty acids, vitamin E, potassium, and fiber. Yum!

QUICK CURRIED CHICKEN AND CUCUMBER SALAD

Chicken is loaded with selenium, an essential mineral that boosts energy, fights free radicals, destroys cancer cells, and repairs damage to DNA. Chicken is also a good source of anti-stress vitamins B6 and B3 and protein to keep your blood sugar levels stable. The antibacterial and antiviral properties of garlic and the healthy fat from the coconut make this immune-strengthening dish filling and energizing as well.

1 teaspoon extra-virgin olive oil or coconut oil
3 teaspoons (6 g) curry powder
1 pound (455 g) free-range chicken breasts, cut into strips
2 cloves garlic, minced
½ cup (80 g) chopped red or brown onion
2 cups (270 g) diced cucumber
1 red bell pepper, sliced into strips
1 green bell pepper, sliced into strips
Salt and pepper

Heat oil in a large skillet over high heat. Add curry powder and cook, stirring, for 30 seconds. Add chicken, garlic, and onions and cook until chicken is no longer pink, about 5 minutes. Reduce heat and add cucumber, red bell pepper, and green bell pepper and cook for 2 to 3 minutes, just until heated through.

YIELD: 2 SERVINGS

EACH WITH: Calories 354.25; Calories From Fat 50.36; Total Fat 4.55 g; Cholesterol 136 mg; Sodium 310.28 mg; Potassium 785.97 mg; Total Carbohydrates 16.48 g; Fiber 5.4 g; Sugar 6.94 g; Protein 57.12 g

BLOOD SUGAR BALANCE RATING: Very High

Health Facilitators	Nutrient Density Rating
Protein	High
Fat	Low
Carbohydrate	Medium
Enzymes	Low
Antioxidants	High
Fiber	Medium

STEADY-ENERGY SALMON SALAD SUPREME

1 can (7.5 ounces, or 210 g) water-packed salmon, drained
½ cup (60 g) diced celery
2 tablespoons (12 g) diced scallions
½ cup (65 g) frozen peas, thawed
1 hard-boiled egg, peeled and chopped
5 large ripe olives
2 tablespoons (30 ml) reduced-fat mayonnaise
2 teaspoons (1.5 g) dried basil
2 cups (40 g) mixed lettuce greens or spinach

Combine the salmon, celery, scallions, peas, egg, olives, mayonnaise, and basil in a large bowl. Divide the contents of the bowl into two portions and serve over mixed lettuce greens or spinach.

YIELD: 2 SERVINGS
EACH WITH: Calories 287.94; Calories From Fat 126.2; Total Fat 14.07 g; Cholesterol 198.18 mg; Sodium 764.09 mg; Potassium 736.47 mg; Total Carbohydrates 10.35 g; Fiber 3.74 g; Sugar 3.6 g; Protein 31.1 g
BLOOD SUGAR BALANCE RATING: Very High

Health Facilitators	Nutrient Density Rating
Protein	High
Fat	Medium
Carbohydrate	Medium
Enzymes	Medium
Antioxidants	High
Fiber	High

Salmon is famous for its omega-3s, which support neurotransmitter and brain function and help balance your blood sugar. Zesty scallions, a member of the allium family like garlic, contain chromium, a mineral that helps regulate blood sugar levels. The vegetables offer fiber, copper, manganese, potassium, and vitamins C, B6, and folate, which provide energy and immune system support with every nourishing bite.

CHUNKY CHICKEN VEGETABLE SOUP

What is more soothing and healing than a yummy bowl of homemade chicken soup? The chicken is loaded with lean protein, while barley and vegetables offer fiber, tryptophan, potassium, magnesium, copper, manganese, chromium, and vitamins C, A, and folate that boost your mood and stabilize your blood sugar levels for hours. Don't limit this recipe to the cold winter months—this homemade chicken soup is a welcome dish to have on hand for year-round health.

1 to 2 tablespoons (15 to 30 ml) extra-virgin olive oil
1 pound (455 g) raw chicken, ground or diced
1 cup (160 g) chopped red or brown onion
5 cups (1.2 L) chicken stock
½ cup (90 g) uncooked whole-grain barley (not pearl barley)
2 cups (360 g) diced tomato
½ teaspoon salt
1 to 2 cloves garlic, minced
1 teaspoon dried basil
½ teaspoon dried thyme
1 teaspoon tomato purée (optional)
¼ teaspoon red pepper flakes
1½ cups fresh vegetables of choice

Heat the olive oil in a 4-quart (3.8-L) saucepan over medium-high heat. Add the chicken and onion and cook until brown, about 5 minutes, stirring constantly. Add the chicken stock and barley to saucepan. Stir in the tomato, salt, garlic, basil, thyme, tomato purée (if using), and red pepper flakes. Adjust seasonings to taste, and bring the mixture to a boil. Reduce heat and simmer for 30 minutes or until barley is tender. Add the mixed vegetables and cook in the soup until crisp-tender.

YIELD: 6 SERVINGS
EACH WITH: Calories 156.34; Calories From Fat 35.73; Total Fat 3.89 g; Cholesterol 7.1 mg; Sodium 845.38 mg; Potassium 476.48 mg; Total Carbohydrates 21.04 g; Fiber 4.69 g; Sugar 4.04 g; Protein 9.89 g
BLOOD SUGAR BALANCE RATING: Very High

Health Facilitators	Nutrient Density Rating
Protein	High
Fat	Medium
Carbohydrate	High
Enzymes	Low
Antioxidants	High
Fiber	High

BLOOD SUGAR–BALANCING BUCKWHEAT WITH CABBAGE AND CORN

2 tablespoons (30 ml) extra-virgin olive oil, coconut oil, or ghee

3 cups (270 g) chopped cabbage (preferably savoy)

2 cups (320 g) corn kernels

1 large red or brown onion, chopped

½ red bell pepper, minced

4 cups (960 ml) vegetable stock or purified water

1 teaspoon sea salt

¼ teaspoon freshly ground black pepper

1 teaspoon mixed herbs, such as oregano, dill, and basil

2 cups (330 g) roasted buckwheat groats

½ cup (30 g) chopped parsley

1 teaspoon horseradish (optional)

Heat the oil in a 2-quart (1.9-L) saucepan over medium-high heat; when hot, sauté the cabbage, corn, onion, and red bell pepper. Add the stock or water, salt, pepper, and mixed herbs and bring to a rolling boil. Add the buckwheat and simmer for 20 minutes. Turn off the heat and fold in parsley and horseradish. Let sit, covered, for 10 minutes. Serve hot.

YIELD: 6 SERVINGS

EACH WITH: Calories 353.91; Calories From Fat (21%); Total Fat 8.41 g; Cholesterol 4.8 mg; Sodium 699.07 mg; Potassium 642.48 mg; Total Carbohydrates 62.18 g; Fiber 8.87 g; Sugar 6.48 g; Protein 13.08 g

BLOOD SUGAR BALANCE RATING: Very High

Health Facilitators	Nutrient Density Rating
Protein	High
Fat	Medium
Carbohydrate	High
Enzymes	Low
Antioxidants	High
Fiber	High

Energizing and nutritious, buckwheat is a cereal grain that is rich in flavonoids, which protect against disease by extending the action of vitamin C. Vitamin C, a powerful antioxidant, improves adrenal gland function, which boosts cortisol production and in turn improves your body's stress-coping abilities. Buckwheat also contains protein and fiber, which help keep blood sugar levels stable. Cabbage is rich in fiber and sulfur, making it a potent ally when it comes to fighting against bacterial infections such as yeast and fungus. It is also abundant in vitamin C and, combined with zesty horseradish, onions, and herbs, will boost your immune system and rev up your metabolism.

REJUVENATING COLESLAW

Cabbage is one of the most nourishing foods for Type 3 sugar addicts because its high sulfur content is highly effective for combating candida infections. Cabbage also improves immune function, thanks to antioxidant phytonutrients (nutrients found in plants) that protect the body from free-radical damage to the cell membranes. The enzymes in cabbage increase digestion and improve your absorption of nutrients. This recipe combines other sulfur-containing vegetables, such as fresh onions and garlic, for a dish that will satisfy your taste buds and rev your metabolism for many hours.

2 cups (140 g) shredded green cabbage
1 cup (70 g) shredded red cabbage
1 cup (120 g) grated carrot
½ cup (50 g) diced olives
½ small onion, diced
2 garlic cloves, minced
½ cup (60 g) slivered almonds (optional)
2 tablespoons (30 ml) mayonnaise
1 tablespoon (15 ml) extra-virgin olive oil or coconut oil
1 teaspoon apple cider vinegar or juice of 1 medium lemon
¼ teaspoon freshly ground black pepper
¼ teaspoon cayenne
Salt

Place cabbage and carrot in a bowl, and mix in olives, onion, garlic, and almonds, if using. In a separate bowl, mix together mayonnaise, oil, vinegar or lemon juice, black pepper, cayenne, and salt to taste, and stir into coleslaw. Refrigerate to chill before serving.

YIELD: 4 SERVINGS
EACH WITH: Calories 180.73; Calories From Fat 117.02; Total Fat 13.63 g; Cholesterol 1.91 mg; Sodium 230.44 mg; Potassium 310.84 mg; Total Carbohydrates 13.34 g; Fiber 4.67 g; Sugar 4.78 g; Protein 4.03 g
BLOOD SUGAR BALANCE RATING: Medium

Health Facilitators	Nutrient Density Rating
Protein	Low
Fat	Low
Carbohydrate	High
Enzymes	High
Antioxidants	High
Fiber	Very High

NUTRITIVE NAVY BEAN SOUP

5 cups (1.2 L) vegetable stock, divided
½ cup (80 g) chopped red or brown onion
1 can (15 ounces, or 430 g) navy beans, drained and rinsed
1 sweet potato, peeled and diced
2 carrots, thinly sliced
½ cup (90 g) barley
1 cup (36 g) shredded red chard
2 tablespoons (32 g) miso
2 tablespoons (30 ml) purified water

Bring ¼ cup (60 ml) of the vegetable stock to a boil in a stockpot. Add the onion and cook for 5 minutes. Add the remaining stock, navy beans, sweet potato, carrots, and barley. Cover and simmer for 30 minutes. (If you are preparing the soup in advance, stop at this step and refrigerate soup. When ready to continue, reheat and follow remaining directions.) Add the chard, lower the heat, and simmer for 1 to 2 minutes, or until the chard wilts. Remove from heat and set aside. Whisk together the miso and water in a small bowl. Stir into the soup and serve.

YIELD: 4 SERVINGS

EACH WITH: Calories 299.47; Calories From Fat 42.74; Total Fat 4.72 g; Cholesterol 9 mg; Sodium 1291.3 mg; Potassium 941.46 mg; Total Carbohydrates 47.22 g; Fiber 8.48 g; Sugar 9.79 g; Protein 17.84 g

BLOOD SUGAR BALANCE RATING: High

Health Facilitators	Nutrient Density Rating
Protein	Medium
Fat	Low
Carbohydrate	High
Enzymes	Low
Antioxidants	High
Fiber	Very High

Navy beans are small, mild, white beans often used in French cooking. In this soup, they are combined with barley and red chard for a varied nutritional profile. It also looks pretty! Miso adds depth of flavor, while the beans stabilize blood sugar levels thanks to their high protein and fiber content. Combine this dish with brown rice for added protein and fiber.

CANDIDA-CLEARING CARAWAY CABBAGE

Not only does this tasty side dish balance your blood sugar, it also promotes an abundance of "good bacteria," which in turn helps heal leaky gut, eliminates toxins, and keeps your metabolism humming.

2 tablespoons (30 ml) coconut oil or extra-virgin olive oil
1 medium red or brown onion, coarsely chopped
1 teaspoon sea salt
½ teaspoon freshly ground black pepper
1 teaspoon allspice
¼ teaspoon cloves (optional)
1 apple, peeled, cored and cubed
1 to 2 pounds (455 to 910 g) finely shredded red cabbage
¼ cup (60 ml) purified water, boiling
½ cup (120 ml) red wine vinegar
½ cup (40 g) juniper berries
1 tablespoon (7 g) caraway seeds

Heat the oil in a large skillet over medium heat. Add the onion and sauté until golden brown, about 5 minutes. Add salt, black pepper, allspice, cloves, apple, and shredded cabbage, stirring to combine well. Add boiling water and simmer for 1 hour, adding more water if necessary to keep moistened. Add the vinegar, juniper berries, and caraway seeds. Simmer for another 10 to 15 minutes. Serve hot.

YIELD: 8 SERVINGS
EACH WITH: Calories 91.8; Calories From Fat 45.21; Total Fat 5.19 g; Cholesterol 0 mg; Sodium 247.73 mg; Potassium 202.25 mg; Total Carbohydrates 10.66 g; Fiber 2.4 g; Sugar 2.45 g; Protein 1.47 g
BLOOD SUGAR BALANCE RATING: High

Health Facilitators	Nutrient Density Rating
Protein	Low
Fat	Low
Carbohydrate	High
Enzymes	High
Antioxidants	High
Fiber	Very High

ENERGY-STABILIZING HUMMUS

5 garlic cloves, peeled and minced
3¼ cups (780 g) cooked garbanzo beans (1⅔ cups, or 335 g dried)
⅔ cup (160 ml) warm purified water
6 tablespoons (90 g) tahini
¼ cup (60 ml) freshly squeezed lemon juice
1 cup (190 g) cooked, well-drained spinach
1 tablespoon (4 g) chopped cilantro

Combine all ingredients in a food processor and process until blended. Serve at room temperature and refrigerate leftovers.

YIELD: 5 SERVINGS
EACH WITH: Calories 308.91; Calories From Fat 90.12; Total Fat 10.77 g; Cholesterol 0 mg; Sodium 603.27 mg; Potassium 489.65 mg; Total Carbohydrates 43.9 g; Fiber 10.08 g; Sugar 0.52 g; Protein 12.71 g
BLOOD SUGAR BALANCE RATING: High

Health Facilitators	Nutrient Density Rating
Protein	Medium
Fat	Moderate
Carbohydrate	High
Enzymes	High
Antioxidants	High
Fiber	Very High

The chief ingredient in hummus, chickpeas (also called garbanzo beans), is loaded with fiber that digests slowly and keeps blood sugar levels from rising too rapidly. Combine this easy dip with whole grains and you have a complete protein in just minutes. Serve with whole-wheat pita wedges, sesame crackers, or raw veggie slices.

ROUSING RADICCHIO AND ENDIVE SALAD

This tangy red, white, and green salad dotted with the orange shreds of carrot is an excellent source of vitamins A and C, folic acid, calcium, and magnesium. Arugula and radicchio are cruciferous vegetables that contain powerful anti-cancer compounds and are loaded with enzymes for detoxifying the body. Endives add a slightly bitter taste and help tone the liver and is effective at eradicating yeast, fungi, and other pathogens within the digestive tract. Enjoy!

3 small bunches of arugula, leaves torn into bite-sized pieces
1 medium head of radicchio, leaves torn into bite-sized pieces
4 heads Belgian endive, cut crosswise into bite-sized pieces
1 carrot, shredded
1 medium tomato, diced
¼ cup (60 ml) coconut oil or extra-virgin olive oil
2 tablespoons (30 ml) freshly squeezed lemon juice
1 tablespoon (3 g) minced fresh chives
Salt and freshly ground black pepper
Tomato wedges (optional)

In a large bowl, toss together the arugula, radicchio, endive, carrot, and tomato. Drizzle the salad with oil and lemon juice. Add chives and salt and pepper to taste. Toss well. Serve with tomato wedges and extra lemon, if desired.

YIELD: 4 SERVINGS
EACH WITH: Calories 264.66; Calories From Fat 130.97; Total Fat 15.21 g; Cholesterol 0 mg; Sodium 206.45 mg; Potassium 2330.56 mg; Total Carbohydrates 29.17 g; Fiber 20.78 g; Sugar 5.43 g; Protein 10.87 g
BLOOD SUGAR BALANCE RATING: Medium

Health Facilitators	Nutrient Density Rating
Protein	Low
Fat	Low
Carbohydrate	High
Enzymes	High
Antioxidants	High
Fiber	Very High

SOOTHING SOLE FLORENTINE

6 sole fillets
1 tablespoon (3 g) fresh oregano
Sea salt
2 tablespoons (30 ml) lemon juice
3 cups (60 g) chopped fresh spinach
¼ teaspoon grated nutmeg
Lemon wedges

Preheat oven to 325°F (180°C, or gas mark 4). Place fillets in baking dish and sprinkle with oregano, salt, and lemon juice. Bake for 5 minutes. Remove from oven and top with spinach and grated nutmeg. Return to oven and bake for an additional 3 to 4 minutes, or until spinach is wilted. Serve with a wedge of lemon.

YIELD: 6 SERVINGS
EACH WITH: Calories 154.66; Calories From Fat 18.41; Total Fat 2.04 g; Cholesterol 86.36 mg; Sodium 145.3 mg; Potassium 531.56 mg; Total Carbohydrates 1.16 g; Fiber 0.56 g; Sugar 0.21 g; Protein 31.16 g
BLOOD SUGAR BALANCE RATING: Very High

Health Facilitators	Nutrient Density Rating
Protein	High
Fat	Medium
Carbohydrate	Medium
Enzymes	Low
Antioxidants	High
Fiber	Medium

Not only is fish healthy for your heart and brain, it also stabilizes blood sugar levels thanks to its high protein content. Flaky white fish such as sole includes several essential vitamins and minerals, along with omega-3 essential fatty acids. Just one cup of spinach contains far more than your daily requirements of vitamins A and K, and almost all of your daily magnesium and calcium requirement. Boost your energy with this recipe on a regular basis!

SUSTAINING SHRIMP CREOLE

A delicious and wonderful combination of tangy taste and crunchy texture, this nutritious dish is bound to delight with every bite. High-protein shrimp balance blood sugar and contain tryptophan, omega-3s, selenium, vitamin D, B12, iron, zinc, and magnesium, which lift mood and help you stay calm in the face of stress. Peppers are excellent sources of vitamin C and vitamin A, two powerful antioxidants that work to neutralize free radicals and give your body a boost in energy. Peppers are also an excellent source of vitamins D and B12, which benefit your immune system. Toss into the mix the lycopene-laden tomatoes, which help protect against breast, prostate, and intestinal cancers, especially when consumed with healthy fats such as avocado and coconut or olive oil, and you have one tantalizing and healthful dish.

4 teaspoons (20 ml) extra-virgin olive oil or coconut oil
½ cup (75 g) chopped green pepper
½ cup (60 g) chopped celery
½ cup (80 g) chopped red or brown onion
1 garlic clove, minced
1 can (28 ounces, or 785 g) whole tomatoes, chopped and undrained
¼ teaspoon red pepper flakes
6 black olives, chopped
1 bay leaf
½ teaspoon finely chopped thyme
20 medium shrimp, peeled and deveined
2 cups (330 g) cooked brown rice
½ cup (70 g) peas, fresh or frozen and thawed
½ avocado, chopped

In medium saucepan, heat oil over medium heat. Add green pepper, celery, onion, and garlic and cook about 5 minutes, or until tender. Add tomatoes and their liquid, red pepper flakes, olives, bay leaf, and thyme; bring to a boil. Reduce heat to low and simmer, uncovered, about 30 minutes or until reduced slightly, stirring often. Add shrimp and cook until shrimp turns pink, about 4 minutes longer. Remove bay leaf and discard. Serve over cooked brown rice with peas chopped avocado.

YIELD: 4 SERVINGS

EACH WITH: Calories 311.98; Calories From Fat 91.55; Total Fat 10.63 g; Cholesterol 45.6 mg; Sodium 635.62 mg; Potassium 759.79 mg; Total Carbohydrates 44.89 g; Fiber 7.65 g; Sugar 10.97 g; Protein 12.58 g

BLOOD SUGAR BALANCE RATING: Very High

Health Facilitators	Nutrient Density Rating
Protein	High
Fat	Medium
Carbohydrate	High
Enzymes	Medium
Antioxidants	High
Fiber	High

HIGH-ENERGY HALIBUT WITH GINGER MAYONNAISE

½ cup (115 g) reduced-fat mayonnaise
2 tablespoons (30 ml) rice or coconut milk
1 tablespoon (15 ml) Dijon mustard
1 teaspoon minced fresh ginger
1 teaspoon freshly ground black pepper
1 ripe tomato, chopped
1 tablespoon (3 g) chopped chives
1 tablespoon (4 g) chopped parsley
Six 6-ounce (170-g) halibut steaks
Juice of 1 lemon (optional)

In a small bowl, whisk together the mayonnaise, rice or coconut milk, mustard, ginger, and black pepper. Mix in the tomato, chives, and parsley. Let stand at room temperature for an hour. Meanwhile, preheat grill or grill pan. Grill the halibut steaks until they reach desired doneness and top with the ginger mayonnaise. Sprinkle with fresh lemon juice, if desired.

YIELD: 6 SERVINGS

EACH WITH: Calories 275.1; Calories From Fat 105.13; Total Fat 11.75 g; Cholesterol 61.43 mg; Sodium 285.44 mg; Potassium 880.96 mg; Total Carbohydrates 5.3 g; Fiber 1.34 g; Sugar 1.46 g; Protein 36.21 g

BLOOD SUGAR BALANCE RATING: Very High

Health Facilitators	Nutrient Density Rating
Protein	High
Fat	Medium
Carbohydrate	Medium
Enzymes	Low
Antioxidants	Medium
Fiber	Medium

Heart-healthy halibut is rich in selenium, magnesium, potassium, vitamin B12, niacin, vitamin B6, and omega-3s. Ginger boosts immunity thanks to its warming effects within the body that promote healthy sweating, which is often helpful during colds and flu because it aids detoxification and protects the skin against invading microorganisms such as *E. coli, Staphylococcus aureus,* and fungus—including candida. Serve with brown rice and avocado or over a bed of fresh salad greens.

CALMING COCONUT CASHEW CURRY

This highly nourishing curry contains numerous antioxidants to support your metabolism and balance your blood sugar. Cashews are loaded with healthy fats ideal for giving you steady energy for hours, along with enzymes and copper, iron, magnesium, and calcium. Cashews are also a rich source of tryptophan, a precursor to the "happiness molecule" serotonin, which improves mood and sleep quality. Make this delicious dish whenever you have trouble sleeping or are feeling blue. The warm spices cumin, coriander, cardamom, and turmeric also improve overall immune health and fight against invading yeast. Add fish, shrimp, or chicken for additional protein, if desired.

Health Facilitators	Nutrient Density Rating
Protein	Medium
Fat	Medium
Carbohydrate	High
Enzymes	Low
Antioxidants	High
Fiber	High

1½ cups (225 g) raw cashews
2 to 3 tablespoons (30 to 45 ml) coconut oil
1 medium red or brown onion, chopped
2 garlic cloves, minced
1 small jalapeno pepper, diced
1 red bell pepper, sliced into slivers
2 large sweet potatoes, diced (and peeled, if desired)
1 medium head cauliflower, cut into florets
1 teaspoon turmeric
1 teaspoon ground cumin
1 teaspoon coriander
½ teaspoon cardamom
2 teaspoons (4 g) peeled and finely minced fresh ginger
1 cinnamon stick
Dash cayenne
1½ cups (360 ml) coconut milk
½ cup (120 ml) vegetable stock
1 cup (140 g) peas, fresh or frozen and thawed
1 to 2 teaspoons (5 to 10 ml) fresh lime juice
1 to 2 cups (165 to 330 g) cooked brown rice

Put cashews in an dry skillet over medium-high heat. Stir or shake almost constantly until cashews are evenly browned and toasted, no more than 5 minutes. Remove from pan immediately and set aside.

In a large nonstick skillet, heat coconut oil over medium-high heat. When hot, add onion, garlic, jalapeno pepper, and red bell pepper. Sauté until softened, about 5 minutes. Add sweet potatoes, cauliflower, turmeric, cumin, coriander, cardamom, ginger, cinnamon stick, and cayenne. Sauté until spices and vegetables are well blended and coated with oil, stirring constantly, about 2 minutes. Add coconut milk and vegetable stock. Bring to a boil. Reduce heat to low and simmer until potatoes are tender and sauce is thickened, about 15 to 20 minutes. Stir in peas and lime juice and cook until heated through. Sprinkle with toasted cashews. Serve over brown rice.

YIELD: 4 SERVINGS
EACH WITH: Calories 794.9; Calories From Fat 415.87; Total Fat 49.46 g; Cholesterol 0.9 mg; Sodium 254.55 mg; Potassium 2120.8 mg; Total Carbohydrates 77.59 g; Fiber 19.1 g; Sugar 20.3 g; Protein 24.53 g
BLOOD SUGAR BALANCE RATING: Very High

NOURISHING MEDITERRANEAN SALMON

¼ cup (60 ml) plus 2 tablespoons (30 ml) extra-virgin olive oil or coconut oil, divided

1 tablespoon (2 g) fresh rosemary, or 1 teaspoon (1.2 g) dried

4 whole black peppercorns

1 bay leaf

4 salmon fillets, about 3 to 4 ounces (85 to 115 g) each

1 tablespoon (15 ml) apple cider vinegar

5 garlic cloves, minced

10 black olives, pitted and chopped

1 large tomato, seeded and chopped

½ medium red onion, chopped

2 tablespoons (17 g) capers, drained

Salt and pepper

4 cups mixed (80 g) salad greens or spinach

1 avocado, sliced into quarters

Whisk ¼ cup (60 ml) oil, rosemary, peppercorns, and bay leaf in a small bowl. Place fish in a single layer in a glass baking dish. Pour oil and herb mixture over fish, and turn fish to coat. Cover and refrigerate at least 2 hours. Whisk remaining 2 tablespoons (30 ml) oil, vinegar, and garlic in a large bowl. Add olives, tomato, red onion, and capers. Prepare grill or preheat broiler. Season fish with salt and pepper to taste. Grill or broil until salmon is opaque in center, about 8 to 10 minutes. Transfer to serving plates and top with tomato mixture. Serve immediately with lettuce or spinach and an avocado wedge.

YIELD: 4 SERVINGS

EACH WITH: Calories 480.1; Calories From Fat 352.83; Total Fat 40.09 g; Cholesterol 61 mg; Sodium 301.96 mg; Potassium 860.3 mg; Total Carbohydrates 10.42 g; Fiber 4.89 g; Sugar 1.21 g; Protein 22.84 g

BLOOD SUGAR BALANCE RATING: Very High

Health Facilitators	Nutrient Density Rating
Protein	High
Fat	Medium
Carbohydrate	High
Enzymes	Medium
Antioxidants	High
Fiber	Medium

Salmon is one of the stars of the Mediterranean diet, famous for its heart-healthy and cholesterol-lowering benefits. Salmon's omega-3s also lower your risk for cancer and diabetes and help fight depression. The blend of protein, healthy fat, and carbohydrates make this dish a winner for balancing blood sugar levels and nourishing your brain and body.

PROTEIN-PACKED AMARANTH PIE

If your goal is to reduce the amount of animal protein you eat, amaranth is a great source of plant protein. It's higher in the amino acid lysine than most other grains are, and it's much richer in iron, magnesium, and calcium, to help keep anemia and osteoporosis at bay. It also provides fiber, mostly insoluble, which is beneficial in preventing or healing a variety of diseases, including heart disease, certain cancers, and digestive tract issues. And, of course, fiber helps balance your blood sugar. Immune-boosting fresh onions, garlic, and mixed herbs make this dish specifically helpful for keeping yeast in check. Did we mention that it also tastes delicious?

Health Facilitators	Nutrient Density Rating
Protein	High
Fat	Low
Carbohydrate	High
Enzymes	Low
Antioxidants	High
Fiber	High

For Crust
2 cups (250 g) amaranth flour
5 tablespoons (70 g or 75 ml) unsalted butter or coconut oil
1 teaspoon sea salt
½ cup (120 ml) purified water

For Sauce
1 tablespoon (14 g or 15 ml) unsalted butter, ghee, or coconut oil
4 to 6 brown onions, thinly sliced
4 cloves garlic, minced
1 tablespoon (4 g) mixed herbs, such as oregano, parsley, rosemary and basil
Dash red pepper flakes
½ cup (95 g) amaranth flour
1 cup (240 ml) purified water
1 teaspoon sea salt
½ red bell pepper, finely chopped
2 to 3 scallions, thinly sliced
1 tablespoon (4 g) finely chopped cilantro
1 avocado, cut into quarters

To make the crust: Preheat oven to 375°F (190°C, or gas mark 5). Combine flour, butter or oil, and salt in a bowl or food processor. Pulse or cut butter into dough until crumbly, gradually adding water until dough begins to form a ball. Remove from bowl or processor and form into a flat ball. Place on waxed paper, sprinkle surface with flour, and cover with another piece of waxed paper. Roll dough to 12 inches (30 cm) diameter. Grease a 12-inch (30-cm) pizza pan with butter. Transfer dough to prepared pan, crimp edges, and bake for 10 minutes.

To make the sauce: Heat butter in a medium saucepan over medium-high heat and sauté the onion, garlic, mixed herbs, and red pepper flakes. Reduce heat, cover, and cook until onions are translucent or soft, about 5 minutes, then add the amaranth, water, and sea salt. Bring to a boil, reduce heat, and simmer, covered, for 15–20 minutes, or until amaranth is tender. Remove lid and boil off excess liquid. Add the pepper, scallions, and cilantro during the last 2–3 minutes of cooking. Pour over the pie crust and sprinkle with additional red pepper flakes. Bake for 20 minutes. Serve with a wedge of avocado.

YIELD: 4 SERVINGS
EACH WITH: Calories 556.03; Calories From Fat (48%) 264.38; Total Fat 29.72 g; Cholesterol 45.8 mg; Sodium 959.28 mg; Potassium 410.96 mg; Total Carbohydrates 63.09 g; Fiber 11.36 g; Sugar 2.68 g; Protein 6.47 g
BLOOD SUGAR BALANCE RATING: Very High

ZESTY ZUCCHINI AND CHICKEN BAKE

2 teaspoons (10 ml) extra-virgin olive oil or coconut oil
2 garlic cloves, minced
1 pound (455 g) boneless, skinless chicken breasts
15 ounces (440 ml) tomato sauce
2 cups (250 g) julienned zucchini
1 tablespoon (4 g) chopped basil
1 tablespoon (4 g) chopped oregano
1 tablespoon (4 g) chopped thyme
1 tablespoon (5 g) grated lemon peel
1 cup (165 g) cooked brown rice
4 teaspoons (12 g) pine nuts

Preheat oven to 375°F (190°C, or gas mark 5). Heat oil in a large skillet over medium-high heat and sauté garlic for 30 seconds. Add chicken, cover, reduce heat, and cook for 30 minutes.

Spray a 9 × 13-inch (23 × 33-cm) baking dish with nonstick cooking spray. Pour tomato sauce into prepared dish. Place the zucchini, basil, oregano, thyme, and chicken on top of tomato sauce. Sprinkle the lemon peel over the top. Cover with foil and bake for 30 minutes.

Serve over brown rice and top with pine nuts.

YIELD: 4 SERVINGS

EACH WITH: Calories 268.56; Calories From Fat 59.83; Total Fat 6.16 g; Cholesterol 68 mg; Sodium 643.83 mg; Potassium 733.61 mg; Total Carbohydrates 21.71 g; Fiber 4.59 g; Sugar 6.18 g; Protein 31.23 g

BLOOD SUGAR BALANCE RATING: Very High

Health Facilitators	Nutrient Density Rating
Protein	High
Fat	Medium
Carbohydrate	Medium
Enzymes	Low
Antioxidants	High
Fiber	High

Zucchini are an excellent source of vitamins C and A, both of which provide excellent protection from yeast overgrowth. Zucchini also contain immune boosters such as the minerals potassium, copper, and magnesium. This dish offers healthy amounts of lean protein from chicken and nutritious herbs that are pleasing to the palate. Pine nuts add crunch and extra protein, and fiber-rich brown rice keeps you satisfied for hours.

CHERRY YOGURT FREEZE

Cherries are considered a "super"' fruit by many health experts because of the amount of disease-fighting antioxidants, vitamins, and minerals they contain. Cherries are the perfect fruit for Type 3 sugar addicts because they are low in sugar, and their high fiber content keeps blood sugar stable. Combine cherries' potassium, magnesium, folate, and vitamin C with yeast-fighting yogurt, and this dessert is a smart and delicious choice.

2 cups (300 g) cherries, fresh or frozen and thawed
1 cup (240 ml) plain low-fat yogurt
2 teaspoons (10 ml) vanilla extract, or more to taste
Freshly grated nutmeg
2 to 3 tablespoons (16 to 24 g) chopped walnuts

Freeze the cherries for several hours or overnight. Place the yogurt and vanilla in a food processor or blender and add the cherries. Process until almost smooth. Then process for several seconds until the mixture is completely smooth. Add nutmeg to taste, add more vanilla, if desired, and serve garnished with chopped walnuts. You may also hold in the freezer for up to 2 hours (it will become too hard if frozen any longer).

YIELD: 2 SERVINGS

EACH WITH: Calories 225.25; Calories From Fat 59.85; Total Fat 7.07 g; Cholesterol 7.35 mg; Sodium 86.28 mg; Potassium 632.29 mg; Total Carbohydrates 32.28 g; Fiber 3.4 g; Sugar 27.04 g; Protein 9.04 g

BLOOD SUGAR BALANCE RATING: Medium

Health Facilitators	Nutrient Density Rating
Protein	Low
Fat	Low
Carbohydrate	High
Enzymes	Very High
Antioxidants	Very High
Fiber	Very High

LET-THE-SUNSHINE-IN BARS

1 cup (240 ml) freshly squeezed orange juice
1 cup (175 g) dried apricots
½ cup (120 ml) molasses
½ cup (120 ml) coconut oil
1 cup (80 g) rolled oats
1 cup (125 g) coconut flour
½ cup (50 g) wheat germ
1 teaspoon cinnamon
½ teaspoon salt
1 cup (145 g) raisins, roughly chopped
⅔ cup (85 g) toasted almond meal

Preheat oven to 350°F (180°C, or gas mark 4). In a small saucepan, heat orange juice to a boil. Add dried apricots, return to a boil, and turn off heat. Cover pan and let apricots absorb juice until tender enough to cut with a sharp knife, but not really soft, about 10 minutes.

Meanwhile, mix molasses and coconut oil and set aside. In a separate bowl, stir together oats, flour, wheat germ, cinnamon, and salt. Drain apricots and add the juice to the honey-oil mixture. Chop apricots coarsely and stir into dry ingredients along with raisins and almond meal. Combine wet and dry ingredients and press mixture into an oiled 9 x 13-inch (23 x 33-cm) baking dish. Bake about 30 minutes, or until lightly browned. (Keep an eye on them! Cookies made with molasses brown quickly.) Let cool completely before cutting.

YIELD: 2 DOZEN BARS
EACH WITH: Calories 157.24; Calories From Fat 60.95; Total Fat 7.14 g; Cholesterol 0 mg; Sodium 52.95 mg; Potassium 271.95 mg; Total Carbohydrates 22.77 g; Fiber 3.72 g; Sugar 11.87 g; Protein 2.8 g
BLOOD SUGAR BALANCE RATING: Medium

Health Facilitators	Nutrient Density Rating
Protein	Low
Fat	Moderate
Carbohydrate	High
Enzymes	High
Antioxidants	High
Fiber	Very High

These treats are delicious and nutritious thanks to their exotic star, coconut oil. Coconut oil contains lauric and caprylic acid, which have antimicrobial, antioxidant, antifungal, and antibacterial properties to defeat yeast. Toss in some mineral-rich dried fruits, and these lightly sweet bars will have you smiling with delight.

CHAPTER 10

Type 4 Sugar Addiction

Depressed and Craving Carbs: Sugar cravings caused by your period, menopause, or andropause

ARE YOU A TYPE 4 SUGAR ADDICT?

Your total score will tell you whether you fit the Type 4 profile.

WOMEN
PMS

_____Do you have a history of PMS (premenstrual syndrome)? (30 points)

Or, in the week before your period, do you have increased and severe . . .

_____ irritability (15 points)

_____ anxiety (15 points)

_____ unhappiness or depression (15 points)

_____ bloating (15 points)

_____ Your total score

If you scored 30 or higher, read the section on PMS that follows.

Perimenopause

Are you older than thirty-eight or have you had a hysterectomy or ovarian surgery? If so:

_____ Do you have decreased vaginal lubrication? (25 points)

_____ Do you have decreased sex drive (libido)? (15 points)

_____ Have your periods been getting irregular or changing in other ways? (15 points)

In the week before and around your period, do you experience noticeably worse . . .

_____ insomnia? (15 points)

_____ headaches? (15 points)

_____ fatigue? (15 points)

_____ hot flashes or sweats? (20 points)

_____ Your total score

If you scored 30 or higher, you likely have symptoms from estrogen or progesterone deficiency; read the section on perimenopause and menopause that follows.

Menopause

Are you older than forty-seven and have your periods stopped, or have you had a hysterectomy? If so, do you have . . .

____ depression? (15 points)

____ vaginal dryness? (15 points)

____ fatigue? (15 points)

____ insomnia? (15 points)

____ loss of libido? (15 points)

____ Your total score

If you scored 30 or higher, you likely have symptoms from hormone deficiency associated with menopause; read the section on perimenopause and menopause that follows.

MEN
Andropause

____ Are you older than forty-five? (15 points)

____ Do you have decreased libido? (20 points)

____ Do you have erectile dysfunction or decrease in erections? (20 points)

____ Do you have hypertension? (20 points)

____ Do you have diabetes? (20 points)

____ Do you have high cholesterol? (20 points)

____ Are you overweight with a "spare tire" around your waist? (20 points)

____ Your total score

If you scored 50 or higher, these symptoms may be the result of an inadequate testosterone level. Ignore the "normal range" for testosterone levels on the lab result (even if your doctor uses it) and instead use the ranges we supply in the "Low Testosterone" section below.

THE TYPE 4 SUGAR ADDICT

When their hormones are in flux, Type 4 sugar addicts reach for sweets to self-medicate. If you are a woman, your estrogen levels fluctuate before and during your period, making you feel blue, tired, irritable, and cranky—so you reach for that cupcake to help you feel better. If you are in perimenopause or menopause, you experience mood swings, hot flashes, fatigue, and headaches along with intense sugar cravings when estrogen, progesterone, and even testosterone levels plummet during the four to seven days around your period. If you are a man older than forty-five, declining testosterone levels (called andropause) can also trigger sugar cravings.

Why Sugar Makes You Feel Better (Temporarily)

One reason we feel blue when either estrogen or testosterone levels decline is because these hormones affect the production of the "happiness molecule" serotonin, along with other brain chemicals (neurotransmitters). We reach for sugar to boost levels of serotonin in an attempt to feel better. The problem? When your sugar high wears off, you are more bummed out, fatigued, and cranky than you were before. So you reach for sugar once again to get that "high," setting you in a pattern of addiction.

In the short term, eating sugar does raise serotonin levels and make you feel happier. When your body releases insulin to process the sugar you've eaten, the insulin drives many amino acids (proteins) into your muscles, but not tryptophan, leaving more tryptophan free to go into your brain to make serotonin. Unfortunately, the more sugar you eat, the less effective insulin becomes over time (leading to insulin resistance), and the antidepressant effect diminishes. In fact, insulin resistance can actually cause a drop in serotonin levels in the brain, leaving you more depressed than when you started and craving even more sugar to get the same "high." So while eating something sweet can temporarily help boost your mood, it leads to even worse blood sugar fluctuations, exacerbation of your symptoms, and ultimately sugar addiction.

REDUCE YOUR SUGAR INTAKE TO FEEL BETTER FOR THE LONG HAUL

While it's incredibly tempting to reach for a sweet treat to increase energy and alleviate depression and anxiety, you now know that relying on sugar sets you up for mood swings, hormonal imbalances, and insulin resistance. Thankfully, eating a healthful diet that supplies you with steady energy and keeps your blood sugar in check will help you feel better even when your hormones are haywire. You'll also decrease insulin resistance and reduce your risk of diabetes, high cholesterol, and heart disease.

To break the cycle of Type 4 sugar addiction, the best solution is to eat a steady and balanced supply of lean protein; low-glycemic carbohydrates like whole grains, fruits, and vegetables; and healthy fats like omega-3s. These foods will cause your blood sugar to rise gradually, preventing a blood sugar roller coaster and calming cravings.

What Is the Glycemic Index?

The glycemic index (GI) is a scale that rates how much or how little foods raise your blood sugar. All foods are rated against glucose, which scores a 100 on the scale. As a sugar addict, you'll want to aim for low-glycemic foods to help keep your blood sugar nice and stable. This is especially important for Type 4 sugar addicts because the combination of fluctuating hormones and sugar highs and lows can make you feel quite miserable. Learn more about the glycemic index in Appendix B.

Foods That Boost Serotonin Naturally

As mentioned above, the amino acid tryptophan is a precursor to the feel-good hormone serotonin. Eating lean, high-protein foods that contain generous levels of tryptophan will make the most difference to your hormone levels, improving how you feel overall and in the long term. Good choices include free-range poultry, fish, shrimp, lamb, organic and grass-fed beef, eggs, beans, kelp, nuts, seeds, whey protein, and cottage cheese.

Your body uses tryptophan best when you consume it in conjunction with a small amount of carbohydrate, such as a serving of low-glycemic vegetables, brown rice or legumes, or a handful of nuts. Carbohydrates increase the amount of tryptophan that gets into the brain to be turned into serotonin, and choosing low-glycemic carbs ensures that your blood sugar stays stable in a healthy way.

Choose Organic Foods to Balance Hormones

If your budget allows, try to choose organic foods when it is convenient. Eating organic reduces your exposure to insecticides and pesticides, which are toxic and can interfere with the normal function of hormones in the body. It's especially important to buy organic when it comes to foods you eat frequently, such as milk, and thin-skinned fruits and vegetables like apples, berries, celery, and bell peppers. The Environmental Working Group website www.foodnews.org provides a list of the foods highest and lowest in pesticides, to help you get the most bang for your buck. Most supermarkets now carry many organic options, including less expensive store brands.

Essential Fatty Acids Stabilize Hormones and Blood Sugar

Healthy fats provide long-lasting energy without raising your blood sugar. Omega-3 fatty acids are especially important for Type 4 sugar addicts because they are building blocks for important players like hormones and neurotransmitters, as well as cell membranes and enzymes. Foods high in omega-3s include cold-water fatty fish such as salmon, mackerel, halibut, herring, trout, sardines, and tuna. You'll also find omega-3s in flaxseed and flaxseed oil, hemp seeds, sesame seeds, walnuts, and sea greens. The best food sources for healthy omega-6 essential fatty acids, which also improve mood and decrease sugar cravings, are beans and nuts, olives, tofu, and dark green leafy vegetables. Foods with omega-9 fatty acids, which are helpful to balance out the omega-3s and -6s for heart health, include olives and olive oil, most nuts, and avocados. You'll want to include all of these essential fatty acids in your diet every day for the best hormone and blood sugar control.

A proper ratio of omega-3 essential fatty acids to omega-6 essential fatty acids is important to prevent sugar cravings caused by anxiety and depression. But, thanks largely to processed and fast foods, the current typical American diet contains fourteen to twenty-five times more omega-6 fatty acids than omega-3s. Keeping your oil intake balanced will also balance your mood and decrease sugar cravings. Consuming more omega-3s will also decrease inflammation, cancer, heart disease, stroke, diabetes, arthritis, and autoimmune conditions aggravated by high sugar intakes, helping you feel better overall.

A healthy ratio of omega-3s to omega-6s is 1:3. You can reach that ratio by increasing foods rich in omega-3s and reducing your intake of unhealthy sources of omega-6s such as baked goods and polyunsaturated vegetable oils such as corn, sunflower, soybean, and safflower.

Fish Oil Supplements

If you don't get enough omega-3s through diet, you might want to supplement. Look for products that provide both EPA (eicosapentaenoic acid) and DHA (docosahexaenoic acid) and are purified to remove toxic contaminants like mercury and PCBs. To minimize the fishy aftertaste, take the capsules frozen and with a meal.

If the fishy taste is still a problem, or if you have trouble swallowing large pills, a new fish oil supplement called Vectomega is available in tablet form rather than capsule, which should help with both concerns. It also claims to deliver EPA and DHA in a form similar to that found in the human brain, and preliminary research suggests that increases its absorption. If you'd like to try it, it's available at some natural foods stores or online.

Enjoy a Daily Dose of Chocolate

You may be surprised to learn that chocolate is an okay food for Type 4 sugar addicts. Women intuitively crave chocolate (especially around their menstrual cycles) because they know it is good for them and their moods. Chocolate boosts PEA (phenylethylamine), a potent mood elevator and antidepressant. Chocolate also contains a mild stimulant called theobromine that gives you a small energy lift, but not enough to trap you on the sugar roller coaster like caffeine does. Dark chocolate is also high in antioxidants and lower in sugar than other kinds of chocolate. Look for varieties that are at least 60 percent cocoa to get the most health benefits (the darker the better!). Not only will small amounts of chocolate (up to an ounce or so a day) improve mood and sugar cravings, but there is another fringe benefit. While excess sugar may increase heart attack risk, consuming small amounts of chocolate (about ½ ounce a day) is associated with a 61 percent reduced risk of heart disease— making it around 40 times as effective as cholesterol blocker medications (called statins)!

Sugar-free chocolates in moderation are an even better option (Godiva, Abdallah, and Russell Stover brands taste the best). These are not low-calorie though, so choose the best tasting chocolate you can find, and savor it in small amounts—up to ½ to one ounce a day.

Drink Filtered Water for Balanced Hormones

Besides choosing the right foods, Type 4 sugar addicts should pay special attention to the water they drink. That's because our public water supply is full of chemicals that can interfere with estrogen, progesterone, and testosterone function. For everyday drinking, use a good quality home water filter.

When you're on the go, fill a reusable glass or stainless steel bottle with filtered water from home (the chemicals in plastic bottles can leach into the water—avoid those made with BPA, and don't leave them in the sun or run them through the dishwasher). If you buy bottled water, a good brand in the U.S. (not in Europe) is Dasani. Overall though, when convenient, start switching from plastic bottles to glass or stainless steel.

The Benefits of Bio-Identical Hormones

Premarin, the brand of synthetic estrogen most commonly prescribed for menopausal women, contains a form of the hormone that comes from pregnant horse urine. This is obviously quite different than human estrogen, and some research shows it increases breast cancer risk by 23 percent. Add the synthetic progesterone Provera to the mix, and you increase that risk by 38 to 67 percent!

The Women's Health Initiative study showed that the combination of Premarin and Provera significantly increased the risk of heart attack and stroke. Natural bio-identical estrogen and progesterone, on the other hand, have been shown in many studies to have an opposite effect— decreasing the risk of heart attack and stroke, and reducing other side effects—while still easing the hormonal transition into menopause. You can read more about bio-identical hormones for women and men and how they can help you kick your sugar addiction holistically in *Beat Sugar Addiction Now!*.

Critical Nutrients for Type 4 Sugar Addicts

Optimizing nutritional support with specific vitamins helps you kick Type 4 sugar addiction in many ways. The recipes that follow provide abundant amounts of these nutrients to make it easy (and delicious!) for you to get off the sugar/ hormonal roller coaster and feel better now. In addition to improving your diet through these recipes, I recommend taking a good multivitamin (my favorite is the Energy Revitalization System vitamin powder by Enzymatic Therapy) to optimize nutrient levels. Look for a product that contains the amounts noted below.

Vitamin B1 (Thiamine) Thiamine is critical for proper brain functioning, and it decreases both anxiety and depression. Research indicates that B1 improves mood, possibly by increasing synthesis of acetylcholine, a neurotransmitter associated with memory, and by making you more clearheaded, composed, and energetic. Take 75 mg daily.

Vitamin B6 If you have PMS, you'll want to stock up on B6. Vitamin B6 eases the deficiency of prostaglandin E1 that causes irritability and drives sugar cravings. If you have PMS symptoms, take 150–200 mg a day for three to six months to alleviate them. Then reduce your dose to 85 mg a day (or start with this lower dose if PMS symptoms are not a concern for you).

Vitamin B12 (Cobalamin) B12 is another mood-boosting B vitamin. A 2005 study published in the *International Journal of Neuropsychopharmacology* found that among people treated for depression with antidepressants, those who had higher levels of vitamin B12 tended to get a greater benefit from the medication. Vitamin B12 is critical for nerve and brain function, and deficiencies become increasingly common as we age. Medications such as acid blockers for indigestion and metformin for diabetes can also interfere with B12 absorption. Take 500 mcg a day.

Vitamin D Vitamin D is essential for increasing bone density and helping prevent osteoporosis and fractures that can be caused by estrogen deficiency in women and low testosterone in men. Vitamin D deficiency is also associated with increased risk of depression and cancer. Few foods contain vitamin D, but your body is quite efficient at making it from sunshine. However, because vitamin D deficiency is so common—even in sunny climates—I recommend supplementing with 1,000–2,000 IUs daily.

Magnesium Magnesium has been called the "anti-stress mineral" because it relaxes muscles, improves sleep, and relieves tension. Like B6, magnesium helps increase the production of prostaglandin E1, minimizing the irritability that triggers sugar cravings. Magnesium also helps to make the three other key "happiness" neurotransmitters that your body needs: serotonin, dopamine, and norepinephrine. Take 150–200 mg daily.

Iodine An iodine deficiency contributes not only to the fatigue and hypothyroidism that can drive Type 1 sugar cravings, but also to irregular periods, breast cysts, and breast tenderness. Research suggests that seaweed, which is high in iodine, may even lower breast cancer risk. Take 200+ mcg/day. If you have breast tenderness or fibrocystic breast disease, talk to your doctor about taking 6,250–12,500 mcg (6.25–12.5 mg) of a supplement called Tri-iodine that balances three key forms of iodine (do not take more than this high dose without a physician's supervision). Unusual side effects include acne and flaring indigestion on these higher doses, so stop taking iodine if these become a problem.

Evening Primrose Oil Evening primrose oil contains GLA, an essential fatty acid the body uses to make another "happiness hormone" called prostaglandin E1 (PGE1), which also calms sugar-induced inflammation. It can also help ease the symptoms of PMS, including mood swings, bloating, and breast tenderness, making you less likely to give in to sugar cravings around your period. Take 3,000 mg a day for three months. After that, you may only need to take it during the week before your period. Once you are feeling better, you can switch to less expensive borage oil and see if it works as well for you.

Green Tea May Ease PMS

If you have anxiety from PMS, theanine, a component in green tea, can help keep you calm and alert during the day, while also helping you sleep at night. That's because theanine stimulates your body's "natural valium," called gamma-aminobutyric acid (GABA), without addiction or side effects. It also increases alpha brainwave activity, creating a state of deep relaxation and mental alertness similar to what is achieved through meditation. Theanine naturally stimulates the release of calming GABA and the feel-good neurotransmitter dopamine as well. Drink a cup or two of green tea daily for a sugar-free mood and energy boost. To supplement, look for theanine made by Suntheanine, which is in the form your body can use. A typical supplement dose is 50–200 mg.

Treating Perimenopause and Menopause Naturally

The most effective remedy for the symptoms of menopause, specifically hot flashes, is black cohosh. (Research indicates the best brand is Remifemin by Enzymatic Therapy, Inc.) Remifemin helps stabilize autonomic function, including your blood pressure, pulse, and sweating, which means it decreases hot flashes associated with low estrogen. You'll also be on less of a sugar roller coaster when your autonomic function is balanced.

Black cohosh contains no estrogen. It's safe for women with breast cancer, and studies suggest it may even decrease the risk of breast cancer. If you'd like to try black cohosh, take two capsules twice a day for two months; then you might be able to lower your dose to one capsule twice a day.

For women in menopause who have low estrogen, it's also smart to get in the habit of eating a handful of soybean pods (called edamame) daily around your period. Eat Well and Enjoy Life now make a delicious edamame hummus, making this even easier. Edamame is a good source of natural estrogen, plus protein, vitamins, minerals, and fiber, and it's low on the glycemic index.

For Men in Andropause: Testosterone Replacement

If you are a healthy man entering andropause, suboptimal testosterone levels can lead to insulin resistance and sugar cravings. Treatment with bio-identical hormones decreases insulin resistance and can lower cholesterol and high blood pressure. This is especially important for diabetics whose illness is a risk factor for heart disease. Treatment with bio-identical hormones may also improve heart health, muscle mass, libido and sexual function, and reduce depression along with your risk of elevated cholesterol, hypertension, and diabetes from the blood-sugar disorder metabolic syndrome. Low testosterone in men (and excessive sugar intake for anyone) are two of the main causes of metabolic syndrome.

You may have heard that treatment with testosterone will increase prostate size or the blood test marker for prostate cancer (PSA). But, in fact, a review of 18 studies published in the *Journal of Urology* in 1998 showed that testosterone treatment does not increase the risk of prostate cancer. It is also important that you not confuse taking safe levels of bio-identical natural testosterone with the high-dose, synthetic, and toxic testosterone that some athletes illegally use. You can learn more about how to use bio-identical hormones safely to curb your sugar cravings and beat your sugar addiction naturally in *Beat Sugar Addiction Now!*

CHAPTER 11

Recipes for Type 4 Sugar Addiction

When hormones are out of balance during PMS, perimenopause, menopause, and andropause (male menopause) it can cause sugar cravings to soar. In order to stop type 4 sugar addiction, we start with a healthy diet. These recipes have been created specifically to address the issues related to Type 4 sugar personality—they will keep your blood sugar levels stable, your hormones balanced, and you, healthy. Use them in combination with the bio-identical hormones and natural remedies described in Chapter 10 to heal your body and feel better than ever before!

BLISSFUL BONE-BUILDING OMELET

4 organic eggs

2 tablespoons (30 ml) heavy cream

Freshly ground black pepper

1 cup (190 g) cooked spinach, well drained and chopped

3 tablespoons (27 g) crumbled goat cheese

2 tablespoons (5 g) finely slivered fresh basil, or 2 teaspoons (1.4 g) dried basil

2 tablespoons (20 g) diced red onion

2 tablespoons (30 ml) extra-virgin olive oil or coconut oil

1 slice whole-grain rye or pumpernickel bread (optional)

Salad greens and alfalfa sprouts for garnish (optional)

In a medium bowl, using a fork, whisk eggs, cream, and black pepper. Set aside.

Combine spinach with crumbled goat cheese, basil, and red onion. Set aside.

Heat oil in a 10-inch (25-cm) skillet or frying pan over medium-high heat. When the oil is hot, pour in the egg mixture. Cook until eggs begin to set. Lift edges to allow uncooked egg to seep underneath. When bottom layer of egg is cooked but top is still moist, spread spinach and cheese mixture over one side of omelet. Gently fold omelet in half. Cook 30 seconds longer until filling is hot. Slide omelet onto a plate and serve immediately with plain or toasted rye bread and salad and sprouts, if desired.

YIELD: 2 SERVINGS

EACH WITH: Amount Per Serving; Calories 449.72; Calories From Fat (69%); Total Fat 34.59 g; Cholesterol 454.8 mg; Sodium 427.87 mg; Potassium 1128.84 mg; Total Carbohydrates 15.13 g; Fiber 4.79 g; Sugar 2.33 g; Protein 22.82 g

BLOOD SUGAR BALANCE RATING: Very High

Health Facilitators	Nutrient Density Rating
Protein	Very High
Fat	High
Carbohydrate	High
Enzymes	Medium
Antioxidants	High
Fiber	Medium

Goat cheese is loaded with mood-boosting tryptophan and, together with spinach, provides calcium to build strong bones. Calcium also keeps you calm and reduces cravings for sweet foods. This omelet is high in vitamins E and C that will keep your hormones and your blood sugar levels stable. Garnish with plenty of salad greens and alfalfa sprouts for added enzymes, antioxidants, and fiber, and you've got power you can feel in your bones.

SUSTAINING SARDINE SALSA WITH AVOCADO ON TOAST

This delicious little fish dish is packed with omega-3s, calcium, and vitamin D to strengthen your bones. This recipe offers the perfect balance of protein, healthy fats, carbohydrates, and antioxidants—a powerful combo that will elevate your mood and balance your hormones.

1 can (3 ounces, or 85 g) water-packed sardines
1 small fresh tomato, chopped (or 3 oil-packed sundried tomatoes, chopped)
1 tablespoon (15 ml) fresh lemon juice
2 tablespoons (8 g) chopped fresh parsley
2 tablespoons (12 g) chopped scallions
Freshly ground black pepper
2 slices ½-inch (1.3-cm) thick sourdough bread
½ avocado, sliced
2 large romaine lettuce leaves
2 tablespoons (30 ml) cottage cheese (optional)

Drain the water from the sardines and place in a bowl. Add the tomatoes, lemon juice, parsley, scallions, and black pepper and use the back of a fork to blend ingredients together. Toast the slices of bread lightly and spread them with avocado. Pile the sardine mixture on top, and sprinkle with more lemon juice and pepper if needed. Serve with romaine lettuce and cottage cheese, if desired.

YIELD: 2 SERVINGS
EACH WITH: Calories 298.57; Calories From Fat 115.31; Total Fat 13.09 g; Cholesterol 36.13 mg; Sodium 689.03 mg; Potassium 699.52 mg; Total Carbohydrates 28.38 g; Fiber 5.27 g; Sugar 3.58 g; Protein 18.37 g
BLOOD SUGAR BALANCE RATING: Very High

Health Facilitators	Nutrient Density Rating
Protein	High
Fat	Very High
Carbohydrate	High
Enzymes	Very high
Antioxidants	Very high
Fiber	High

MIGHTY MEDITERRANEAN FRITTATA

1 tablespoon (15 ml) olive oil, butter, or ghee
2 broccoli crowns, cut into bite-sized pieces
1 medium yellow bell pepper, chopped
1 medium red bell pepper, chopped
2 cups (40 g) chopped spinach
½ cup (50 g) pitted and halved ripe olives
6 organic eggs, lightly beaten
½ cup (120 ml) rice, almond, goat, or cow's milk
2 tablespoons (5 g) chopped fresh basil or 1 teaspoon dried basil
1 teaspoon dried oregano
Sea salt and pepper
1 to 2 tablespoons (5 to 10 g) finely grated Parmesan cheese
¼ cup (30 g) finely ground cashews

Preheat oven to 350°F (180°C, or gas mark 4). Grease a 9-inch (23-cm) round pan with the butter or oil. Evenly arrange broccoli, yellow and red peppers, spinach, and olives in the pan. Beat together eggs, milk, basil, oregano, and salt and pepper to taste in a small bowl and pour over vegetables. Bake for 35 to 40 minutes, or until the center has set. Broil for the last two minutes to brown the top. Cool, slice into wedges, and serve warm or cold garnished with Parmesan cheese and ground cashews.

YIELD: 4 SERVINGS

EACH WITH: Calories 334.77; Calories From Fat 223.62; Total Fat 25.71 g; Cholesterol 320.79 mg; Sodium 396.88 mg; Potassium 396.52 mg; Total Carbohydrates 13.82 g; Fiber 3.88 g; Sugar 4.11 g; Protein 15.15 g

BLOOD SUGAR BALANCE RATING: Very High

Health Facilitators	Nutrient Density Rating
Protein	High
Fat	Medium
Carbohydrate	High
Enzymes	Low
Antioxidants	High
Fiber	High

The health benefits of broccoli and spinach make them mealtime winners, especially when it comes to keeping hormones balanced. Both are loaded with antioxidants, vitamin C, folic acid, and magnesium to nourish and support healthy hormone levels. Plus, the high-fiber variety of vegetables helps stabilize blood sugar levels.

ENERGY-GIVING GRANOLA

This simple-to-make version of an old favorite will satisfy your sweet tooth and keep your blood sugar levels stable at the same time. The addition of omega-3–rich walnuts and flaxseed oil feed your brain cells as well as balance your hormones, and coconut oil boasts additional healing essential fatty acids. Sunflower seeds are loaded with zinc, which boosts your immune system, while the raw oats are full of filling fiber to keep your digestive system working properly.

6 cups (480 g) rolled oats
1¼ cups (85 g) unsweetened chopped coconut
½ cup (60 g) chopped almonds
½ cup (60 g) chopped walnuts
1 cup (225 g) raw, shelled sunflower seeds
½ cup (60 g) sesame seeds
Dash of cinnamon
Pinch of salt
½ cup (120 ml) raw honey
½ cup (120 ml) organic coconut oil
2 to 3 tablespoons (30 to 45 ml) flaxseed oil

Preheat oven to 325°F (170°C, or gas mark 3). Mix oats, coconut, almonds, walnuts, sunflower seeds, sesame seeds, cinnamon, and salt together in a large bowl. Combine honey and coconut oil in a saucepan over medium heat and heat to a thin liquid. Pour over dry ingredients and mix well. Spread onto a baking pan and flatten with moist hands. Bake for 15 to 20 minutes. Cool and store in an airtight container. Drizzle with flaxseed oil and serve with almond or rice milk and/or fresh fruit.

YIELD: 6 TO 8 SERVINGS
EACH WITH: Calories 981.88; Calories From Fat 602.9; Total Fat 71.01 g; Cholesterol 0 mg; Sodium 60.74 mg; Potassium 607.37 mg;Total Carbohydrates 76.74 g; Fiber 16.9 g; Sugar 21.86 g; Protein 20.18 g;
BLOOD SUGAR BALANCE RATING: High

Health Facilitators	Nutrient Density Rating
Protein	Medium
Fat	High
Carbohydrate	High
Enzymes	High
Antioxidants	High
Fiber	Very High

GOOD OIL' AVOCADO TUNA SALAD

1 ripe medium avocado
Dash of lemon or lime juice
2 cans (8 ounces, or 225 g) water-packed light tuna
2 tablespoons (8 g) chopped parsley
2 tablespoons (12 g) chopped scallions
½ teaspoon sea salt (optional)
¼ to ½ teaspoon freshly ground black pepper
2 cups (40 g) spinach or mixed greens

Mash avocado with lemon or lime juice. Flake tuna and add to avocado along with parsley, scallions, salt (if using), and black pepper. Serve over spinach or mixed greens.

YIELD: 2 SERVINGS
EACH WITH: Calories 257.78; Calories From Fat 119.45; Total Fat 14.19 g; Cholesterol 25.52 mg; Sodium 791.45 mg; Potassium 867.35 mg; Total Carbohydrates 10.73 g; Fiber 6.95 g; Sugar 0.93 g; Protein 24.56 g
BLOOD SUGAR BALANCE RATING: Very High

Health Facilitators	Nutrient Density Rating
Protein	High
Fat	High
Carbohydrate	High
Enzymes	High
Antioxidants	High
Fiber	Medium

Make this salad when you want a nutritious, tasty lunch and don't have much time for preparation. Avocadoes and tuna contain omega-3 essential fatty acids that balance blood sugar levels and hormones. Calcium from the spinach helps you stay calm and stabilizes hormones. Swap tuna for halibut, salmon, or sea bass, if you prefer. This salad is also good with rice crackers or whole-grain bread.

KICKIN' CHICKEN AND QUINOA SALAD

Quinoa is high in plant protein, which stabilizes blood sugar, and tryptophan, which lifts mood. It's also packed with magnesium and iron to keep hormones and blood sugar in balance. The delicious blend of vegetables and herbs contains numerous vitamins and minerals and dozens of antioxidants.

⅓ cup (60 g) quinoa
2 cups (220 g) cooked boneless, skinless chicken, cubed
1 medium apple, peeled and chopped
1 medium red onion, chopped
2 stalks celery, chopped
1 medium carrot, shredded
¼ cup (15 g) cilantro
¼ cup (30 g) chopped walnuts
¼ cup (35 g) raisins
3 tablespoons (45 ml) organic mayonnaise (with no hydrogenated oils)
2 tablespoons (30 ml) lime or lemon juice
1 teaspoon cumin
Freshly ground black pepper
1 teaspoon sea salt
4 large lettuce leaves (for serving)
1 avocado, sliced in quarters

Rinse quinoa well and add to ⅔ cup (160 ml) purified water in a 2-quart (1.9-L) saucepan. Bring to boil, then immediately reduce heat to low. Simmer, covered, for 10 to 15 minutes or until all water has been absorbed. Toss quinoa with chicken and next 12 ingredients (through salt), and chill. Serve over lettuce leaves with avocado.

YIELD: 4 SERVINGS

EACH WITH: Calories 441.74; Calories From Fat 204.52; Total Fat 23.45 g; Cholesterol 63.25 mg; Sodium 621.73 mg; Potassium 780.68 mg; Total Carbohydrates 33.5 g; Fiber 7.52 g; Sugar 11.52 g; Protein 26.96 g

BLOOD SUGAR BALANCE RATING: Very High

Health Facilitators	Nutrient Density Rating
Protein	High
Fat	Medium
Carbohydrate	High
Enzymes	High
Antioxidants	High
Fiber	High

LOW-GLYCEMIC LAMB KEBOBS WITH MINT PARSLEY PESTO

For Kebobs

½ cup (120 ml) olive oil

Juice of 2 lemons

2 garlic cloves, peeled and minced

¼ cup (15 g) chopped mint leaves

2 tablespoons (4 g) chopped fresh rosemary

2 tablespoons (5 g) chopped fresh thyme

¼ teaspoon sea salt

1 pound (455 g) boneless leg of lamb (can substitute other meat or extra-firm tofu)

12 cremini mushrooms, cut in half

20 pearl onions, peeled

2 cups (300 g) cherry tomatoes

2 cucumbers, peeled and cut into ½-inch (1.3-cm) rounds

12 metal skewers (if using wood, soak the skewers for 30 minutes)

Sea salt and black pepper

For Mint Parsley Pesto

½ cup (48 g) mint

½ cup (32 g) parsley

⅓ cup (80 ml) extra-virgin olive oil

2 tablespoons (30 ml) fresh lemon or lime juice

¼ teaspoon sea salt

To make the kebobs: In a large mixing bowl combine olive oil, lemon juice, garlic, mint, rosemary, thyme, and sea salt. Clean and chop lamb into ½-inch (1.3-cm) cubes. Add lamb to olive oil mixture and toss to coat evenly. Marinate in the refrigerator 4 to 6 hours or overnight. Preheat grill or oven to 375°F (190°C, or gas mark 5). Assemble kebobs by threading one piece of mushroom, onion, meat, tomato, and cucumber onto a skewer. Repeat with remaining ingredients and skewers. Season with salt and pepper. Grill 3 to 5 minutes on each side, or bake in the oven for 5 minutes on each side, or until lamb reaches desired doneness.

To make the pesto: Combine all ingredients in a food processor or blender and process until smooth. Adjust seasonings to taste, and serve with kebobs.

YIELD: 4 SERVINGS

EACH WITH: Calories 745.26; Calories From Fat 496.07; Total Fat 56.08 g; Cholesterol 122.47 mg; Sodium 516.24 mg; Potassium 1163.9 mg; Total Carbohydrates 22.89 g; Fiber 7.47 g; Sugar 3.16 g; Protein 42.86 g

BLOOD SUGAR BALANCE RATING: Very High

Lamb is not only an excellent source of high-quality protein, it is also a good source of zinc, a mineral essential for immune function. Zinc helps stabilize blood sugar levels as well and is important for maintaining men's prostate health. This meal also contains lots of vitamin B12, which helps your cells metabolize protein, carbohydrate, and fat. The mint and parsley pesto packs an added nutrient and antioxidant punch.

Health Facilitators	Nutrient Density Rating
Protein	Very High
Fat	Medium
Carbohydrate	Low
Enzymes	High
Antioxidants	High
Fiber	Medium

HORMONE-BALANCING TOFU STIR-FRY

Soy foods are an excellent source of plant protein and are loaded with tryptophan to stabilize blood sugar levels and hormones. Tofu easily takes on the flavor of its surrounding ingredients, making it quite versatile. Tempeh is made from fermented soybeans, which are high in protein, vitamins, minerals, and isoflavones, and fiber. Filling vegetables and a flavorful sauce make this dish satisfying and incredibly healthy.

2 ounces (55 g) soft tofu
8 ounces (170 g) tofu or tempeh, cut into cubes
1 large red or brown onion
1 cup (70 g) fresh (or reconstituted dried) shiitake mushrooms
2 carrots, sliced on diagonal
½ to 1 cup (120 to 240 ml) vegetable stock
3-inch (7.6-cm) piece of kombu, soaked and thinly sliced
1 cup (70 g) broccoli florets
½ cup (62 g) sliced water chestnuts
1 cup (50 g) bean sprouts
1 clove garlic, minced
2 tablespoons (16 g) grated fresh ginger
Tamari (wheat-free) or soy sauce to taste
3 tablespoons (45 ml) toasted sesame oil
Dash of cayenne

If using tempeh, bake or steam for 10 minutes before sautéing. Cut onion into ¼-inch (0.6-cm) pieces. Remove stems from mushrooms and reserve to make stock, if desired. Slice mushrooms. In a wok or large skillet, sauté onion over medium heat until it starts releasing its juices. Add mushrooms, cover, and simmer for 5 minutes. Add carrots and sauté for a few minutes, adding stock as necessary to prevent sticking or drying out of other ingredients. Then add the sliced kombu. Add tofu or tempeh, broccoli, water chestnuts, bean sprouts, and garlic. Sauté a few more minutes or until broccoli is bright green. Add ginger, and stir and cook 1 minute more. Remove from heat, and season with tamari, toasted sesame oil, and cayenne.

YIELD: 4 SERVINGS
EACH WITH: Calories 240.49; Calories From Fat 113.58; Total Fat 12.79 g; Cholesterol 1.8 mg; Sodium 489.48 mg; Potassium 610.18 mg; Total Carbohydrates 24.97 g; Fiber 6.5 g; Sugar 6.45 g; Protein 8.41 g
BLOOD SUGAR BALANCE RATING: High

Health Facilitators	Nutrient Density Rating
Protein	High
Fat	Medium
Carbohydrate	High
Enzymes	Medium
Antioxidants	High
Fiber	High

BEAT SUGAR ADDICTION NOW! COOKBOOK

DAILY-SUSTENANCE SALAD

For Salad

1 large carrot
½ bunch watercress
4 scallions
¼ cup (20 g) dried arame, soaked
2 celery stalks
2 cups (330 g) cooked brown rice
½ cup (70 g) peas, fresh or frozen and thawed

For Creamy Parsley Dressing

1 handful washed parsley
2 tablespoons (30 ml) tahini
½ cup (120 ml) purified water
2 tablespoons (30 ml) lemon juice
½ teaspoon sea salt
Freshly ground black pepper

To make the salad: Shred carrot with a potato peeler. Remove the stems from the watercress. Chop scallions, arame, and celery stalks. Combine the vegetables in a salad bowl, then stir in the rice and peas.

To make the dressing: Place all ingredients in a blender and purée until creamy. Pour approximately ¼ cup (60 ml) of the dressing on the salad and toss well.

YIELD: 4 SERVINGS

EACH WITH: Calories 203.79; Calories From Fat 44.57; Total Fat 5.3 g; Cholesterol 0 mg; Sodium 333.2 mg; Potassium 375.11 mg; Total Carbohydrates 33.75 g; Fiber 6.3 g; Sugar 3.71 g; Protein 7.2 g

BLOOD SUGAR BALANCE RATING: Very High

Health Facilitators	Nutrient Density Rating
Protein	High
Fat	Medium
Carbohydrate	High
Enzymes	High
Antioxidants	High
Fiber	Very high

Simple and easy to prepare, this salad works well served on its own or as a side dish. For higher protein and omega-3 content, just add a can of tuna or salmon into the mix. Arame, a mild-tasting type of seaweed that is packed with zinc, vitamin C, and iodine, blends nicely with the parsley dressing and helps keep your thyroid and adrenal glands healthy. This salad is loaded with antioxidants, vitamins, minerals, and fiber that will boost your metabolism and keep your blood sugar balanced for several hours.

SATISFYING TEX-MEX SALAD

A truly unique blend of Southwest cuisine and south-of-the-border ingredients, this salad contains macro- and micronutrients that are beneficial for hormone health, including the omega-3s in the flaxseed and lemon dressing. This delicious mix of flavors will keep your appetite, your hormones, and your blood sugar levels stable and satisfied for hours.

2 cups (40 g) shredded red leaf lettuce
1 cup (90 g) shredded red cabbage
1 pound (455 g) cooked chicken breast, turkey, fish, or shrimp, chopped
½ red bell pepper, cut julienne
1 cup (130 g) jicama, cut julienne
1 small avocado, peeled and diced
¼ cup (55 g) canned black beans, drained and rinsed
¼ red onion, thinly sliced
¼ cup (55 g) pumpkin seeds
¼ cup (60 ml) flaxseed oil
2 to 3 tablespoons fresh lemon or lime juice
Dash cayenne
Freshly ground black pepper

Combine lettuce and next 8 ingredients (through pumpkin seeds) in a large serving bowl. Whisk together flaxseed oil, lemon juice, cayenne, and black pepper. Toss with salad.

YIELD: 4 SERVINGS
EACH WITH: Calories 885.17; Calories From Fat 442.36; Total Fat 50.64 g; Cholesterol 192.78 mg; Sodium 342.86 mg; Potassium 1549.25 mg; Total Carbohydrates 30.77 g; Fiber 13.38 g; Sugar 3.59 g; Protein 77.77 g
BLOOD SUGAR BALANCE RATING: Very High

Health Facilitators	Nutrient Density Rating
Protein	High
Fat	High
Carbohydrate	High
Enzymes	High
Antioxidants	High
Fiber	High

BLOOD SUGAR–STABILIZING SESAME-COCONUT CRUSTED SALMON

1 tablespoon (15 ml) maple syrup

¼ cup (60 ml) purified water

¼ cup (60 ml) tamari sauce (wheat-free) or Bragg's liquid amino acids

1 tablespoon (6 g) peeled, chopped fresh ginger

1 garlic clove, chopped

4 salmon steaks, about 3 to 4 ounces (85 to 115 g) each

3 tablespoons (24 g) coconut flour

¼ cup (30 g) sesame seeds

2 tablespoons (9 g) desiccated coconut

2 tablespoons (30 ml) coconut oil

2 tablespoons (30 ml) sesame oil

4 cups (80 g) spinach, steamed

Combine maple syrup, water, tamari, or liquid amino acids ginger, and garlic in a bowl. Add fish to bowl and marinate 45 minutes or overnight in the refrigerator. In a resealable plastic bag, combine flour with sesame seeds and desiccated coconut. Drop marinated fish into the bag and coat with flour and seeds. Heat coconut and sesame oils in a frying pan over medium-high heat. Sauté fish 2 to 3 minutes on each side, or until desired doneness. Serve over steamed spinach.

YIELD: 4 SERVINGS

EACH WITH: Calories 426.4; Calories From Fat 273.52; Total Fat 31.17 g; Cholesterol 61 mg; Sodium 1086.3 mg; Potassium 645.62 mg; Total Carbohydrates 13.83 g; Fiber 4.39 g; Sugar 4.32 g; Protein 25.49 g

BLOOD SUGAR BALANCE RATING: Very High

Health Facilitators	Nutrient Density Rating
Protein	High
Fat	High
Carbohydrate	Medium
Enzymes	Low
Antioxidants	High
Fiber	Medium

Enjoy the nutty flavor of this delicious salmon coated with calcium-rich sesame seeds. Coconuts contain both lauric and caprylic acid, which are soothing as well as antimicrobial and antifungal. And the omega-3s in the salmon benefit your hormones and your blood sugar levels.

ALL-STAR ASPARAGUS SPEARS

Asparagus is both succulent and tender, and it's especially nourishing for Type 4s because it's high in tryptophan, potassium, fiber, and vitamins B6, A, and C. Asparagus fights inflammation and is a natural diuretic, which helps when you are feeling the effects of bloating with PMS. This healthful side dish complements any protein you care to try.

1 pound (455 g) asparagus, tough ends trimmed
2 tablespoons (30 ml) fresh lemon or lime juice
1 teaspoon Dijon mustard
2 garlic cloves, minced
2 tablespoons (30 ml) flaxseed oil
3 tablespoons (45 ml) extra-virgin olive oil
1 tablespoon (5 g) Parmesan cheese, grated
Dash cayenne
Freshly ground black pepper
½ teaspoon sea salt
1 tablespoon (8 g) sesame seeds

In a large skillet, bring 1 inch (2.5 cm) of water to a boil over medium-high heat. Add asparagus and cook until tender, about 3 to 6 minutes. Remove from pan, drain, and arrange on a serving platter. In a blender or food processor, blend lemon or lime juice and next 8 ingredients (through salt) until smooth (or place ingredients in a jar with a tight-fitting lid and shake vigorously until well blended). Pour over asparagus, sprinkle with sesame seeds, and serve immediately.

YIELD: 4 SERVINGS
EACH WITH: Calories 195.8; Calories From Fat 163.65; Total Fat 18.61 g; Cholesterol 1.1 mg; Sodium 272.83 mg; Potassium 259.26 mg; Total Carbohydrates 6.24 g; Fiber 2.75 g; Sugar 2.35 g; Protein 3.56 g
BLOOD SUGAR BALANCE RATING: High

Health Facilitators	Nutrient Density Rating
Protein	Low
Fat	Medium
Carbohydrate	High
Enzymes	High
Antioxidants	High
Fiber	High

SATISFYING TAHINI-GREENS STEAMER

4 to 5 carrots, chopped
1 bunch dark leafy greens (kale, collards, spinach)
2½ cups (600 ml) purified water, divided
¼ cup (60 ml) tahini
1½ tablespoons (22 ml) maple syrup
Juice of 1 lemon
2 to 3 tablespoons shoyu
1 tablespoon (8 g) sesame seeds (optional)

Place a steamer basket in a pot with 2 cups (480 ml) water. Bring water to a boil. Add carrots and steam 5 to 7 minutes. Remove carrots. Repeat with kale or other greens. Combine tahini, maple syrup, lemon juice, shoyu, and remaining ½ cup (120 ml) water. Toss with vegetables, sprinkle with sesame seeds, and serve.

YIELD: 4 SERVINGS

EACH WITH: Calories 179.14; Calories From Fat 74.15; Total Fat 8.87 g; Cholesterol 0 mg; Sodium 439.54 mg; Potassium 857.04 mg; Total Carbohydrates 22.36 g; Fiber 5.93 g; Sugar 9.17 g; Protein 6.78 g

BLOOD SUGAR BALANCE RATING: High

Health Facilitators	Nutrient Density Rating
Protein	Low
Fat	Medium
Carbohydrate	Medium
Enzymes	Medium
Antioxidants	High
Fiber	High

This combination of ingredients can't be beat for balancing your hormones and keeping your overall metabolism happily humming. Kale is one of the most nutrient-dense vegetables and is loaded with vitamins C, A, K, B6, and tryptophan, which keeps hormones and blood sugar stable. The lemon tahini dressing balances the flavors out nicely. Sprinkle with sesame seeds for added calcium and crunch.

BLOOD SUGAR–BALANCING BRUSSELS SPROUTS

Brussels sprouts. You either love them or hate them. If you fall in the latter category, this dish may just win you over. Here, the sprouts are mingled with roasted red peppers and baked into sweetness that is sure to satisfy. Packed with fiber, vitamin C, iron, beta carotene (a precursor to vitamin A) and the antioxidant quercetin, these small cruciferous veggies benefit your blood sugar and your hormones.

2 red peppers, halved and seeded
½ tablespoon (7 ml) extra-virgin olive oil
1½ pounds (680 g) brussels sprouts, steamed
1 clove garlic, peeled and minced
Salt and freshly ground black pepper
1 tablespoon (4 g) minced fresh dill
Dash cayenne

Preheat oven to 350°F (180°C, or gas mark 4). Place the peppers on a baking sheet and brush with the oil. Bake for 30 minutes. Remove the peppers from the oven, let cool, and then peel and seed. Cut the peppers into ¼-inch (0.6-cm) strips. Place the brussels sprouts in a glass or ceramic baking dish. Stir in the pepper strips. Season with garlic, salt, and black pepper, tossing to mix well. Bake, uncovered, for 10 minutes and garnish with fresh dill and cayenne.

YIELD: 6 SERVINGS

EACH WITH: Calories 67.9; Calories From Fat 16.29; Total Fat 1.87 g; Cholesterol 0 mg; Sodium 294.56 mg; Potassium 481.26 mg; Total Carbohydrates 11.44 g; Fiber 4.05 g; Sugar 4.01 g; Protein 3.51 g

BLOOD SUGAR BALANCE RATING: Medium

Health Facilitators	Nutrient Density Rating
Protein	Low
Fat	Medium
Carbohydrate	High
Enzymes	Low
Antioxidants	High
Fiber	High

SUPER-FAST STIR-FRIED BROCCOLI

2 heads fresh broccoli
2 tablespoons (30 ml) dark sesame oil
2 scallions, cut in 1-inch (2.5-cm) sections (both white and green parts)
1½ teaspoons Bragg's liquid amino acids
2 tablespoons (16 g) sesame seeds
1 tablespoon (15 ml) flaxseed oil

Wash the broccoli and break it into small florets with some of the stem attached. Peel the larger stems and cut into ½-inch (1.3-cm) rounds. Heat a wok or skillet over high heat for 30 seconds and swirl in the sesame oil. Briskly stir-fry the broccoli florets, stems, and scallions for 4 to 5 minutes, or until tender. Add the Bragg's liquid amino acids to the broccoli and cook over medium heat for another 10 minutes, adding a little water if necessary to steam and soften the broccoli. Toss with sesame seeds and flaxseed oil. Serve immediately.

YIELD: 6 SERVINGS
EACH WITH: Calories 85.6; Calories From Fat 6.93; Total Fat 8.38 g; Cholesterol 0 mg; Sodium 87.55 mg; Potassium 105.33 mg; Total Carbohydrates 52.33 g; Fiber 0.49 g; Sugar 0.13 g; Protein 156.33 g
BLOOD SUGAR BALANCE RATING: Medium

Health Facilitators	Nutrient Density Rating
Protein	Low
Fat	Low
Carbohydrate	High
Enzymes	Low
Antioxidants	High
Fiber	Very High

This is one of most versatile and tasty ways to serve broccoli, the workhorse of the cruciferous vegetable group. Not only does broccoli contain vitamins C, A, and E, zinc, potassium, calcium, beta carotene, folate, and amino acids, it is also rich in fiber and contains some omega-3s. A stir-fry is fast, delicious, and lends itself to endless variations limited only by your imagination. Add cubed tofu or chicken strips and serve it with brown rice for a complete meal.

CALMING BEANS AND KALE

Beans are quick and
easy to prepare and are
an excellent source of
tryptophan, which helps
balance blood sugar
levels and hormones, and
improves mood and sleep.
Beans are also extremely
high in folate (which helps
stabilize blood sugar), iron,
plant protein, fiber, vitamin
B1, copper, and potassium.
As a bonus, they are low in
calories. Makes a great side
dish or a small meal.

2 to 3 kale leaves, cleaned and chopped into bite-sized pieces
1 cup (240 ml) vegetable stock
1½ cups (340 g) cooked white beans (cannellini or Great Northern)
2 garlic cloves, peeled and thinly sliced
¼ teaspoon sea salt
Dash cayenne
1 tablespoon (15 ml) flaxseed oil

Put kale and vegetable stock into a sauté pan and cook on medium-high
heat for 3 to 5 minutes or until wilted. Add white beans, garlic, and sea salt.
Cover and cook on medium heat 5 to 7 minutes. Add water or more stock if
needed. Add a dash of cayenne and serve drizzled with flaxseed oil.

YIELD: 4 SERVINGS
EACH WITH: Calories 196.12; Calories From Fat 69.1; Total Fat 7.8 g; Cholesterol 1.8 mg;
Sodium 208.76 mg; Potassium 518.25 mg; Total Carbohydrates 23.52 g; Fiber 4.77 g;
Sugar 1.25 g; Protein 8.76 g
BLOOD SUGAR BALANCE RATING: High

Health Facilitators	Nutrient Density Rating
Protein	High
Fat	Medium
Carbohydrate	High
Enzymes	High
Antioxidants	High
Fiber	Very High

STRESS-FIGHTING BEEF STIR-FRY

1 pound (455 g) organic grass-fed steak (or extra-firm tofu)
⅓ cup (80 ml) mirin rice wine
2 tablespoons (30 ml) shoyu or tamari sauce (wheat-free)
1 teaspoon maple syrup
Cornmeal
2 tablespoons (30 ml) sesame or coconut oil, divided
1 brown or red onion, peeled and sliced into thin crescents
1 inch (2.5 cm) ginger, peeled and minced
2 cloves garlic, minced
⅓ cup (80 ml) purified water
1 bunch broccoli, cut into florets and stems
½ cup (45 g) purple cabbage, cut into thick strips

Cut steak (or tofu) into thin strips and place in a mixing bowl. Combine mirin, shoyu (or tamari), and maple syrup and marinate 35 to 40 minutes. Remove steak from the marinade (reserving leftover marinade) and coat with cornmeal. Heat 1 tablespoon (15 ml) oil in a frying pan over medium-high heat. Add steak and cook 2 to 3 minutes, or until desired doneness. Remove from the pan and set aside. (If using tofu, cook until lightly browned on each side.) Add remaining 1 tablespoon (15 ml) oil to the pan and sauté onion, ginger, and garlic for 1 to 2 minutes. Add the purified water, the broccoli stems and florets, and cabbage and cook 3 to 4 minutes. Return cooked beef (or tofu) to the pan with the leftover marinade, and cook on medium-high heat for 2 to 3 minutes, or until boiling.

YIELD: 4 SERVINGS
EACH WITH: Calories 227.5; Calories From Fat 114.3; Total Fat 13.04 g; Cholesterol 0 mg; Sodium 789.42 mg; Potassium 278.29 mg; Total Carbohydrates 19.2 g; Fiber 1.82 g; Sugar 9.32 g; Protein 10.71 g
BLOOD SUGAR BALANCE RATING: Very High

Health Facilitators	Nutrient Density Rating
Protein	High
Fat	Low
Carbohydrate	Medium
Enzymes	Low
Antioxidants	High
Fiber	High

In addition to being an excellent source of tryptophan and protein, lean beef provides plenty of selenium, zinc, iron, and B complex vitamins to help you fight stress. Choose organic, grass-fed beef if you can to avoid pesticides and hormones that potentially can interfere with your own.

SUSTAINING SIZZLING SHRIMP

A wonderfully nutritious alternative to meat proteins, low-fat, low-calorie shrimp are a perfect choice for managing blood sugar levels. Another benefit? Research shows that eating shrimp actually raises HDL, or "good" cholesterol. Lime juice and a splash of hot pepper sauce adds calorie-free zest and plenty of antioxidants, such as vitamin C and selenium.

2 pounds (910 g) medium shrimp, cleaned, peeled, and deveined
¼ cup (56 g or 60 ml) unsalted organic butter or coconut oil
4 cloves garlic, minced
1 cup (100 g) minced scallions
¼ cup (60 ml) freshly squeezed lime juice
Coarsely ground black pepper
Hot pepper sauce
¼ cup (15 g) chopped fresh parsley
2 to 4 cups (40 to 80 g) mixed lettuce greens

Prepare the shrimp and set aside. In a large sauté pan, melt the butter or coconut oil. Add the garlic and scallions and sauté until the scallions turn bright green. Add the shrimp and lime juice. Maintain the heat and cook just briefly, until shrimp turns pink (be careful not to overcook). Stir in the black pepper, hot pepper sauce, and parsley. Serve over mixed greens.

YIELD: 4 TO 6 SERVINGS

EACH WITH: Calories 252.54; Calories From Fat 102.64; Total Fat 11.79 g; Cholesterol 229.82 mg; Sodium 230.06 mg; Potassium 388.88 mg; Total Carbohydrates 4.64 g; Fiber 0.85 g; Sugar 0.6 g; Protein 31.44 g

BLOOD SUGAR BALANCE RATING: Very High

Health Facilitators	Nutrient Density Rating
Protein	High
Fat	Medium
Carbohydrate	Medium
Enzymes	Medium
Antioxidants	High
Fiber	High

HEALING CHICKEN STIR-FRY

1 tablespoon (15 ml) extra-virgin olive oil
1 garlic clove, minced
1 large brown onion, chopped
4 small chicken breasts, about 3 to 4 ounces (85 to 115 g) each, cut into
    1-inch (2.5-cm) cubes
4 carrots, sliced
1 can (15 ounces, or 420 g) whole tomatoes, chopped
1 teaspoon cinnamon
Pinch cayenne
1 teaspoon ground cumin
2 tablespoons (30 ml) chunky peanut butter
1½ cups (360 ml) chicken stock or broth
Salt and pepper

Heat olive oil in a large pan, then sauté garlic and onion until translucent, about 5 minutes. Add chicken and brown on all sides. Add carrots, tomatoes, cinnamon, cayenne, cumin, and peanut butter. Stir until blended. Add stock or broth and season with salt and pepper to taste. Cook over medium-low heat until sauce thickens, about 30 to 45 minutes.

YIELD: 4 SERVINGS

EACH WITH: Calories 353.07; Calories From Fat 5.08; Total Fat 10.88 g; Cholesterol 90.67 mg; Sodium 755.46 mg; Potassium 770.93 mg; Total Carbohydrates 423.75 g; Fiber 4.53 g; Sugar 5.12 g; Protein 1279.33 g

BLOOD SUGAR BALANCE RATING: Very High

Health Facilitators	Nutrient Density Rating
Protein	High
Fat	Medium
Carbohydrate	Low
Enzymes	Low
Antioxidants	High
Fiber	Low

High in protein and tryptophan, this dish is both grounding and balancing—with a spicy kick. The garlic and spices boost your immune system and your metabolism. Garlic contains compounds that protect your heart, as well as sulfur to improve liver and immune system function. And cayenne contains vitamin C and strengthens immunity.

COMFORTING QUINOA-CRAB CASSEROLE

Busy night? Try this easy dish that's high in calcium, magnesium, and selenium to calm you while keeping your blood sugar levels stable. Quinoa is a nutrient-dense grain that contains nearly twice the amount of protein per cup found in other grains. Pair this recipe with a side of tossed greens and a medley of your favorite veggies for extra nutrients.

½ pound (225 g) cooked crabmeat
2 celery stalks, finely chopped
1 red bell pepper, diced
⅓ cup (35 g) chopped black olives
¼ cup (15 g) finely chopped cilantro
1 medium brown or red onion, finely chopped
2 large garlic cloves, minced
1 teaspoon fresh basil, chopped
1 teaspoon fresh oregano, chopped
Salt and pepper
Dash cayenne pepper
1 egg
1 cup (185 g) cooked quinoa
1 cup (240 ml) plain yogurt
Juice of ½ lemon
1 tablespoon (15 ml) extra-virgin olive oil or coconut oil

Preheat oven to 350°F (180°C, or gas mark 4). Mix crab, celery, red bell pepper, olives, cilantro, onion, garlic, basil, oregano, salt, pepper, and cayenne in a bowl. Whisk egg in a separate bowl and blend with quinoa, yogurt, and lemon juice. Gradually stir egg mixture into crab mixture. Place in a lightly oiled 10-inch (25-cm) casserole dish. Bake for 15 to 20 minutes.

YIELD: 4 SERVINGS
EACH WITH: Calories 248.96; Calories From Fat 74.95; Total Fat 8.56 g; Cholesterol 99.64 mg; Sodium 397.94 mg; Potassium 685.1 mg; Total Carbohydrates 22.55 g; Fiber 3.55 g; Sugar 7.84 g; Protein 20.61 g
BLOOD SUGAR BALANCE RATING: Very High

Health Facilitators	Nutrient Density Rating
Protein	High
Fat	Medium
Carbohydrate	Medium
Enzymes	Low
Antioxidants	High
Fiber	High

MOOD-BOOSTING MEATLOAF WITH A KICK

1 to 2 tablespoons (15 to 30 ml) extra-virgin olive oil or coconut oil
2 pounds (910 g) ground turkey, veal, or chuck steak
1 cup (185 g) cooked quinoa
¾ cup (120 g) chopped brown or red onion
2 cloves garlic, chopped
2 tablespoons (30 ml) horseradish
2 tablespoons (8 g) chopped cilantro
2 tablespoons (8 g) chopped parsley
½ cup (70 g) raisins
1 teaspoon salt (optional)
¼ teaspoon pepper
1 teaspoon dry mustard
1 teaspoon cumin powder
½ cup (120 ml) ketchup
2 eggs, lightly beaten

Preheat oven to 350°F (180°C, or gas mark 4). Coat an 8 × 4 × 2-inch (20 × 10 × 5-cm) glass loaf pan with olive oil. Combine remaining ingredients, blending by hand to mix thoroughly. Shape and place in prepared loaf pan. Bake for 1 hour.

YIELD: 5 TO 6 SERVINGS

EACH WITH: Calories 381.92; Calories From Fat 155.75; Total Fat 17.34 g; Cholesterol 189.95 mg; Sodium 798.44 mg; Potassium 677.55 mg; Total Carbohydrates 25.79 g; Fiber 2.11 g; Sugar 14.1 g; Protein 31.18 g

BLOOD SUGAR BALANCE RATING: Very High

Health Facilitators	Nutrient Density Rating
Protein	High
Fat	High
Carbohydrate	Medium
Enzymes	Low
Antioxidants	High
Fiber	High

This is real comfort food that is not only great for your hormones but for your blood sugar levels too. It's loaded with protein and calming tryptophan and has a deliciously sweet and spicy kick thanks to the raisins and herbs such as garlic (a great antioxidant). This dish is delightfully easy and simple to prepare and goes straight into the oven for an hour after the prep work is complete. It tastes great as leftovers, for breakfast, lunch, or dinner, or even as a quick snack. Serve it with salad or steamed vegetables to round out the meal.

BALANCING BASIL APRICOT TURKEY BREAST

Turkey is high in tryptophan, which makes it a great mood enhancer and natural antidepressant. This alone is often enough to prevent you from reaching for a sugar fix to feel better. You'll feel wonderfully nourished as well as calm and relaxed after this well-balanced and easy meal. It's savory, yet simple to make and perfect for festive occasions.

4 turkey breasts
4 garlic cloves
1 tablespoon (15 ml) extra-virgin olive oil or coconut oil
Salt and pepper
1 teaspoon chopped fresh rosemary
1 teaspoon chopped fresh basil
20 dried apricot halves
¾ cup (115 g) dried cranberries
3 large carrots, cut into ½-inch (1.3-cm) slices
1 cup (70 g) broccoli florets
1½ cups (360 ml) turkey broth

Preheat oven to 325°F (170°C, or gas mark 3). Make a slit in each turkey breast with a knife and insert a garlic clove in each one. Rub turkey breast with oil, then sprinkle with salt and pepper. Place turkey breast in a shallow roasting pan and season with rosemary and basil. Create a nest around the turkey with apricots, cranberries, carrots, and broccoli. Pour the turkey broth over. Cover and bake for 30 to 45 minutes, or until meat is done, basting often.

YIELD: 4 SERVINGS

EACH WITH: Calories 619.76; Calories From Fat (11%); Total Fat 7.85 g; Cholesterol 48.76 mg; Sodium 1495.09 mg; Potassium 941.78 mg; Total Carbohydrates 115.07 g; Fiber 10.88 g; Sugar 16.24 g; Protein 23.09 g

BLOOD SUGAR BALANCE RATING: Very High

Health Facilitators	Nutrient Density Rating
Protein	High
Fat	Medium
Carbohydrate	Low
Enzymes	Low
Antioxidants	High
Fiber	Low

METABOLISM-MASTERING COCONUT CURRY

2 pounds (910 g) chicken, veal, or turkey, cut into 2-inch (5-cm) cubes

1 tablespoon (5 g) coriander

1 teaspoon curry powder

½ teaspoon chili powder (optional)

¼ teaspoon black pepper

¼ teaspoon turmeric

¼ teaspoon cumin

¼ teaspoon anise

¼ teaspoon cinnamon

¼ teaspoon ground cloves

¼ teaspoon cardamom

2 cloves garlic, pounded

1-inch (2.5-cm) piece ginger, shredded

1 teaspoon lemon or lime juice

2 fresh green chiles, slit open (optional)

Salt

½ cup (120 ml) water

2 tablespoons (30 ml) coconut oil

1 large onion, sliced finely

2 ripe tomatoes, quartered

1 cup (240 ml) coconut cream mixed with 1½ cups (360 ml) purified water

Put meat in a large saucepan, and add coriander and the next 15 ingredients (through water). Mix well. Bring to a boil, reduce heat and simmer, covered, until meat is cooked, about 10 minutes.

Heat coconut oil in a frying pan over medium-high heat, add sliced onion and fry until golden brown. Add tomatoes, stirring for 5 seconds, then add coconut cream and water mixture and stir again. Bring to a boil and remove from heat. Pour over meat mixture and stir to combine.

YIELD: 4 TO 6 SERVINGS

EACH WITH: Calories 417.23; Calories From Fat 133.65; Total Fat 14.36 g; Cholesterol 90.67 mg; Sodium 127.93 mg; Potassium 426.48 mg; Total Carbohydrates 32.46 g; Fiber 1.83 g; Sugar 27.81 g; Protein 37.59 g

BLOOD SUGAR BALANCE RATING: Very High

The blend of herbs and spices in this delicious curry are packed with antioxidants, which protect your cells from free radicals, harmful oxygen molecules that rob your body of energy. When you increase your intake of antioxidants, you boost metabolism and promote longevity. This dish is high in calcium, magnesium, selenium, tryptophan, manganese, copper, chromium, fiber, and vitamins C, B6, B1, A, and E that help keep your metabolism running efficiently. The balance of proteins and healthy fat make this meal a perfect choice to stabilize blood sugar. Serve it over brown rice and with a salad.

Health Facilitators	Nutrient Density Rating
Protein	High
Fat	High
Carbohydrate	Low
Enzymes	Low
Antioxidants	High
Fiber	Medium

COLONIAL BAKED APPLES WITH CHERRIES

Easy is the operative word here. This dessert is easy to make—and even easier to eat. Try these cherry- and nut-filled baked apples for breakfast, brunch, or dessert. Cherries are low on the glycemic index and contain an abundance of antioxidants, such as vitamin C. Apples are also high in vitamin C, which stabilizes blood sugar levels and minimizes sugar cravings.

Nonstick vegetable spray
2 tablespoons (30 ml) freshly squeezed lemon juice
⅓ cup (60 g) dried cherries
3 tablespoons (25 g) chopped walnuts
1 teaspoon grated lemon zest
2 tablespoons (30 ml) honey or maple syrup
6 apples, cored

Preheat the oven to 350°F (180°C, or gas mark 4). Spray a baking sheet with nonstick vegetable spray. In a bowl, mix together the lemon juice, cherries, walnuts, lemon zest, and honey or maple syrup. Place the cored apples on the baking sheet. Fill each apple with the cherry-nut mixture. Bake until the apples are soft, about 30 to 40 minutes.

YIELD: 6 SERVINGS

EACH WITH: Calories 141.75: Calories From Fat 23.45; Total Fat 2.8 g; Cholesterol 0mg; Sodium 3.23 mg; Potassium 184.63 mg; Total Carbohydrates 31.19 g; Fiber 4.06 g; Sugar 18.54 g; Protein 1.17 g

BLOOD SUGAR BALANCE RATING: Medium

Health Facilitators	Nutrient Density Rating
Protein	Medium
Fat	Medium
Carbohydrate	High
Enzymes	Low
Antioxidants	Medium
Fiber	High

COOL COCONUT SPICE COOKIES

2 cups (250 g) coconut flour
1 cup (80 g) rolled oats
Pinch of salt
¼ teaspoon allspice
¼ teaspoon nutmeg
¼ teaspoon ground ginger
½ teaspoon cinnamon
½ cup (120 ml) purified water
½ cup (120 ml) coconut oil
½ cup (120 ml) maple syrup
⅓ cup (40 g) walnuts, coarsely chopped
½ cup (90 g) carob or chocolate chips (optional)

Preheat oven to 375°F (190°C, or gas mark 5). Combine flour, oats, salt, allspice, nutmeg, ginger, and cinnamon in a bowl. Mix water, oil, and maple syrup together using a whisk. Add liquid ingredients to dry ingredients and mix together well to form dough. Stir in walnuts and carob or chocolate chips (if using). Shape pieces of dough into cookies and bake for 10 to 12 minutes.

YIELD: 2 DOZEN COOKIES
EACH WITH: Calories 133.9; Calories From Fat 65.89; Total Fat 7.63 g; Cholesterol 0.03 mg; Sodium 15.8 mg; Potassium 49.71 mg; Total Carbohydrates 15.16 g; Fiber 4.58 g; Sugar 4.93 g; Protein 2.23 g
BLOOD SUGAR BALANCE RATING: High

Health Facilitators	Nutrient Density Rating
Protein	Medium
Fat	High
Carbohydrate	High
Enzymes	Medium
Antioxidants	Medium
Fiber	High

These coconut spice cookies are rich in protein as well as healthy fats that support blood sugar metabolism and balanced hormones. Coconut is loaded with fiber, supports your thyroid and your metabolism, and offers antiviral, antifungal, antibacterial properties that destroy harmful bacteria like *H. Pylori* and *Giardia*. Walnuts add omega-3 essential fatty acids, and the oats provide fiber to balance both blood sugar and hormone levels.

CHAPTER 12

Recipes for All Sugar-Addiction Types

The healing properties in the recipes in this section make them suitable for all four types of sugar addicts. Supplying your body with essential nutrients is your best bet for keeping your blood sugar levels stable and weaning yourself off sugar. In fact, when you start eating these low-sugar, healthful recipes, you will be surprised at how quickly you lose your interest in sweets—most people are freed from their sugar cravings in a relatively short amount of time . . . just a few days! Start by using the recipes for your specific type(s), and add in these recipes once you start to feel better. After a few months, you'll be amazed at how balanced your blood sugar is and how good you feel. You are healing your sugar addiction bite by bite!

BERRY-NUTTY SMOOTHIE

1 cup (155 g) frozen blueberries
¼ cup (75 g) frozen strawberries
4 to 6 tablespoons (60 to 90 ml) plain yogurt
2 tablespoons (30 ml) flax oil
2 to 4 tablespoons (30 to 60 ml) crunchy peanut butter or almond butter
2 to 4 scoops (⅔ to 1⅓ cups, or 80 to 160 g) protein powder
1¾ cups (420 ml) purified water
1 cup (240 ml) ice (optional)

Place ingredients in a blender. Blend until rich and creamy, approximately 2 to 3 minutes.

YIELD: 2 SERVINGS

EACH WITH: Calories 497.19; Calories From Fat (56%); Total Fat 32.58 g; Cholesterol 1.84 mg; Sodium 252.51 mg; Potassium 394.87 mg; Total Carbohydrates 26.01 g; Fiber 7.23 g; Sugar 14.66 g; Protein 36.75 g

BLOOD SUGAR BALANCE RATING: High

Health Facilitators	Nutrient Density Rating
Protein	High
Fat	High
Carbohydrate	Medium
Enzymes	High
Antioxidants	Very High
Fiber	Medium

High in vitamin C (one serving contains 14 mg, or 25 percent of your daily requirement), fiber, manganese, and antioxidant power, the tiny blueberry is one of the healthiest fruits around. Strawberries also contain vitamin C, along with folic acid, potassium, and fiber. Protein powder, rich peanut or almond butter, and yogurt make this smoothie a balancing meal or snack and a favorite you'll make again and again.

STABILIZING EGGS SUPREME

You'll feel full for hours after you eat this delicious, blood sugar–stabilizing dish that provides protein and good fats and contains vitamins A, D, B12, and riboflavin for strengthening your immune system. Switch out the dairy for tofu if you're dairy intolerant, and you won't miss a nutritional thing.

4 eggs
2 tablespoons (30 ml) heavy cream
Freshly ground black pepper
Dash cayenne
1 tablespoon (15 ml) extra-virgin olive oil or coconut oil
1 small red onion, chopped
1 garlic clove, minced
1 tablespoon (14 g) unsalted butter
3 tablespoons (45 g) cream cheese, cut into small cubes
1 sliced ripe avocado
2 cups (40 g) spinach or mixed salad greens

Preheat broiler. In a medium bowl, using a fork, whisk eggs, cream, black pepper, and cayenne. Set aside. In a nonstick skillet, melt oil over medium-high heat. When oil is hot, sauté the onions and garlic until onions are translucent, about 5 minutes. Remove from skillet and set aside.

Melt butter in skillet and add egg mixture. As eggs cook, lift edges to allow uncooked egg to seep underneath. When bottom is set but top is still moist, place cream cheese cubes and onion mixture over eggs and place under broiler. Broil 1 to 2 minutes, checking frequently, until top is golden and puffed up. Top with sliced avocado. Serve over a bed of spinach or salad greens.

YIELD: 2 TO 3 SERVINGS
EACH WITH: Calories 369.96; Calories From Fat 285.36; Total Fat 32.8 g; Cholesterol 321.83 mg; Sodium 162.27 mg; Potassium 524.41 mg; Total Carbohydrates 10.41 g; Fiber 5.05 g; Sugar 0.83 g; Protein 11.92 g
BLOOD SUGAR BALANCE RATING: Very High

Health Facilitators	Nutrient Density Rating
Protein	High
Fat	High
Carbohydrate	Medium
Enzymes	Low
Antioxidants	High
Fiber	Low

BEAT SUGAR ADDICTION NOW! COOKBOOK

BLOOD SUGAR–BALANCING BUCKWHEAT BREAD

1¼ cups (150 g) buckwheat pancake mix
1 cup (140 g) polenta or maize meal
2 teaspoons (9 g) baking powder
1 teaspoon salt
1 egg
1 cup (240 ml) coconut or rice milk
⅓ cup (80 ml) purified water
¼ cup (60 ml) extra-virgin olive oil, plus more for pan

Preheat oven to 350°F (180°C, or gas mark 4). Brush an 8-inch (20-cm) loaf pan with olive oil. Then line with parchment paper and brush this with oil also. Place the pancake mix, polenta, baking powder, and salt in a large bowl and combine thoroughly. In a small bowl, beat egg and add coconut or rice milk, water, and oil. Add egg mixture to dry ingredients and stir until well blended. Pour into prepared loaf pan and bake for 30 minutes. Rotate the pan and bake for a further 12 to 15 minutes. It is done when a skewer comes out clean. Remove from pan immediately and peel off paper lining. Cool on a wire rack in fresh air to develop crust. Best served the same day or toasted over the next couple of days.

YIELD: 6 TO 8 SERVINGS
EACH WITH: Amount Per Serving; Calories 314.37; Calories From Fat (39%); Total Fat 14.16 g; Cholesterol 26.44 mg; Sodium 689.84 mg; Potassium 131.22 mg; Total Carbohydrates 41.68 g; Fiber 5.11 g; Sugar 1.42 g; Protein 6.42 g
BLOOD SUGAR BALANCE RATING: High

Health Facilitators	CNutrient Density Rating
Protein	Medium
Fat	Medium
Carbohydrate	High
Enzymes	Low
Antioxidants	Low
Fiber	High

This nutritious loaf is a fabulous golden yellow, and the texture reminds you of how bread should taste: filling and delicious. Slice it thinly and add your favorite low-glycemic toppings (such as avocado, hummus, or mashed bananas) for extra nutrient density and to increase blood sugar balance. This bread is a great accompaniment to soups and salads too. It is gluten-, dairy-, and wheat-free and will keep for up to three days.

STRENGTHENING MINESTRONE

Minestrone is the "everything but the kitchen sink" of soups and is a nourishing and satisfying dish for all of the four types. A little of this and a little of that add up to a quick and easy Italian classic. The combination of vitamins and minerals are strengthening and boost immune function. Feel free to add your favorite meat or some lentils for added protein. A sprinkling of freshly grated Parmesan cheese is a wonderful finishing touch and a calcium-rich blood sugar–balancer.

1 tablespoon (15 ml) extra-virgin olive oil
4 medium cloves garlic, minced
1 small onion, diced
2 medium stalks celery, diced
2 medium carrots, cut into ½-inch (1.3-cm) slices
¼ teaspoon finely chopped thyme
¼ teaspoon finely chopped parsley
⅛ teaspoon black pepper
⅛ teaspoon salt
3 cups (720 ml) vegetable stock, divided
½ cup (120 ml) canned diced tomatoes, drained
½ cup (35 g) shredded savoy cabbage
3 cups (720 ml) vegetable juice
½ cup (112 g) cooked red kidney beans
½ cup (85 g) brown rice

In a soup pot, heat the oil over medium heat and sauté the garlic and onion until the onion is translucent, about 5 minutes. Add the celery, carrots, thyme, parsley, black pepper, and salt. Moisten with 3 tablespoons (45 ml) of the stock and cook for 5 minutes. Add the tomatoes, cabbage, vegetable juice, and remaining stock and bring to a boil. Lower the heat, stir in beans and brown rice, and simmer, covered, for 20 to 30 minutes.

YIELD: 8 SERVINGS
EACH WITH: Calories 143.81; Calories From Fat 29.63; Total Fat 3.34 g; Cholesterol 2.7 mg; Sodium 426.73 mg; Potassium 567.6 mg; Total Carbohydrates 24.62 g; Fiber 3.76 g; Sugar 6.46 g; Protein 5.38 g
BLOOD SUGAR BALANCE RATING: High

Health Facilitators	Nutrient Density Rating
Protein	Medium
Fat	Medium
Carbohydrate	High
Enzymes	Low
Antioxidants	High
Fiber	High

SATISFYING CILANTRO SALMON CAKES

3 teaspoons (15 ml) extra-virgin olive oil or coconut oil, divided
1 small brown or red onion, finely chopped
1 stalk celery, finely diced
2 tablespoons (8 g) fresh parsley, chopped
2 tablespoons (8 g) fresh cilantro, chopped
15 ounces (420 g) canned salmon, drained, or 1½ cups cooked salmon
1 large egg, lightly beaten
2 tablespoons (30 ml) Dijon mustard
1¾ cups (290 g) cooked brown rice
½ teaspoon freshly ground black pepper
Dash cayenne
1 avocado, sliced into quarters
1 lemon, cut into wedges
4 large romaine lettuce leaves

Preheat oven to 400°F (200°C, or gas mark 6). Coat a baking sheet with cooking spray or coconut oil. Heat 1½ teaspoons (7 ml) oil in a large nonstick skillet over medium-high heat. Add onion and celery; cook, stirring, until softened, about 3 minutes. Stir in parsley and cilantro; remove skillet from heat.

Place salmon in a medium bowl. Flake apart with a fork; remove any bones and skin. Add egg and mustard, and mix well. Add the onion mixture, rice, pepper, and cayenne; mix well. Shape the mixture into 8 patties, about 2½ inches (6.5-cm) wide. Heat remaining 1½ teaspoons (7 ml) oil in the same skillet over medium heat. Add 4 patties and cook until the undersides are golden, 2 to 3 minutes. Using a wide spatula, turn them over onto the prepared baking sheet. Repeat with the remaining patties. Bake the salmon cakes until golden on top and heated through, 15 to 20 minutes. Serve salmon cakes with avocado and lemon wedges over romaine lettuce.

YIELD: 4 TO 6 SERVINGS
EACH WITH: Calories 307.62; Calories From Fat 150.96; Total Fat 17.16 g; Cholesterol 79.9 mg; Sodium 131.87 mg; Potassium 531.95 mg; Total Carbohydrates 19.48 g; Fiber 4.05 g; Sugar 1.77 g; Protein 19.46 g
BLOOD SUGAR BALANCE RATING: High

This delicious dish will boost your intake of omega-3 essential fatty acids and keep blood sugar levels stable for hours. Serve these tasty cakes with a tossed salad or eat as a snack. They're easy to prepare and a great way to use convenient canned (or leftover) salmon. They taste great eaten cold too!

Health Facilitators	Nutrient Density Rating
Protein	High
Fat	Medium
Carbohydrate	Medium
Enzymes	Low
Antioxidants	High
Fiber	High

TRYPTOPHAN-RICH TURMERIC TURKEY BURGERS

Turkey is not only low in fat and good for your waistline, it's high in tryptophan, which will keep your mood and your blood sugar levels stable. It's also highly nutritious, with selenium and B vitamins, as well as zinc, making it ideal for keeping your immune system strong. The health benefits of curcumin, the active ingredient in turmeric, are well documented. Not only does it contain numerous antioxidants, it is also anti-inflammatory and improves digestion, circulation, and energy. It may even help in fat metabolism and weight management and prevent premature aging.

1 pound (455 g) ground turkey
1 teaspoon turmeric
1 teaspoon cumin
½ red or brown onion, chopped
1 clove garlic, finely chopped
¼ cup (16 g) chopped cilantro
¼ cup chopped parsley
¼ teaspoon salt
Black pepper
Dash cayenne
1 egg, beaten
2 tablespoons (30 ml) extra-virgin olive oil or coconut oil
3 cups (60 g) mixed greens or spinach

Mix the first 11 ingredients (through egg) in a bowl. Form this mixture into four patties. Heat oil in a skillet over medium heat, add patties, and sauté until cooked through and no longer pink, about 7 to 10 minutes. Serve over a bed of mixed salad or spinach greens.

YIELD: 4 SERVINGS

EACH WITH: Calories 265.01; Calories From Fat 158.05; Total Fat 17.69 g; Cholesterol 142.46 mg; Sodium 292.84 mg; Potassium 491.56 mg; Total Carbohydrates 3.57 g; Fiber 1.16 g; Sugar 0.91 g; Protein 22.54 g

BLOOD SUGAR BALANCE RATING: Very High

Health Facilitators	Nutrient Density Rating
Protein	Very High
Fat	Low
Carbohydrate	Low
Enzymes	Low
Antioxidants	High
Fiber	Low

BEAT SUGAR ADDICTION NOW! COOKBOOK

SUPERCHARGED CHICKEN AND GREENS

1½ pounds (680 g) cooked chicken breast, cubed or stripped
1 cup (100 g) chopped scallions
¾ cup (75 g) chopped celery
1 cup (100 g) green beans, raw or lightly steamed
2 tablespoons (16 g) golden sesame seeds
Salt and pepper
¼ cup (60 ml) extra-virgin olive oil or coconut oil
2 tablespoons (30 ml) fresh lemon or lime juice
1 tablespoon (15 ml) Dijon mustard
2 tablespoons (30 ml) purified water
6 cups (120 g) chopped green leaf lettuce
6 walnuts or macadamia nuts, chopped

Mix chicken, scallions, celery, green beans, and sesame seeds in a large bowl. Season with salt and pepper to taste. In a separate bowl, make vinaigrette by whisking oil, lemon or lime juice, Dijon mustard, and water together. Toss greens and vinaigrette in a large bowl; arrange a single serving on each plate. Top each serving with chicken mixture and a sprinkling of chopped nuts.

YIELD: 6 SERVINGS
EACH WITH: Calories 340.98; Calories From Fat 157.37; Total Fat 17.98 g; Cholesterol 96.39 mg; Sodium 136.33 mg; Potassium 598.49 mg; Total Carbohydrates 6.79 g; Fiber 3.25 g; Sugar 1.85 g; Protein 38 g
BLOOD SUGAR BALANCE RATING: Very High

Health Facilitators	Nutrient Density Rating
Protein	High
Fat	Medium
Carbohydrate	Medium
Enzymes	High
Antioxidants	High
Fiber	High

Enjoy the delicious flavors and textures in the nutrient-dense and blood sugar–stabilizing salad. Perfect for all four sugar addiction types, it contains just the right amount of protein plus omega-3 essential fatty acids (from the nuts). The vegetables and herbs add a nice zing and are full of antioxidants for greater energy, making you less likely to reach for sugar to pep you up!

PEPPY PAPAYA TUNA

1 pound (455 g) water-packed white tuna, drained and separated into chunks
4 large garlic cloves, minced
1½ teaspoons (4 g) ground cumin
1 teaspoon fresh basil, chopped
1 teaspoon fresh parsley, chopped
Salt and pepper
1 teaspoon Dijon mustard
2 shallots, finely chopped
4 cups (80 g) mixed salad greens or spinach
4 radishes, flowered
1 large avocado, peeled and sliced lengthwise into quarters
1 large cucumber, peeled and sliced into ¼-inch (0.6-cm) pieces
1 large papaya, peeled and quartered
2 small tomatoes, quartered

Put drained tuna chunks, garlic, cumin, basil, parsley, salt, and pepper into a bowl and blend well. Stir in mustard and chopped shallots. Place salad greens or spinach leaves in the center of a serving plate. Top with four individual scoops of herbed tuna, placing a flowered radish in the center of each scoop. Arrange avocado slices opposite each other around each tuna scoop. Fill in avocado gaps by alternating 2 to 3 cucumber slices with papaya and tomato slices.

YIELD: 4 SERVINGS
EACH WITH: Calories 270.27; Calories From Fat 92.18; Total Fat 10.72 g; Cholesterol 47.63 mg; Sodium 482.25 mg; Potassium 1070.31 mg; Total Carbohydrates 14.53 g; Fiber 5.99 g; Sugar 5.45 g; Protein 30.28 g
BLOOD SUGAR BALANCE RATING: Very High

Health Facilitators	Nutrient Density Rating
Protein	High
Fat	High
Carbohydrate	High
Enzymes	High
Antioxidants	High
Fiber	High

Papaya are packed full of natural digestive enzymes, including papain and chymonpapin, making them excellent for improving your digestion. The papaya is also rich in antioxidant nutrients such as vitamins A and C. The delicious flavors of avocado and herbs and the omega-3-rich tuna all combine to make this a totally scrumptious salad that keeps blood sugar levels balanced. Best of all, it's easy to prepare so you are in and out of the kitchen in a flash.

CREAMY CARROT AND GENTLE GINGER SOUP

2 pounds (910 g) organic carrots, roughly chopped
2 tablespoons (30 ml) extra-virgin olive oil or coconut oil
6 garlic cloves, chopped
2 medium brown onions
2 cups (480 ml) organic chicken broth
1⅓ cups (320 ml) coconut milk
⅓ cup (80 ml) rice or almond milk
2 teaspoons grated fresh ginger
½ teaspoon sea salt
½ teaspoon black pepper
Dash cayenne (optional)
2 tablespoons (8 g) dried parsley

Steam the carrots until soft. While the carrots are steaming, heat the oil in a small skillet over medium-high heat. Sauté the garlic and onions until they are softened and slightly browned, about 5 minutes. Combine steamed carrots, cooked garlic and onions, broth, coconut milk, rice or almond milk, ginger, salt, pepper, and cayenne (if using) in a blender. Blend on the purée setting until smooth. Pour the blended soup into a large saucepan over medium heat and cook, stirring occasionally, until heated through. Serve garnished with dried parsley.

YIELD: 6 SERVINGS

EACH WITH: Calories 239.26; Calories From Fat 138.09; Total Fat 16.29 g; Cholesterol 0 mg; Sodium 524.94 mg; Potassium 747.22 mg; Total Carbohydrates 21.92 g; Fiber 5.1 g; Sugar 9.18 g; Protein 4.87 g

BLOOD SUGAR BALANCE RATING: High

Health Facilitators	Nutrient Density Rating
Protein	Low
Fat	Medium
Carbohydrate	Medium
Enzymes	Low
Antioxidants	High
Fiber	High

Carrots are an excellent source of antioxidants and are the richest vegetable source of beta carotenes, compounds that promote cardiovascular health and good vision. Ginger is not only gentle on digestion but adds a pleasing flavor, which is highlighted by the good fats in the coconut milk. This soup contains no dairy, but it is so creamy that you'd never know it was missing. This recipe also offers lots of dietary fiber to balance your blood sugar levels.

BONE-BUILDING COTTAGE CHEESE SALAD

Calcium- and protein-rich cottage cheese combines with vegetables in this salad to provide vitamins A, C, E, B6, and folic acid, zinc, selenium, potassium, and magnesium to help boost your immune system and keep you strong. Don't skip the flaxseed oil. Not only is it delicious, it also fights inflammation and balances your hormones.

2 organic carrots, finely diced
3 scallions, finely chopped
1 small red bell pepper, finely chopped
3 celery stalks, finely chopped
2 tablespoon (8 g) fresh parsley, minced
1 tablespoon (3 g) fresh chives, minced
2 cups (480 ml) cottage cheese
2 tablespoons (30 ml) flaxseed oil
Freshly ground black pepper
Dash cayenne
4 cups (80 g) mixed salad greens or spinach

In a medium bowl, using a fork, mix all ingredients except salad greens or spinach. Line 4 individual plates with mixed salad greens. Mound the cottage cheese salad on top. Serve immediately.

YIELD: 4 SERVINGS
EACH WITH: Calories 206.74; Calories From Fat 83.04; Total Fat 9.41 g; Cholesterol 9.04 mg; Sodium 541.81 mg; Potassium 615.58 mg; Total Carbohydrates 13.29 g; Fiber 3.49 g; Sugar 4.86 g; Protein 17.65 g
BLOOD SUGAR BALANCE RATING: Very High

Health Facilitators	Nutrient Density Rating
Protein	High
Fat	High
Carbohydrate	High
Enzymes	High
Antioxidants	High
Fiber	High

ANTIOXIDANT-RICH RATATOUILLE

3 tablespoons (45 ml) extra-virgin olive oil or coconut oil

1 large onion, chopped

3 minced garlic cloves

1 large eggplant, (peeled, if desired) and cut into ½-inch (1.3-cm) cubes

1 red bell pepper, cut into ½-inch (1.3-cm) pieces

1 green bell pepper, cut into ½-inch (1.3-cm) pieces

1 large zucchini, cut into ¼-inch (0.6-cm) half circles

1 cup (100 g) green beans, ends trimmed, and sliced diagonally into 1-inch (2.5-cm) pieces

6 large ripe tomatoes, chopped

2 tablespoons (30 ml) tomato paste

¼ cup (16 g) chopped fresh parsley

¼ cup (60 ml) red wine

½ cup (120 ml) water

2 tablespoons (5 g) slivered fresh basil, or 2 teaspoons (1.5 g) dried basil

½ teaspoon dried thyme

½ teaspoon dried rosemary

½ teaspoon dried marjoram

1 bay leaf

1 tablespoon (15 ml) balsamic vinegar

Finely ground black pepper

In a large Dutch oven, heat oil over medium high heat. When oil is hot, add onion and garlic and sauté until softened, about 5 minutes. Add eggplant and bell peppers and cook until softened, about 8 minutes more. Add zucchini and next 11 ingredients (through bay leaf). Mix well. Bring to a boil. Reduce heat and simmer, uncovered, 20 minutes, stirring occasionally. Add balsamic vinegar and black pepper. Taste and adjust seasonings. Simmer 15 minutes more. Serve hot, warm, or cold.

YIELD: 4 TO 6 SERVINGS

EACH WITH: Calories 154.07; Calories From Fat 65.75; Total Fat 7.47 g; Cholesterol 0 mg; Sodium 62.12 mg; Potassium 856.52 mg; Total Carbohydrates 19.41 g; Fiber 7.09 g; Sugar 9.83 g; Protein 3.89 g

BLOOD SUGAR BALANCE RATING: High

Ratatouille, with the delicate flavor and soft texture of eggplant, bell pepper, and zucchini, has been long prized by the French and Italians as a favorite Mediterranean dish. The vegetables are loaded with antioxidants, vitamins B and C, numerous minerals, and tons of fiber. The antioxidants protect brain cells as well as strengthen your immune system. And the oil adds healthy fats to keep blood sugar levels stable.

Health Facilitators	Nutrient Density Rating
Protein	Medium
Fat	Low
Carbohydrate	High
Enzymes	High
Antioxidants	High
Fiber	High

CURRIED CAULIFLOWER WITH A KICK

Cauliflower is loaded with vitamin C and is a cruciferous vegetable, which are highly prized for their immune-boosting power. The yogurt adds a good helping of probiotics, or "friendly bacteria," that improve digestion, and the garlic, ginger, onion, and turmeric further strengthen immunity. This dish is also high in fiber and healthy fats to keep your blood sugar steady for hours.

1 cup (240 ml) purified water
1 large head cauliflower, separated into florets
2 tablespoons (28 g) unsalted butter
2 tablespoons (30 ml) extra-virgin olive oil or coconut oil
1 large onion, diced
1 teaspoon mustard seeds
2 minced garlic cloves
2 teaspoons peeled and finely minced fresh ginger
1 teaspoon ground coriander
1 teaspoon ground cumin
1 teaspoon turmeric
1 to 2 teaspoons (2 to 4 g) curry powder
Freshly ground black pepper
Dash cayenne
1 tablespoon (15 ml) fresh lemon or lime juice
1 cup (240 ml) whole-milk plain yogurt
1 tablespoon (4 g) chopped fresh cilantro

In a large saucepan, bring water to a boil. Add cauliflower florets and cook until barely tender, about 5 minutes. Drain and set aside. In a large nonstick skillet, heat butter and oil over medium-high heat. When hot, add onion and sauté until softened, about 5 minutes. Add mustard seeds and stir until seeds begin to pop, about 1 minute. Add garlic, ginger, coriander, cumin, turmeric, curry powder, black pepper, and cayenne. Stir and cook until well mixed, about 2 minutes. Reduce heat to low. Add lemon or lime juice and yogurt, and mix well. Add cooked cauliflower. Stir until well blended and evenly coated with curry spices. Taste and adjust seasonings. Sprinkle with chopped cilantro before serving.

YIELD: 4 SERVINGS
EACH WITH: Calories 204.91; Calories From Fat 124.73; Total Fat 14.19 g; Cholesterol 18.94 mg; Sodium 83.45 mg; Potassium 598.15 mg; Total Carbohydrates 15.68 g; Fiber 4.11 g; Sugar 8.56 g; Protein 6.48 g
BLOOD SUGAR BALANCE RATING: Medium

Health Facilitators	Nutrient Density Rating
Protein	Low
Fat	Medium
Carbohydrate	High
Enzymes	High
Antioxidants	High
Fiber	Very High

LUSCIOUS LOW-GLYCEMIC LENTILS

1 cup (225 g) lentils, picked over and rinsed
3 cups (720 ml) vegetable stock or purified water
2 tablespoons (28 g or 30 ml) unsalted butter, ghee, or coconut oil
2 tablespoons (12 g) peeled and finely minced fresh ginger
½ teaspoon cardamom
½ teaspoon ground cumin
½ teaspoon ground turmeric
½ teaspoon red pepper flakes
2 to 3 tablespoons (8 to 12 g) minced fresh cilantro
1 to 2 tablespoons (15 to 30 ml) fresh lemon juice

In a medium saucepan, bring lentils and stock or water to a boil over medium-high heat. Reduce heat to low and simmer, covered, about 30 minutes or until lentils are tender, stirring occasionally. In a small nonstick skillet, melt butter over medium-high heat. When butter is hot and bubbly, add ginger, cardamom, cumin, turmeric, and red pepper flakes. Sauté until spices are well coated with butter, about 3 minutes. Add spices, cilantro, and lemon juice to cooked lentils. Simmer 10 minutes over low heat. Taste and adjust seasonings.

YIELD: 4 SERVINGS
EACH WITH: Calories 182.18; Calories From Fat 45.33; Total Fat 5.15 g; Cholesterol 12.21 mg; Sodium 9.1 mg; Potassium 408.21 mg; Total Carbohydrates 24.32 g; Fiber 12 g; Sugar 0.93 g; Protein 10.15 g
BLOOD SUGAR BALANCE RATING: Very High

Health Facilitators	Nutrient Density Rating
Protein	High
Fat	Low
Carbohydrate	Medium
Enzymes	High
Antioxidants	High
Fiber	Very High

Lentils are quick and easy to prepare since they don't require pre-soaking like beans and other legumes. Lentils are loaded with minerals and vitamins like folate and potassium and are very high in the essential amino acid tryptophan, which makes them especially helpful for keeping your blood sugar levels and your moods balanced. High in plant protein and low in fat, lentils are an excellent choice for vegetarians and vegans. Lentils are also very high in fiber, which benefits your hormones. Tasty herbs like cumin and turmeric add to the nutrient density of this delicious dish!

SIMPLE ROAST CHICKEN WITH HEALING HERBS

Ideal for all four sugar addiction types, this dish is simple, easy, delicious, and nutritious. High in tryptophan and protein, it keeps you looking on the bright side and off the sugar roller coaster. Leftovers are wonderful for lunch the next day!

1 (3½- to 4-pound, or 1.6- to 1.8-kg) chicken, 4 bone-in chicken breasts, or 1 large turkey breast
1 head of garlic, cut in half
2 lemons, sliced in thirds
1 bunch rosemary
1 bunch marjoram
½ cup (120 ml) purified water
2 tablespoons (30 ml) extra-virgin olive oil

Preheat oven to 350°F (180°C, or gas mark 4). If using a whole chicken, discard giblets and rinse and pat dry. Place chicken on a roasting pan and stuff the cavity with garlic, lemon pieces, rosemary, and marjoram. If using the chicken or turkey breasts, in a shallow baking dish, scatter the garlic, lemons, and herbs evenly across the bottom. Place the chicken or turkey on top. Add the water to the pan and baste the chicken or turkey with the oil. Bake until juices run clear when pierced with a fork, about 1½ to 2 hours for the whole chicken, or until internal temperature reaches 160°F (71°C), or about 30 minutes for chicken or turkey breasts.

YIELD: 4 SERVINGS
EACH WITH: Amount Per Serving; Calories 123.8; Calories From Fat 62.89; Total Fat 7.22 g; Cholesterol 15.12 mg; Sodium 460.88 mg; Potassium 166.77 mg; Total Carbohydrates 11.09 g; Fiber 3.08 g; Sugar 0.18 g; Protein 8.54 g
BLOOD SUGAR BALANCE RATING: Very High

Health Facilitators	Nutrient Density Rating
Protein	High
Fat	Medium
Carbohydrate	Low
Enzymes	Low
Antioxidants	Low
Fiber	Low

HIGH-ENERGY GARLIC SHRIMP

For Spicy Garlic Sauce

2 to 3 garlic cloves, peeled and minced

1 cup (240 ml) plus 3 tablespoons (45 ml) purified water, divided

⅓ cup (80 ml) toasted sesame oil

1 tablespoon (15 ml) hot pepper sauce

1 tablespoon (15 ml) maple syrup

3 tablespoons (45 ml) shoyu

1 teaspoon red pepper flakes

1 tablespoon (8 g) kudzu or arrowroot starch

For Shrimp

¼ cup (60 ml) purified water

½ teaspoon coconut oil

1 red or brown onion, sliced thinly

1 bunch broccoli, florets and stems (cut stems into thin rounds)

1 carrot, sliced thinly on the diagonal

1 pound (455 g) wild-caught shrimp, peeled and deveined

To make the garlic sauce: Mix all ingredients except kudzu and 3 tablespoons (45 ml) water in a small saucepan and cook over medium heat for 3 minutes. Dilute kudzu in 3 tablespoons (45 ml) water and slowly add to the pan. The sauce will begin to thicken. Cook for 3 to 5 minutes or until kudzu becomes clear.

To make the shrimp: Add water, oil, and red onion to a frying pan and cook over medium heat for 1 to 2 minutes. Add broccoli stems and carrot and cook for 2 minutes. Add broccoli florets and shrimp, cover pan and steam for 2 to 3 minutes. Add Spicy Garlic Sauce to the pan. Cover and cook over medium heat for 5 minutes.

YIELD: 2 TO 4 SERVINGS

EACH WITH: Calories 369.6; Calories From Fat 215.07; Total Fat 24.32 g; Cholesterol 172.37 mg; Sodium 873.85 mg; Potassium 500.23 mg; Total Carbohydrates 12.81 g; Fiber 1.21 g; Sugar 5.45 g; Protein 25.67 g

BLOOD SUGAR BALANCE RATING: Very High

Low-calorie, high-protein shrimp are rich in B vitamins and are a super source of omega-3s, which offer powerful protection against depression and help to elevate your mood. Shrimp also contain iodine to support your thyroid naturally, and their protein make them a go-to choice for stabilizing blood sugar levels. This scrumptious seafood is also a good source of magnesium, which studies suggest can help prevent the development of type 2 diabetes. Serve with a large mixed green salad.

Health Facilitators	Nutrient Density Rating
Protein	High
Fat	High
Carbohydrate	Low
Enzymes	Low
Antioxidants	Medium
Fiber	Low

MEGA-OMEGA DEEP-SEA DELIGHT

A perfect food for all four sugar-addiction types, halibut is packed with omega-3s and is an excellent source of protein. It's chock full of vitamins B6, B12, and folic acid that lower homocysteine levels and boost heart health. It also contains magnesium, which improves the flow of blood, oxygen, and nutrients throughout the body. Fresh herbs and spices, including ginger (anti-inflammatory), antioxidant-rich garlic (antibacterial, antiviral, and antifungal), and cilantro (an appetite stimulant) combine to complement the delicate, sweet flavor of halibut. Add a delicious green salad or some steamed asparagus and broccoli to this dish to round out the flavors and further stabilize your blood sugar levels.

½ green bell pepper, chopped
3 tablespoons (24 g) chopped cilantro or parsley
1 teaspoon cumin
½ teaspoon chili powder
½ teaspoon chopped fresh ginger
2 to 4 tablespoons (30 to 60 ml) fresh lemon or lime juice
2 to 4 cloves fresh garlic, chopped
1 teaspoon salt
2 tablespoons (30 ml) apple cider vinegar
2 pounds (910 g) whole halibut
2 tablespoons (28 g or 30 ml) butter or ghee (clarified butter)

Preheat oven to 350°F (180°C, or gas mark 4). Mix the first 9 ingredients (through vinegar). Stuff the fish with this mixture, rubbing some on the outside as well. Tie the fish with a string or wrap in aluminum foil. (If wrapping in foil, dot fish with butter or pour ghee over the fish before sealing.) Put in greased baking dish and bake for 40 to 45 minutes. If baking unwrapped, baste with butter and turn over when fish turns red to finish cooking.

YIELD: 4 TO 8 SERVINGS

NOTE: When fish is cooked, you can pour off the gravy into a saucepan and add a little flour, cooking over low heat and stirring until thickened.

NOTE: If you are using fillets rather than whole fish, place the pepper and herb mixture around the fish and bake it.

EACH WITH: Calories 189.87; Calories From Fat 56.12; Total Fat 6.31 g; Cholesterol 54.13 mg; Sodium 101.38 mg; Potassium 693.59 mg; Total Carbohydrates 1.26 g; Fiber 0.29 g; Sugar 0.33 g; Protein 30.53 g

BLOOD SUGAR BALANCE RATING: Very High

Health Facilitators	Nutrient Density Rating
Protein	High
Fat	Low
Carbohydrate	Low
Enzymes	Low
Antioxidants	Medium
Fiber	Low

TRANSFORMING TEMPEH

3 tablespoons (45 ml) peanut oil or coconut oil
3 cloves garlic, finely chopped or minced
½ red onion, chopped
1 tablespoon (6 g) fresh ginger, peeled and finely chopped
½ teaspoon red pepper flakes
4 medium zucchini, cut into ¼-inch (0.6-cm) circles
2 red bell peppers, slivered
1 pound (455 g) tempeh, cut into ½-inch (1.3-cm) squares
2 tablespoons (30 ml) tamari sauce (wheat-free), or Bragg's liquid amino acids
2 tablespoons (30 ml) sesame oil
1 tablespoon (15 ml) fresh lime juice
2 tablespoons (12 g) chopped scallions,
2 tablespoons (8 g) chopped fresh cilantro

In a wok or a large nonstick skillet, heat the peanut oil over medium to high heat. When oil is hot, add garlic, onions, and ginger and cook for 30 seconds, stirring constantly. Add red pepper flakes, zucchini, red bell pepper and tempeh, and stir-fry about 7 minutes, until vegetables are tender. In a separate bowl, combine the tamari or liquid amino acids, sesame oil, lime juice, scallions, and cilantro. Pour over tempeh and vegetables and cook, stirring, until heated through. Taste and adjust seasonings.

YIELD: 4 SERVINGS

EACH WITH: Calories 441.66; Calories From Fat 257.78; Total Fat 29.84 g; Cholesterol 0 mg; Sodium 539.32 mg; otassium 1220.25 mg; Total Carbohydrates 25.28 g; Fiber 4.35 g; Sugar 6.95 g; Protein 25.63 g

BLOOD SUGAR BALANCE RATING: Very High

Health Facilitators	Nutrient Density Rating
Protein	High
Fat	Medium
Carbohydrate	Medium
Enzymes	Medium
Antioxidants	High
Fiber	High

Tempeh is an excellent choice for all four types who have difficulty digesting plant-based high-protein foods such as beans and legumes or soy foods such as tofu. That's because the process of fermentation makes the soybeans softer and easier to digest. High in calcium, zinc, and iron, along with the dozens of antioxidants from the vegetables, this dish is packed with nutrients to keep blood sugar levels stable. Serve over steamed brown rice.

SPICE-IT-UP SAUSAGES WITH LENTILS AND LEEKS

Leeks are a small but mighty member of the onion family. Packed with plant protein, rich in vitamins C, B6, and folate, plus iron and manganese, leeks balance blood sugar and even raise HDL or "good" cholesterol. Leeks are particularly high in tryptophan, which means mellow moods and a good night's sleep. Combined with tasty sausage, fresh herbs, and garlic, this dish is a go-to meal for all four types. Enjoy this one for lunch or dinner or as a hearty snack, served with brown rice.

2 tablespoons (30 ml) olive oil
½ brown onion, chopped
2 garlic cloves, peeled and minced
1 large leek, cleaned and chopped
2 cups (40 g) spinach, cleaned and chopped
2 tablespoons (5 g) fresh thyme
2 tablespoons (8 g) chopped cilantro
2 cups (385 g) dried lentils, soaked overnight
3½ cups (840 ml) purified water
2 bay leaves
1½ pounds (680 g) chicken sausage links (or pork, turkey, or tofu), diced
1 teaspoon sea salt
Freshly ground black pepper
Dash cayenne

Heat oil in a large skillet over medium-high heat. Sauté onion, garlic, and leek 1 to 2 minutes. Add spinach and cook until wilted, about 3 to 5 minutes. Add thyme, cilantro, lentils (drained from soaking water), purified water, and bay leaves. Bring to a boil, cover, and simmer over low heat for 30 minutes. Add diced sausage, salt, black pepper, and cayenne. Continue cooking 30 more minutes, or until lentils are soft.

YIELD: 4 TO 6 SERVINGS

EACH WITH: Calories 331.44; Calories From Fat 70.4; Total Fat 7.8 g; Cholesterol 18.75 mg; Sodium 528.8 mg; Potassium 727.26 mg; Total Carbohydrates 42.74 g; Fiber 20.62 g; Sugar 2.36 g; Protein 22.78 g

BLOOD SUGAR BALANCE RATING: Very High

Health Facilitators	Nutrient Density Rating
Protein	High
Fat	Medium
Carbohydrate	High
Enzymes	Low
Antioxidants	Medium
Fiber	High

NOURISHING APPLE NUT CAKE

4 large apples, cored, peeled, and sliced
2 tablespoons (16 g) chopped walnuts
4 teaspoons (10 g) cinnamon
6 dates, chopped
1 cup (145 g) raisins
3 cups (375 g) coconut flour
1 tablespoon (14 g) baking powder
½ cup (120 ml) coconut oil
4 large eggs
½ cup (120 ml) freshly squeezed orange juice
1 tablespoon (15 ml) melted butter

Preheat the oven to 350°F (180°C, or gas mark 4). Grease a 10-inch (25-cm) tube pan or loaf pan. In a medium bowl, blend the apples, walnuts, cinnamon, dates, and raisins. In a separate bowl, combine the flour, baking powder, oil, eggs, orange juice, and butter. Beat 4 to 5 minutes with an electric mixer, until batter is smooth. Pour half the batter into the pan and spread half the apple mixture on top. Repeat the procedure and bake for 30 minutes. Then lower the oven temperature to 300°F (150°C, or gas mark 2) and bake 1 hour more, or until a toothpick inserted into the center comes out clean.

YIELD: 4 TO 6 SERVINGS

EACH WITH: Calories 645.8; Calories From Fat 272.81; Total Fat 31.41 g; Cholesterol 146.09 mg; Sodium 308.64 mg; Potassium 464.39 mg; Total Carbohydrates 85.49 g; Fiber 29.02 g; Sugar 33.19 g; Protein 14.09 g

BLOOD SUGAR BALANCE RATING: High

The combination of the healthy fat in coconuts (lauric acid), the high fiber and antioxidants in apples, and heart-healthy walnuts means this dessert is nourishing and blood sugar–balancing. The orange juice makes this cake moist and delicious. You're sure to want more of this tasty treat!

Health Facilitators	Nutrient Density Rating
Protein	Medium
Fat	High
Carbohydrate	High
Enzymes	Low
Antioxidants	Medium
Fiber	High

FRESH STRAWBERRIES CHANTILLY GONE NUTS

The sweet juiciness and deep red color of strawberries can brighten up both the flavor and look of any meal. Strawberries are loaded with antioxidants, especially vitamin C, which protect against harmful free radicals. The tasty fruit is also high in fiber, potassium, and iodine, which makes them effective at boosting thyroid function. The walnuts add omega-3 essential fatty acids, and the delicious healthy fats in crème fraîche help stabilize your blood sugar levels. This dish makes a perfect snack or sweet ending to a meal!

8 cups (880 g) fresh strawberries, washed, dried, hulled, and quartered
¼ cup (35 g) chopped dates
¼ cup (60 ml) freshly squeezed orange juice
1½ cups (360 ml) crème fraîche
3 to 4 tablespoons (24 to 32 g) walnuts, chopped
8 mint sprigs

Divide the strawberries among 8 serving bowls. In a mixing bowl combine the chopped dates, orange juice, and the crème fraîche, and mix well. Place 3 tablespoons (45 ml) of the date mixture on top of each serving of strawberries and garnish with walnuts and a sprig of mint.

YIELD: 8 SERVINGS

EACH WITH: Calories 214.96; Calories From Fat 20.07; Total Fat 13.11 g; Cholesterol 26.89 mg; Sodium 2.32 mg; Potassium 383.95 mg; Total Carbohydrates 23.42 g; Fiber 4.74 g; Sugar 15.5 g; Protein 2.83 g

BLOOD SUGAR BALANCE RATING: High

Health Facilitators	Nutrient Density Rating
Protein	Low
Fat	High
Carbohydrate	High
Enzymes	High
Antioxidants	High
Fiber	High

BEAT SUGAR ADDICTION NOW! COOKBOOK

Special Supplements

In this appendix you'll find information about many combination products that can simplify treatment for your type of sugar addiction, along with specific brands we recommend. You'll find a more extensive list of supplements in *Beat Sugar Addiction Now!* Unless noted, the natural supplements suggested here can be found in most natural foods stores, at www.Vitality101.com (or by calling 800-333-5287), or at most online natural pharmacies. In Appendix D you'll find the addresses, phone numbers, and websites for the companies who make and/or distribute the products recommended here. You'll also find information about compounding pharmacies, finding the best water filter, and more.

When taking the supplements that are right for your individual condition and/or sugar addiction type, I usually suggest the following:

1. Begin to slowly taper off most treatments when you have felt well for six months. I recommend the vitamin powder (#1, on the following page) for long-term use to maintain optimal nutritional support.

2. Stop supplements one item at a time, so you can see whether you still need them.

3. If need be, any or all of these can be used forever, although this is usually not necessary.

I encourage people who recommend either prescription or natural products to disclose financial ties they may have to the makers of the products they recommend. A word about Fatigued to Fantastic! products: I direct any company making my formulas to donate to charity all of the money that I would have received. I also never accept money from any natural supplement or pharmaceutical product companies. I do make money from products sold on my website (www.Vitality101.com).

OPTIMAL OVERALL NUTRITIONAL SUPPORT FOR ALL SUGAR ADDICTS

Energy Revitalization System multivitamin powder (berry or citrus flavor by Enzymatic Therapy or Integrative Therapeutics): Take one-half to one scoop a day (as feels best) blended with milk, water, or yogurt. If diarrhea occurs, mix the powder with milk and/or start with a lower dose and work your way up to the dose that feels best; or, divide the daily dose into smaller doses and take two to three times a day. It's available at www.Vitality101.com and most natural foods stores.

SUPPLEMENTS FOR TYPE 1 SUGAR ADDICTION

To Increase Energy

Ribose (from Corvalen by Bioenergy Life Science, Inc.): Take one 5-gram scoop of powder three times a day for three weeks, then twice a day. If this is too energizing, take it with milk or food, or lower the dose. Effects are usually seen within two to three weeks for energy and six weeks for heart disease. You can find it at natural foods stores, www.vitality101.com, or at www.corvalen.com.

To Treat Insomnia

Revitalizing Sleep Formula (from Enzymatic Therapy or Integrative Therapeutics): This formula contains 200 mg of valerian, 90 mg of passionflower, 50 mg of L-theanine, 30 mg of hops, 12 mg of piscidia (Jamaica dogwood), and 28 mg of wild lettuce. Take two to four capsules each night, thirty to sixty minutes before bedtime. It can also be used during the day for anxiety. If valerian energizes you (which occurs in 5 to 10 percent of people), use the other components. Do not take more than eight capsules a day.

Magnesium and More

Sustained-Release Magnesium (from Jigsaw Health): If you find that taking magnesium supplements causes diarrhea, use this form (it contains 125 mg per tablet, plus other helpful nutrients). You can find it at www.jigsawhealth.com.

SUPPLEMENTS FOR TYPE 2 SUGAR ADDICTION

For Adrenal Support

Adrenal Stress-End (from Enzymatic Therapy or Integrative Therapeutics, Inc.): This combination product contains important nutrients for adrenal health. Take one to two capsules each morning (or one to two in the morning and another at noon). Lower the dosage or take with food if it upsets your stomach (which is unusual).

SUPPLEMENTS FOR TYPE 3 SUGAR ADDICTION

To Promote Healthy Gut Flora

Acidophilus Milk Bacteria, Acidophilus Pearls, or Probiotic Pearls (from Enzymatic Therapy or Integrative Therapeutics): Take two twice a day for five months, then consider taking one a day to help maintain healthy bowels. The Enzymatic Therapy and the Integrative Therapeutics Inc. acidophilus and probiotic pearls actually contain about 2.8 billion units per pearl, even though the box says only 1 billion. The protective "pearl" coating prevents your stomach acid from killing nearly all of the bacteria, which would have made them useless for fighting yeast.

Anti-Yeast (from NutriElements): This excellent combination of natural products aids in fighting yeast (*Candida*) overgrowth; it also provides important protection for the liver during yeast treatment with Diflucan. Take two capsules two to three times daily, before meals. Available at www.vitality101.com.

SUPPLEMENTS FOR TYPE 4 SUGAR-ADDICTION

For Nutritional Support

Fish Oil (Vectomega from EuroPharma): Take one tablet a day. For depression, consider taking two a day for three to six months, then reducing your dose to one a day.

To Treat Hot Flashes

Black Cohosh (Remifemin from Enzymatic Therapy, Inc.): Take two tablets twice a day for two months, then you can lower the dose to one tablet twice a day. Note: This treatment can take six weeks to work.

SUPPLEMENTS FOR SPECIFIC CONDITIONS COMMON IN SUGAR ADDICTION

Anxiety

Calming Balance (from Health Freedom Nutrition): Start with three capsules, three times a day. After maximum benefit has been achieved (usually in one to six weeks, though it begins to work within thirty minutes), decrease to the minimum dose that provides the same benefit (e.g., two capsules twice a day).

Depression

Fish Oil (VectOmega from EuroPharma): Take one tablet a day. For depression, consider taking two a day for three to six months, then reducing your dose to one a day.

Happiness 1-2-3! (from Health Freedom Nutrition) or In Harmony (from NutriElements): Take two tablets two to three times a day.

If depression persists despite following the recommended treatments above, or if depression is severe, consult your doctor about taking prescription antidepressants.

Heart Disease

Caution: If you have kidney failure, take magnesium only with your physician's approval.

Ribose (from Corvalen): See supplements for Type 1 Sugar Addiction, above.

Coenzyme Q10: Coenzyme Q10 (CoQ10) is critical for energy production. This nutrient is especially important for anyone on cholesterol-lowering statin medications (e.g., Lipitor) because these medications cause CoQ10 deficiency. Take 400 mg a day for six weeks, then 200 mg a day. Use the 200 mg chewable wafers from Enzymatic Therapy.

Magnesium Orotate: Take 6,000 mg a day for one month, then 3,000 mg a day.

Magnesium Glycinate Take 150–200 mg a day (you can find this and the B vitamins in the Energy Revitalization System multivitamin powder from Enzymatic Therapy or Integrative Therapeutics, Inc.).

Acetyl-l-Carnitine: Take 1500–3000 mg a day.

B Complex: Choose a supplement with at least 400 mcg folic acid, 50 mcg B12, and 50 mg of the other B vitamins.

Fish Oil (Vectomega from EuroPharma): Take one tablet a day.

Hypothyroidism

BMR Complex (thyroid glandular plus tyrosine, iodine, and other thyroid-supporting nutrients, available from Integrative Therapeutics): Take one or two capsules three times daily between meals, or as feels best.

Iodine (Tri-iodine from Terry Naturally by EuroPharma): Breast cysts, cancer, or tenderness suggest that iodine deficiency is contributing to your low thyroid condition Take one capsule a day for two to four months. Each capsule contains 12.5 mg iodine. If you develop acne, lower the dose to 6.25 mg. If you develop severe indigestion, stop taking the iodine. Available at www.europharmausa.com.

IBS/Spastic Colon

Peppermint Oil (Peppermint Plus from Enzymatic Therapy or Mentharil from Integrative Therapeutics): Take one to two enteric–coated 0.2 cc capsules three times a day between meals (not with food) for spastic colon.

Simethicone (Mylicon, available over-the-counter in most pharmacies or supermarkets): Chew 40 to 80 mg three times a day as needed for abdominal gas pains.

Indigestion

A great heartburn trio!

Immediate Heartburn Relief chewable antacids (from EuroPharma): Supplies a safe mix of calcium, magnesium, vitamin D, and vitamin K. (Plain calcium—as found in most antacid chews—increases heart attack risk by 31 percent; adding vitamin D and magnesium solves that problem.) Chew one tablet as needed for indigestion.

DGL Licorice (Gut Soothe from EuroPharma): Take two a day for one to two months, and then as needed. This product also contains probiotics.

Limonene (Advanced Heartburn Rescue from EuroPharma): Take this to treat an *H. pylori* infection (a common problem aggravating indigestion). Once your indigestion is better as a result of taking DGL licorice, take one pill of limonene daily for 30 days to clear the infection. This formula also contains sea buckthorn oil, which can help heal the stomach's mucus lining.

To Optimize Digestion

Digestive Enzymes (CompleteGest from Enzymatic Therapy): Take two capsules with each meal to help you digest your food properly. Also drink warm (not cold) liquids with meals, since digestive enzymes (including those made by your body) work only in warm temperatures. Only use plant-based (not animal-based) digestive enzymes to aid digestion.

Migraines and Tension Headaches

To Treat or Prevent Migraines

Butterbur (Petadolex from Enzymatic Therapy): Take 50 mg three times a day for one month, and then 50 mg twice a day thereafter to prevent migraines. You can take 100 mg every three hours to eliminate an acute migraine.

To Prevent Migraines

Energy Revitalization System multivitamin powder: This supplies riboflavin, magnesium, and other nutrients that can markedly decrease the frequency of migraine headaches. Note: Give this product six weeks to work.

Fish Oil (Vectomega by EuroPharma): Take one a day.

Riboflavin (Vitamin B2): Take 300 mg a day (in addition to the vitamin powder).

General Pain

Curamin (from EuroPharma): This product has been a pain relief miracle for many kinds of pain. Take one tablet three times a day until your pain resolves (allow six weeks, but you'll usually see an effect within hours to days), then take one to two tablets a day as needed.

End Pain (from Enzymatic Therapy) or Pain Formula (from Integrative Therapeutics): For ongoing pain, such as arthritis, take one to two tablets three times a day, allowing six weeks to see the full effect (but relief usually begins within hours to days). After six to twelve weeks, use as needed.

Note that the Curamin and End Pain can be taken together.

Osteoporosis

OsteoStrong (Terry Naturally from EuroPharma): Take four tablets each night plus two strontium capsules each morning. Available at www.vitality101.com, or see www.europharmausa.com for natural foods stores near you.

Sinusitis

Sinusitis Nose Spray (prescription-only): This formula contains fluconazole, xylitol, mupirocin, and triamcinolone. Squirt one to two sprays into each nostril twice a day for six to twelve weeks. Use with the silver nose spray below. Available by prescription from ITC Compounding Pharmacy (www.itcpharmacy.com, 303-663-4224).

Silver Nose Spray (Argentyn 23 from Natural-Immunogenics Corp.): Squirt five to ten sprays into each nostril three times a day for seven to fourteen days, until the sinusitis resolves.

Glycemic Index of Common Foods

The glycemic index (GI) tells you which foods raise your blood glucose fastest and highest. This is especially important for sugar addicts to keep in mind. Pure glucose gets a GI score of 100, and all other foods are measured in relation to glucose. A food with a glycemic index above 85 raises blood sugar rapidly, but a food with a glycemic index below 30 does not raise your blood sugar much at all. As a sugar addict, you'll want to eat foods that score low on the glycemic index as often as possible!

Classification	GI Range	Examples
Low GI	55 or below	Most fruits and vegetables (except potatoes, watermelon), grainy breads, pasta, legumes/pulses, milk, products extremely low in carbohydrates (fish, eggs, meat, some cheeses, nuts, cooking oil), brown rice
Medium GI	56–69	Whole wheat products, sweet potatoes, table sugar, most white rices (e.g. jasmine, basmati)
High GI	70 and above	Cornflakes, baked potatoes, watermelon, croissants, white bread, extruded breakfast cereals (e.g., Rice Krispies), straight glucose (100)

Fresh Fruit		Glycemic Index
	Cherries	63
	Blueberries (fresh or frozen)	53
	Grapes	53
	Bananas	52
	Oranges	42
	Peaches	42
	Strawberries (fresh or frozen)	40
	Pears	38
	Apples	38

Starchy Vegetables

These tend to be largely sugar and starch with low protein content to balance the starch, so limit your intake of these to 4 ounces (115 g) or less on most days, using those with a lower glycemic index whenever possible.

Fresh Vegetables		Glycemic Index
	Parsnips	97
	Potato	High 80s
	Rutabaga	72
	Beets	64
	Sweet Potato	61
	Corn	53
	Carrots	47

Other Vegetables

Most other vegetables, particularly green leafy ones, usually score zero or near zero on the glycemic index. Try to eat three to five portions a day, but you can have as much as you like. Use vinaigrette or oil and vinegar dressings on salads as desired.

Meats, Eggs, Poultry, and Seafood

Because they are predominantly high-protein foods, they generally have a zero glycemic index value, and you can eat as much of these as you like. Make these the main component in most of your meals whenever possible, adding beans/legumes, vegetables, and greens for balance.

Beans and Legumes

Although some beans and legumes score high on the glycemic index, they also are high in protein, vitamins, minerals and fiber, making them a healthy choice for sugar addicts—especially vegetarians. Enjoy up to two to three servings a day.

Unless otherwise noted, the following GI scores refer to dried beans or peas that have been boiled. Canned beans tend to have a higher glycemic index value.

Beans and Legumes	Glycemic Index
Black-eyed peas	33–50
Butter beans	28–36, average 31
Chickpeas (garbanzo beans)	31–36
Chickpeas, canned	42
Kidney beans	13–46, average 34
Kidney beans, canned	52
Lentils	18–37
Lentils, canned	52
Navy beans (white beans, haricot)	30–39
Navy beans, pressure cooked	29–59
Peas, dried, split	32
Pinto beans	39
Pinto beans, canned	45
Soy beans	15–20
Soy beans, canned	14

Dairy Products

It's okay to eat up to four servings a day.

Dairy Products	Glycemic Index
Milk, regular (full fat)	11–40, average 27
Milk, skim	32
Yogurt without added sugar	14–23

Breads

As you can see, bread has a high glycemic index. Limit your intake to one or two slices a day or less. I recommend whole-grain products, because they have not lost most of their vitamins and minerals through processing.

Breads	Glycemic Index
White bread	71
Whole wheat bread	71
Wheat bread made with 50% cracked wheat kernels	58
Wheat bread made with 75% cracked wheat kernels	48

Cold Cereals

These tend to have a high glycemic index score. Though a breakfast of eggs and meat (skip the potatoes or grits) is preferable, if you don't have time to prepare this, a bowl of cereal for breakfast is okay as long as it does not contain more than 14 grams of sugar per serving (equal to 3½ teaspoons of sugar; read the nutrition information on the box). Cheerios, Life cereal, and shredded wheat are good choices.

Cold Cereals	Glycemic Index
All-Bran	42
Cornflakes	81
Corn Chex	83
Crispix	87
Fruit Loops	69
Golden Grahams	71
Grape Nuts	71
Life	66
Puffed Wheat	73
Rice Krispies–type cereals	88
Rice Chex	89
Shredded wheat	75
Special K	69
Total	76

Pasta

The glycemic index scores for standard wheat pastas depends on the thickness (the thicker the pasta, the lower the GI), and the way it is cooked (al dente—somewhat firm—has the lowest GI). The longer you cook pasta, the softer it is, and the higher the GI. Eat these sparingly (up to four servings a week).

Pasta	Glycemic Index
Most wheat pastas	35–60

Nuts

These have a low GI score, and you can eat as much as you like. Nuts make good snacks.

Nuts		Glycemic Index
	Cashews	22
	Peanuts	14
	Almonds	0
	Brazil nuts	0
	Hazelnuts	0
	Macadamia nuts	0
	Pecans	0
	Walnuts	0

Finding a Health Practitioner

PHYSICIAN ORGANIZATIONS

Holistic physicians are much more likely to be familiar with the treatments and principles discussed in this book. The following organizations include more than 3,000 practitioners throughout North America who take a holistic approach to medicine.

To find a holistic M.D. or D.O. (Doctor of Osteopathy), the American Board of Integrative and Holistic Medicine, www.holisticboard.org, certifies physicians as having advanced training in the use of natural therapies. Its website lists more than 1,500 board-certified holistic physicians.

To find a naturopath who has completed a four-year training equivalent to medical school, visit the American Association of Naturopathic Physicians website, www.naturopathic.org.

More and more states are wisely allowing naturopaths, physicians with four-year training from one of the seven naturopathic colleges in North America the legal authority to prescribe and treat like other physicians.

IF YOU HAVE CHRONIC FATIGUE SYNDROME OR FIBROMYALGIA

Instead of trying to teach your doctor how to treat chronic fatigue syndrome/ fibromyalgia syndrome (CFS/FMS), go to specialists. The Fibromyalgia and Fatigue Centers have offices throughout the United States and see people from all over the world. Their physicians are excellent, well trained in the SHINE Protocol, stay well versed in new CFS/FMS research and treatments. To find the center nearest you, go to www.fibroandfatigue.com or call 866-443-4276. Holistic physicians (see above) are also more likely to be able to help you.

In addition, the free "Symptom Analysis" program at www.vitality101.com will analyze your medical history (and your laboratory test results, if available) to determine the most likely underlying problems in your case. The program will also create a treatment protocol tailored to your case. This will allow you to begin the natural parts of the protocol on your own, and will assist and support your doctor in giving you the best possible care.

FOR OVERALL HEALTH OPTIMIZATION DURING PERIMENOPAUSE, MENOPAUSE, OR ANDROPAUSE

Recognizing that "55 is the new 35," I recommend these two new programs for health optimization for those aged 45 to 65.

For women, the Well Optimized Woman (WOW) program can offer you a "major tune up," focusing on 14 key areas of health using the principles incorporated in this book. These are:

Energy/overall vitality

Adequacy of estrogen and progesterone

Sexual function

Mental clarity

Mood, motivation, and happiness

Sleep disturbances

Breast health

Identifying silent diseases, such as hypertension, diabetes, hyperlipidemia (high cholesterol), metabolic syndrome, sleep apnea, and anemia

Scalp hair loss or facial hair growth

Pain

Bone health

Thyroid and adrenal health

Weight optimization

Healthy skin

For men, The Optimized Male (TOM) program focuses on treating ten key health issues:

Fatigue

Decreased stamina

Loss of motivation

Depression

Loss of libido

ED (erectile dysfunction)

Metabolic syndrome (high cholesterol, hypertension, diabetes)

Prostate symptoms (slow urine flow, frequent nighttime waking to urinate)

Troublesome arthritis, muscle aches, pain

Memory loss

To find a practitioner near you, see www.WellOptimizedWoman.com or www.TheOptimizedMale.com.

FOR WEIGHT LOSS

The Optimized Weight Loss program includes diet and exercise along with targeted approaches to help maximize your metabolism by providing:

Thyroid support

Adrenal support

Candida elimination

Insulin resistance and metabolic syndrome treatment

Metabolism-boosting nutrients

Improved sleep

Visit www.OptimizedWeightLoss.com to find a practitioner.

APPENDIX D

Resources

This appendix offers many helpful resources, including how to find medications (at the best price) and supplements (retail and wholesale), water filters, excellent compounding pharmacies, and much more.

Also see Appendix A for a list of commonly recommended products (usually mixes of natural products), where we've organized them according to addiction type and specific medical conditions to simplify treatment of sugar addiction and its related problems. Most of these are available from my website at www.vitality101.com or from natural foods stores.

I encourage people who recommend either prescription or natural products to disclose financial ties they may have, so I will also do so. I direct any company making my formulas to donate to charity all the money that I would have received. I also never accept money from natural or pharmaceutical product companies. I do make money from products sold at my website (www.vitality101.com).

Allergy Elimination
NAET
714-532-0800 or 714-523-8900, www.NAET.com
Supplies information about the Nambudripad allergy elimination technique (NAET), including help with locating practitioners worldwide.

Compounding Pharmacies
ITC Pharmacy
303-663-4224 or 888-349-5453, www.itcpharmacy.com
This national mail-order compounding pharmacy does a superb job of quality control and makes a wide range of bio-identical hormones, topical pain formulas, the Sinusitis Nose Spray, and much more. Although there are many excellent compounding pharmacies, this is the one I recommend first.

Cape Apothecary

800-248-5978, 410-757-3522, or 410-974-1788

An excellent holistic compounding pharmacy in Maryland, that fulfills mail orders and also makes medications for injections.

Prescription Medications

Consumers Discount Drugs

323-461-3606

This mail-order pharmacy has the best prices I've found for mail-order prescription medications.

Costco Pharmacy

www.costco.com

Costco has excellent prices on generic prescriptions. To see what a medication should cost, go to the website above. Click on "Pharmacy" and then search using the phrase "Price Checker." You do not have to be a Costco member to fill prescriptions at its pharmacies.

Saunas

High Tech Health

800-794-5355, www.hightechhealth.com

Sweating can remove toxins—especially if you shower immediately after taking a sauna—and can be very helpful for health. Many of the newer saunas are called "far infrared", and a half-hour session three to seven times a week can aid detoxification. I use and recommend the ones from High Tech Health.

Sinusitis Treatment

Sinus Survival by Dr. Robert Ivker

888-434-0033 or 303-771-0033, www.sinussurvival.com

Dr. Ivker's website contains tools such as nasal steamers to help heal chronic sinusitis, as well as many other helpful tools and resources.

Water Filters

Pure Water

443-949-0409, www.jacobsonhealth.com

Contact: Bren Jacobson

Consultant on health and environmental concerns, especially water, and distributor of Multi-Pure water filters, Bren Jacobson also does personal counseling for those seeking to find the best mix of natural and standard treatments for their medical problems (available in person or by phone).

Information and Supplements

Jacob Teitelbaum, M.D.

800-333-5287 or 410-573-5389, www.vitality101.com

Many of the products recommended in this book, especially hard-to-find ones, are available through the website above. At our website, you can sign up for free e-mail newsletters that will keep you on the cutting edge of developments in health care—especially issues related to sugar addiction, pain, and fatigue. There is also a free computerized "Symptom Analysis" program for those with chronic fatigue (CFS) or fibromyalgia that will analyze your symptoms (and your lab results, if available) to tailor a treatment protocol to your case

Wholesale Products for Health Care Practitioners

Most of the products recommended in the book can be found at www.vitality101.com or in most natural foods stores. Health practitioners or natural foods stores that would like to carry these products wholesale for the public can contact the following providers.

Bioenergy Life Science, Inc.

866-267-8253, www.corvalen.com

Email: info@bioenergy.com

Or

800-245-4440, www.douglaslabs.com/corvalen

This company is a source for wholesale purchases of ribose (Corvalen) or ribose with magnesium and and malic acid (CorvalenM) by practitioners. It is to be especially commended for its commitment to quality, in both finished products and extensive patient-focused research. Ribose is available to the public (retail) from www.vitality101.com.

Enzymatic Therapy

800-783-2286, www.enzymatictherapy.com

This company sells to natural foods stores and produces many excellent products, including the Fatigued to Fantastic product line I developed. This line includes Fatigued to Fantastic Energy Revitalization System vitamin powder (which includes the B complex), Fatigued to Fantastic Daily Energy B-Complex, End Pain, Adrenal Stress End, and Revitalizing Sleep Formula. The products I've recommended in this book can be found in most natural foods stores as well as at www.vitality101.com.

Integrative Therapeutics, Inc. (ITI)

For general information, 800-931-1709

For medical professional and practitioners only;

Representative: Cathy Leet (sales representative "in the field"),

920-737-8828, www.integrativeinc.com

I feel this is the best company in the United States making products for health practitioners only, and I am so impressed with them that I asked them to make my End Fatigue line of products (available to health practitioners). These include the Energy Revitalization System "Daily Energy Enfusion" vitamin powder and B complex (which can replace more than thirty-five different vitamin tablets a day), Daily Energy B-Complex, Pain Formula Herbal Mix, Adrenal Stress End, and Revitalizing Sleep Formula. ITI voluntarily registered with the FDA, so its products have to go through the same testing for potency and purity as pharmaceuticals. They have many excellent products, and Cathy Leet is great to work with.

EuroPharma

920-406-6500, www.europharmausa.com

This company is owned by Terry Lemerond, one of my favorite thought leaders in the natural products field. (He brought glucosamine to the American market.) The company's Vectomega fish oil has remarkably high absorption, allowing one-tablet-a-day dosing. I especially recommend the following products:

- Curamin, an amazing herbal pain mix
- Bos-Cur, a special boswellia/curcumin mix that is excellent for colitis and asthma
- Vectomega fish oil supplements; one to two tablets replaces 10 to 20 regular fish oil capsules
- OsteoStrong and Strontium, which, together, are outstanding to improve bone density
- Hydra-7, an omega-7 oil supplement of sea buckthorne oil for dry eyes and mouth
- Tri-Iodine for iodine supplementation
- Gut Soothe, Immediate Heartburn Relief, and Advanced Heartburn Rescue for indigestion

These products are available at www.vitality101.com, or visit the website above for retail locations near you.

Other Products

Body Ecology

800-4-STEVIA (800-478-3842), www.stevia.net

They have the best-tasting stevia I have found. They also offer stevia cookbooks.

Health Freedom Nutrition

800-980-8780, www.HFN-USA.com

This mail-order company offers herbals for anxiety and depression. They also make Calming Balance and Happiness 1-2-3! (also available at www.vitality101. com) and have an informative newsletter.

The BSAN Weight Loss Program: Optimizing Weight Loss in Post-Sugar Addicts

Congratulations! You've made it off the roller coaster of sugar addiction, you're feeling better, and many of you have already begun to shed some of the extra pounds you've been carrying. If you're ready to lose more weight, the next step is repairing your metabolism so you can finally burn off those extra pounds. Here are the tools that can help you do it.

EXERCISE

No matter how much you restrict your calorie intake, you've got to get moving and keep moving for your metabolism to stay high. Otherwise you may as well be in hibernation with your body saying, "Hold on to the fat!' A simple approach to help you move more throughout the day is to get a pedometer that tracks the number of steps you've walked, and work your way up to at least 10,000 steps a day. The trick is to ease into it. Wear the pedometer for three days and write down how many steps you walked each day. Then add 500 steps a day and maintain that level for two weeks. If you feel okay, keep adding 500 steps to your daily goal every other week. Once you reach 10,000 steps, you can stay at that level, or you can keep increasing your step goal or do a more intense workout to help you burn additional calories.

RAISE YOUR METABOLISM'S FIRE

Once you've treated your sugar addiction, review these next steps to boosting metabolism and saying goodbye to persistent pounds. (You can find most of the following supplements at natural foods stores or at www.vitality101.com.)

Optimize Thyroid Function

A slow thyroid equals slow metabolism, which makes it more difficult for you to lose excess weight. Even if your test results are normal, you may still need supplemental thyroid hormone, because traditional thyroid tests are unreliable. Look for a health care practitioner who will prescribe thyroid hormone based on your signs and symptoms rather than test results. Holistic physicians are a good bet, or check with the OWL Program (Optimized Weight Loss by Chronicity Inc; www.OptimizedWeightLoss.com). They have centers all around the United States, and their physicians are familiar with the principles in this book and are comfortable adding thyroid hormone when needed.

If you need to treat a sluggish thyroid on your own, take 6.25 mg of iodine a day (I recommend Tri-iodine by EuroPharma). Don't take more than 12.5 mg a day without a health practioner's supervision or you may block thyroid function. You may also wish to take BMR Complex, a thyroid glandular from Integrative Therapeutics, Inc. These will boost thyroid function and metabolism. Most people can stop taking Tri-iodine after three to twelve months, at which point the iodine in the Energy Revitalization System multivitamin powder from Enzymatic Therapy is sufficient.

Balance Your Adrenal Function

Adrenal fatigue causes some major "feed-me-now-or-I'll-kill-you" sugar cravings. If this sounds like you, add adrenal glandulars, licorice (the herb, not the candy), and other key nutrients to support your adrenal glands. These can be found in combination in the excellent product Adrenal Stress-End by Enzymatic Therapy. See Chapter 6 and *Beat Sugar Addiction Now!* for more information.

Get Rid of the "Yeastie Beasties"

Yeast makes you crave sugar. If you have sinusitis, spastic colon, or recurrent vaginal yeast infections, you likely have a problem with excess yeast. Follow the directions for treating yeast overgrowth in Chapter 8. The most important treatments include probiotics and Anti-Yeast, an excellent natural antifungal mix from Nutri-Elements (see Appendix A). Your holistic physician may also add the medication Diflucan (fluconazole) at a dose of 200 mg a day for six weeks.

Get Enough Sleep

Sleep helps you lose weight by increasing key appetite-suppressing hormones like leptin and ghrelin and boosting levels of growth hormone, which helps build muscle and burn fat. Trouble sleeping? Take the Revitalizing Sleep Formula herbal mix from Enzymatic Therapy (see Appendix A).

Treat Insulin Resistance

If insulin resistance persists despite following the *Beat Sugar Addiction Now!* program, talk to a holistic doctor about taking a very safe, low-cost, and effective medication for boosting insulin sensitivity called metformin (take 500 mg in the morning and at noon). It can cause B12 deficiency, so be sure you also take a multivitamin, such as the Energy Revitalization System vitamin powder from Enzymatic Therapy. Hormones can also play a role in insulin resistance. Men should check that their testosterone levels are high enough, and women should verify that your thyroid is optimized and that DHEA (dehydroepiandrosterone) and testosterone are not too high.

Get Overall Nutritional Support

Nutrient deficiencies can trigger sugar cravings, so I recommend supplementing daily with the Energy Revitalization System vitamin powder to fill in any nutritional gaps.

Give Your Metabolism a Boost

Boost your metabolism with the Turbo Boost Pack by Nutri-Elements. This is an amazing mix of natural fat busters that can get your metabolism fired up. Take three capsules before breakfast and again at lunch. Six capsules contain:

Item	Amount	Action
L-Carnitine	700 mg	Stimulates fat burning
Acetyl-L-Carnitine	500 mg	The acetyl form passes more effectively into cells' mitochondria
TMG	200 mg	May lower homocysteine and increase fat loss
Milk Thistle Extract	500 mg	Liver protection during weight loss
Folinic Acid	100 mcg	B vitamin support to maintain energy production
Methylcobalamin B12	300 mcg	B vitamin support to maintain energy production
Coleus Forskolin Extract	200 mg	Activation of adenyl cyclase with weight loss
Hydroxy Citric Acid	1000 mg	Increased fat burning
Chromium (polynicotinate)	1000 mcg	Insulin cofactor to decrease insulin resistance
PEA (phenylethylamine)	500 mg	Mood elevator (found in chocolate)
Iodine (50% each iodine and iodide)	1000 mcg	Increases thyroid function
Ribose	200 mg	Increases calorie burning
Vitamin B6 (P5P)	25 mg	Special form of vitamin B6 support to maintain energy production
Riboflavin B2	25 mg	B vitamin support to maintain energy production
Calcium Pantothenate B5	100 mg	B vitamin for adrenal support
Rhodiola	400 mg	Blunts excessive cortisol response in chronic stress and improves energy
Green Tea Extract		Increases calorie burning

A SIMPLE DIET FOR MAINTENANCE

Once you have eliminated the causes of your sugar addiction and given your body what it needs to restore balance and optimize metabolism, most people find they can ease up on many of the dietary restrictions. However, this does not mean dumping sugar and white flour back into your diet, which will just make you fat and sick again. Most of you will find that having small amounts of sugar in desserts, fruit, and chocolate (savoring up to an ounce a day) will happily satisfy your sweet tooth. Some of you may find that you need the discipline of all-or-nothing approach to sugar. See what works for you.

Meanwhile, my wife, Laurie (who is a nutritionist and has not consumed added sugars for over 20 years), is happy to share a simple maintenance diet for weight loss that you can do incrementally as needed to shed pounds. Use it when you have finished treating your sugar addiction type. It's easy and effective!

The Can-Do Diet!

By Laurie Teitelbaum, M.S.

The first major step in reaching and maintaining your desirable weight is to handle any sugar addiction problems, as discussed in this cookbook and in *Beat Sugar Addiction Now!* After you have gotten a handle on your sugar addiction, you will very likely start seeing weight loss naturally. However, if you would like to speed up the process, here is an easy weight-loss program that works for many people. Why the Can-Do Diet works:

- The Can-Do Diet is very easy to remember. There are no hassles and no decisions, yet the diet is satisfying and the rewards are gratifying!
- You can eat and enjoy the foods you love every single day.
- You get the nourishment you need.
- You will see your weight drop by up to five pounds in the first week! (After that, weight loss should continue at a safe, healthy rate of one to two pounds per week.)

The Basics of the Can-Do Diet

1. Eat two to three eggs, depending on your activity level, as your first meal of the day. Eat them when you are hungry or when it is convenient. It is okay to add a small pat of butter to these eggs and some vegetables. You may want to try cutting up hard-boiled eggs and eating them with a bit of butter, salt, and pepper.
2. Take the Energy Revitalization System with B Vitamins supplement from Enzymatic Therapy along with an omega-3 fatty acid supplement (we like the Vectomega brand) any time before 2 p.m.
3. Drink all the iced tea, hot tea, or water that you want all day long. The tea should only be sweetened with stevia or another natural (non-sugar)

sweetener. It's best to switch to caffeine-free tea after the first or second cup or to drink all of your tea very diluted.

4. Have a normal, wholesome meal (using the recipes in this book, for example) later in the day. It's best to schedule this meal after 2 p.m. when you are hungry.

That is the diet! Is that easy to remember, or what?

Optional Additions

- You may eat two raw pieces of fruit and a raw vegetable any time during the day. These may be helpful if you do feel any hunger pangs.
- You may have one stevia-sweetened soda sometime during the day. One brand we like is Zevia, often available at natural foods stores.
- Enjoy up to four Emergen-C 1,000 mg Vitamin C drink mixes each day. If you have loose stools or diarrhea, reduce the dose until your loose stools go away.
- You may drink up to two glasses of wine with your normal meal, but preferably not every day. Alcohol consumption will make your weight loss less dramatic, but if it helps you stay on the diet, it may be worth it.
- If you're hungry, enjoy a handful (½ cup [50 g]) of walnuts, filberts, or almonds once a day.

Additional Guidelines

The most effective diets are "diets for life". A diet you can continue long-term is a diet that works. After you reach your desired weight, it's okay to relax these rules or go back to eating three meals a day plus snacks to help keep your blood sugar stable (see Chapter 8). You can always go back to this simple plan if you gain a few pounds!

Base your one regular meal a day on whole, natural foods as much as possible. It is okay to eat what you love and what satisfies you, but whole foods contain the nutrients your body needs. When you eat your regular meal, eat until you are totally satisfied, but do not overeat. Try to regularly include a raw salad and another vegetable in this meal.

Many people eat because they are thirsty or depleted in vitamins. To help you lose weight or maintain your weight loss, take your vitamins and drink a lot of liquids. Drinking calorie-free liquids such as iced tea or water keeps you busy so you won't need to eat for "something to do," keeps your stomach full, and ushers nutrients in and toxins out of your cells. Note: Drink purified water (including the water you use to make tea).

A good brand of stevia is very helpful in this diet. Our office completed a taste test for various brands of stevia, and Stevia Liquid Concentrate by Body Ecology won hands-down. (Available at www.bodyecology.com). Sweet Leaf, available at most natural foods stores, is also excellent.

Be patient while you enjoy the flexibility and ease of this diet. However, if you are not seeing the weight loss you desire, you may need to slightly alter the one normal meal you are consuming daily. Try reducing the carbohydrate content or fat content of that meal and see if that makes a difference. Also consider your activity level. If you find yourself being sedentary (sitting for more than 45 minutes at a time), try adopting a few new habits to get you moving. Perhaps take a daily walk someplace attractive, or consider cleaning the house or stretching while you watch TV.

And finally, if you cheat now and then, it is okay! Simply, and with no guilt, ease yourself back into diet the next day.

ACKNOWLEDGEMENTS

Jacob Teitelbaum: So many special people helped make this book possible that I cannot possibly list them all. In truth, I have created nothing new; I have simply synthesized the wonderful work done by an army of hardworking and courageous physicians and healers.

I would like to extend my sincerest thanks to:

First and foremost, Laurie, my wife, for her immense patience with me during the writing of this book.

My mom and dad, who continue to inspire me despite having passed on long ago.

My staff, especially Cheryl Alberto, who keeps everything handled while I'm busy writing and teaching. Their hard work, compassion, and dedication (and, I must admit, patience with me) are what make my work possible.

My wonderful, amazing, and dedicated publicist and friend, Dean Draznin, and his staff, including Terri Slater, Diane Chojnowski, and Joy Bolster, who are my teammates in making effective treatment and health available to everyone. A special thanks also to Richard Crouse and Rich Mendelson, my computer "genies." Whenever I wish for stuff, they make it happen!

The Anne Arundel Medical Center librarian, Joyce Miller. Over the last thirty years, I have often wondered when she would politely tell me to stop asking for so many studies. So far, she has not. In fact, she always smiles when I ask her for more.

Bren Jacobson and Dr. Alan Weiss, who keep me intellectually, emotionally, and spiritually honest while reminding me to reclaim my sense of humor.

Special thanks to Chrystle—great job! Also to the Fair Winds Press editors and publishers, including Jill Alexander, Will Kiester, Skye Alexander, Karen Levy, Julia Maranan, and Tiffany Hill.

I would especially like to thank the wonderful holistic nutritionist Deirdre Rawlings, N.D., Ph.D., for her recipes and valuable assistance. Deirdre is a rising star in the area of "eating your way to health," and I happily recommend her website, www.foodsforfibromyalgia.com, and the wealth of information available there.

Chrystle Fiedler: Special thanks go to Dr. Teitelbaum for his expertise and enthusiasm, to Deirdre Rawlings for her commitment and creativity, and to Marilyn Allen for her savvy and support. Thanks also to the editorial team at Fair Winds Press, especially publisher Will Kiester, senior editor Jill Alexander, and editor Julia Maranan.

Deirdre Rawlings: My thanks goes to everyone on this project for their vision and their hard work: Jacob Teitelbaum, Chrystle Fiedler, Jill Alexander, and Will at Fair Winds Press. I'd like to thank all of the people involved, including the editors. It's been a pleasure and an honor to work with you, and thank you for allowing me this opportunity to participate and share my knowledge.

ABOUT THE AUTHORS

Jacob Teitelbaum, M.D., is medical director of the Chronicity and Fibromyalgia and Fatigue Centers nationally, author of the popular free iPhone application "Cures A-Z," and author of *Beat Sugar Addiction Now!*, *From Fatigued to Fantastic!*, *Real Cause, Real Cure*, and *Pain Free 1-2-3—A Proven Program for Eliminating Chronic Pain Now*. Dr. Teitelbaum makes frequent media appearances, including *Good Morning America*, CNN, Fox News Channel, the *Dr. Oz Show*, and *Oprah and Friends*. He lives in Kona, Hawaii. His website is www.vitality101.com.

Chrystle Fiedler: Chrystle Fiedler has written more than a hundred articles on alternative and mainstream health topics for national publications including *Natural Health*, *Prevention*, *Remedy*, *Vegetarian Times*, *The Health Monitor Network*, *Woman's Day*, *Better Homes and Gardens* and *Health Magazine*. Chrystle is also the co-author of *Beat Sugar Addiction Now!*. and *The Country Almanac to Home Remedies*. She is also the author of *Death Drops: A Natural Remedies Mystery (Gallery/Simon & Schuster 2012). Visit her author website at www. chrystlefiedler.com.*

Deirdre Rawlings, Ph.D., N.D.: Deirdre's passion for holistic medicine was ignited by her success in healing her own sugar addiction, fatigue, adrenal exhaustion, food allergies, digestive issues, and Candida.

From a chronically exhausted twenty-something to over fifty and fabulous, Deirdre combines over two decades experience in living vibrantly and sharing the latest scientific health principles and practices to help you on your journey to vibrant living.

A traditional naturopath, certified nutritionist, sports nutritionist, speaker, author, and healthy-cooking coach. She holds a Ph.D. in holistic nutrition, a Master's in holistic nutrition, and a master's in herbal medicine. Deirdre specializes in fibromyalgia, chronic fatigue syndrome, digestive challenges, food allergies, and immune rebalancing. She is the author of *Food That Helps Win the Battle Against Fibromyalgia* (Fair Winds 2008). Visit her websites at: www.Nutri-Living.com and www.FoodsForFibromyalgia.com.

INDEX